Talking About Rakugo

The Japanese Art of Storytelling

(Second Edition)

KRISTINE OHKUBO

with **Kanariya Eiraku**

Copyright © 2022 by Kristine Ohkubo.

All rights reserved. No part of this publication may be reproduced, distributed, or transmitted in any form or by any means, including photocopying, recording, or other electronic or mechanical methods, without the prior written permission of the author, except in the case of brief quotations embodied in critical reviews and certain other noncommercial uses permitted by copyright law. For permission requests, contact the author using the webpage address provided below.

https://kristineohkubo.wixsite.com/nonfiction-author

Talking About Rakugo/Kristine Ohkubo. —2nd ed.

ISBN 978-1-0880-2360-0

To *Katsura Shijaku II* (August 13, 1939–April 19, 1999) and the ever-increasing number of amateur and professional rakugo performers who endeavor to entertain us in the English language.

Acknowledgements

I owe an immeasurable debt of gratitude to those individuals who openly welcomed me into the unique and highly captivating world of *rakugo*. Each person served as my guide, teacher, mentor, and resource without hesitation, and for that I am eternally grateful.

I would also like to acknowledge *Masayuki Ohkubo* and *Julie Webb* for their tireless efforts in helping me to revise and reshape this manuscript, and to ensure that nothing was lost in translation.

"Rakugo is a highly distinctive genre of comic monologue that can be called Japan's 'talking art.' It is one of the keys to understanding Japanese culture."

"Rakugo: Japan's Talking Art"

JapanEcho, September 11, 2018

i. The Story of Shinigami (The God of Death) by Kei Ohsuga

Table of Contents

Introduction i

The Evolution of Rakugo 1

1. Otoshibanashi 2
2. The Early Performers 22
3. Kairakutei Black 51

The Transformation of Rakugo 69

4. Rakugo During the War Years 70
5. Rakugo Beyond the Yose 85
6. Tatekawa Danshi V 100
7. Sanyutei Enraku V 109
8. Kokontei Shincho III 117
9. Tachibanaya Enzo VIII 124
10. Hayashiya Sanpei 132
11. Mainstream Comedians Who Trained as Rakugoka 139
12. Female Rakugoka 152
13. Amateur vs. Professional Rakugoka 160
14. Rakugo on the Internet 169
15. Sign Language Rakugo 174

Rakugo in Other Languages 179

16. Katsura Shijaku II 180
17. Katsura Kaishi 188
18. Rakugo with Subtitles 192

In the Words of the Rakugoka 197

    19. *Katsura Sunshine* 198
    20. *Sanyutei Koseinen* 209
    21. *Tatekawa Shinoharu* 218
    22. *Yanagiya Tozaburo* 231
    23. *Kanariya Eiraku* 239
    24. *Kanariya Eishi* 247
    25. *Kanariya Ichirin* 256

English Rakugo Scripts 263

    Another Bottle of Sake (*Kawarime*) 271
    The Summer Burglar (*Natsu Doro*) 280
    Browsing in the Pleasure Quarter (*Nikai Zomeki*) 287
    Faceless Ghost (*Nopperabo*) 298
    The Father and Son Who Love Drinking (*Oyako Zake*) 305
    Foxes in Oji (*Oji no Kitsune*) 311
    Gonbei and the Racoon Dog (*Gonbei Danuki*) 323
    Gonsuke's Lantern (*Gonsuke Jochin*) 331
    Okiku's Dishes (*Okiku no Sara*) 340
    Peach Boy (*Momotaro*) 350
    Test Sake (*Tameshi Zake*) 360
    Time Noodles (*Toki Soba*) 370
    King Lear *(Lear Oh)* 380
    The Replacement of Enma (*Enma no Irekawari*) 391
    Scary Hamburgers (*Hanbaga Kowai*) 398
    Japan Milk Corporation (*Nihon Miruku Kosha*) 408

Appendix 421

Glossary 429

Illustrations and Photos 435

Works Cited 437

About Us 452

Introduction

While most Westerners today are acquainted with the traditional Japanese performing arts of Noh and kabuki, very few have heard of *rakugo*.

What is rakugo? While some people simply refer to it as Japanese "sit down," or "kneel down comedy," this 400-year-old art of storytelling is more complex than those over-simplified descriptions imply. Although it is true that rakugo is performed by a seated storyteller, unlike stand-up comedy, it is not just a series of jokes being fired off one after the other. Rakugo is a continuous story that often incorporates humorous monologues and builds up to the punchline at the end. It also requires the raconteur to portray multiple parts. Professional rakugo performers, like Noh and kabuki practitioners, endure a long and arduous apprenticeship with an experienced master storyteller in order to learn and perfect their art.

It is natural to think of rakugo as a comedic art because it was originally called *otoshibanashi* (stories with a punchline). However, the word "rakugo" is used as a general term to describe various types of stories including *kokkeibanashi* (funny stories), *ninjobanashi* (tragicomic human-interest stories), and *kaidanbanashi* (scary ghost stories).

When discussing rakugo, it is important to point out that there are two distinct performance styles. The first style is known as *Kamigata* (Osaka) rakugo and the second style is known as *Edo* (Tokyo) rakugo. The formats are practically the same and stories are shared between the two; however, there are some key differences to be aware of.

Both Kamigata rakugo and Edo rakugo emerged during the seventeenth century, but Edo rakugo was performed indoors while Kamigata rakugo was performed outdoors. As a result, the *rakugoka* (storytellers) performing in the Kamigata style had to devise ways through which they could attract people passing by and hold their attention throughout the performance. This is why Kamigata rakugo tends to be more colorful and cheerful than Edo rakugo. Furthermore, Kamigata rakugo storytellers place greater emphasis on entertaining an audience and making them laugh. Often, they will repeat a joke until they elicit laughter from the audience.

Since Edo rakugo was performed indoors, patrons were required to pay a fee before being admitted into the theater to watch the performance. With Kamigata rakugo, the performers collected money from the audience members who were still standing around after the performance had concluded. For this reason, it was imperative for Kamigata rakugo performers to engage their audience members and keep them laughing all the way until the end.[1]

Other distinguishing characteristics of Kamigata rakugo include the use of a small wooden table known as a *kendai*, on which the storyteller strikes a wooden clapper called a *kobyoshi* to signal the beginning of a story or a scene change. There is a small screen placed in front of the wooden table to hide the performer's knees, which is called a *hizakakushi*. This style of rakugo also sometimes employs sound effects during the performance to help punctuate the story.

All of these outdoor techniques were retained by the Kamigata storytellers long after the performances were moved indoors during the eighteenth century with the establishment of vaudeville type theaters known as *seki*. And since the Kanto ("to" meaning "east") region starkly differs in terms of language, food, and culture from the Kansai ("sai" meaning "west") region, the theaters are known as *yose* in the eastern part of Japan where the Edo storytelling tradition originated.

Even though the style of performance and presentation of rakugo has changed very little since the art form was formally established in the late eighteenth century, calling it Japan's traditional art gives

---

[1] 上方落語史 (Kamigata Rakugo-Shi). YouTube, 2017.
https://www.youtube.com/watch?app=desktop&v=R6MWif8kZQk&t=45s.

it a sense of inflexibility.² On the contrary, rakugo, unlike Noh and kabuki, is very adaptable.

Rakugo's collection of more than 500 classical stories, which date back to the Edo era, have been updated and altered through the years to include references to current events and situations in an attempt to help audience members better identify with the narratives. Rakugo also includes a vast assortment of original modern stories that are being written every day and constantly altered and updated to suit the audience, the time, and the place. In this regard, rakugo performers are not simply good comedians, but gifted, well-studied, and highly intuitive master storytellers.

There are as many reasons why people want to become rakugo performers as there are rakugoka performing in Japan today. Each person has his or her own unique story recalling why they followed the path leading to the world of rakugo. Perhaps the most unique reason comes from a performer known as Yanagiya Fukumaru II (born in 1954). Born into an affluent family, he always fancied living a poor man's lifestyle. After joining the world of rakugo, he succeeded in that endeavor.³

Though rakugo itself is not yet well-known in the West, thanks to the manga *Showa Genroku Rakugo Shinju* (English title, *Descending*

---

² Oshima, Kimie. "Japanese Sit-Down Comedy." Rakugo. Humor & Health Journal (Vol. XII, Number 3), May 1998. http://www.angelfire.com/vamp/shoopshoop/Rakugo.html.
³ "噺家を夢見た青春時代　落語家・柳家蝠丸さん (Hanashika Wo Yumemita Seishun Jidai - Rakugoka Yanagiya Fukumaru)."The Mainichi, October 12, 2018.

Stories) and English rakugo events organized to foster cultural exchanges, Westerners are slowly becoming better acquainted with the art form.

The Evolution of Rakugo

1. Otoshibanashi

> "
> *"Rakugo was the quintessential plebian art…"*
> —Andrew L. Markus
> *The Journal of Japanese Studies, 1992*

During the thirteenth century in Japan, there were a group of men who served the *daimyo* (feudal lords) as both entertainers and advisors. Because these men originated from a Buddhist sect, they were known as *doboshu* (monks who specialized in the arts). As Japan advanced toward the sixteenth century, the roles of these monks evolved, and they honed their skills as storytellers and conversationalists. As such, they became known as *otogishu* or *hanashishu*.

The sixteenth century in Japan was an era of civil strife known as the *Sengoku* period (the Warring States period). The hanashishu of this period were not mere storytellers; they also served as the sounding boards for military strategies and engaged in battles alongside their lords.[4] Toyotomi Hideyoshi, a feudal lord and

---

[4] "Taikomochi." Wikipedia. Wikimedia Foundation, May 31, 2020. https://en.wikipedia.org/wiki/Taikomochi.

politician of the late Sengoku period, employed as many as 800 hanashishu whom he mobilized for his campaigns in Korea.[5]

When Japan finally achieved peace during the seventeenth century, the role of the hanashishu changed once again and they became entertainers exclusively. Some worked alongside the *oiran* (the high-class Japanese courtesans) and helped them entertain their clientele.[6] Because storytelling was so popular around that time, various collections of favorite stories emerged, including *Gigen yokishu* (*Anthology of Humorous Remarks*) and *Kino wa kyo no monogatari* (*Today's Tales of Yesterday*).[7]

Throughout the seventeenth century, humorous anecdotes were also used during long Buddhist sermons as an effective way to keep people awake and alert. In 1623, through the urging of Kyoto governor Itakura Shigemune, a monk named Anrakuan Sakuden (1554-1642) compiled over 1,000 anecdotes in a book titled *Seisuisho* (*Laughs to Wake You Up*).[8] Today, he is regarded as the father of rakugo, even though he was not a full-time storyteller.

Before it became recognized as rakugo, this type of storytelling was known as *karuguchi* (軽口, frivolous talk), where the kanji 口 (pronounced "kuchi") represents the word "mouth." The earliest

---

[5] Morioka, Heinz, and Miyoko Sasaki. Rakugo, the Popular Narrative Art of Japan. Cambridge, MA: Council on East Asian Studies, Harvard University, 1990. Page 418.
[6] "Taikomochi." Wikipedia.
[7] Morioka and Miyoko, Rakugo.
[8] Brau, Lorie. Rakugo: Performing Comedy and Cultural Heritage in Contemporary Tokyo. Lanham, MD: Lexington Books, 2008. Page 61.

appearance of this particular set of kanji was recorded in 1787. However, the characters together were read *otoshibanashi* (落とし噺), the term which originally identified the storytelling traditions of Kyoto and Osaka (cities in the Kansai region). Otoshibanashi can be traced back to the parodied kabuki plays staged in Osaka's Tenmangu Shrine and in Shijo Kawaramachi in central Kyoto toward the end of the Edo period (1603-1867).[9]

The term "rakugo" first entered into usage during the middle of the Meiji period (1868–1912), and became common during the Showa period (1926–1989).[10]

The first permanent yose theaters where rakugo was performed were established in Edo (Tokyo) in 1798 by the storytellers Okamoto Mansaku (dates unknown) and Sanshotei Karaku (1777-1833). A rakugoka's *kozamei* (stage name) may sound somewhat unusual because it is often taken from a pun. Sanshotei Karaku's stage name, for instance, came from the words *sansho* (Japanese pepper) and *karai* (hot). In other words, his stage name meant "hot pepper." Similarly, Sanyutei Ensho's name was derived from the words *sanyu* (playing on the mountain) and *ensho* (born a monkey). Therefore, the original meaning of his name was "monkey playing on the mountain." The ending *tei* signifies a group or family.

---

[9] Yu, A. C. "Karukuchi." Japanese Wiki Corpus. https://japanese-wiki-corpus.github.io/culture/Karukuchi.html.
[10] "Rakugo." languagehatcom, November 24, 2018. http://languagehat.com/Rakugo/.

These storytelling theaters provided affordable entertainment for ordinary citizens; and at the height of their popularity in 1855, there were 175 yose operating in Edo alone. [11] Until the introduction of these theaters, groups of amateur otoshibanashi storytellers gathered in restaurants or rented halls on specific days to present their stories.

As rakugo took hold in the cities of Edo, Kyoto, and Osaka, it evolved into three distinctive styles. Edo rakugo is still performed in Tokyo, and Osaka rakugo became known as Kamigata rakugo, while Kyoto rakugo eventually faded away. Today, there are only four yose still operating in Tokyo (the Suzumoto Engeijo in Ueno, the Shinjuku Suehirotei in Shinjuku, the Asakusa Engei Hall in Asakusa, and the Ikebukuro Engeijo in Ikebukuro), one in Osaka (the Tenma Tenjin Hanjo Tei), and one each in Kobe (the Kobe Shinkaichi Kirakukan), Nagoya (the Osu Engeijo), and Sendai (the Hanaza).[12]

The popularity of the yose enabled them to grow and expand until the Tenpo era (1841-1843), when a set of highly conservative reforms were initiated by Mizuno Tadakuni, the chief adviser to the shogun. These reforms not only emphasized frugality; they also went so far as to censor and ban works of art and literature

---

[11] Morioka and Miyoko. Rakugo. Page 419.
[12] "Rakugo (The Art of Storytelling)." nippon.com, May 30, 2020. https://www.nippon.com/en/features/jg00045/.

deemed to be lewd in nature. As a result, all but 24 yose theaters throughout Japan were demolished during this period.

But the reforms were highly unpopular and Tadakuni was eventually ousted. The end of the Tenpo era signaled the reemergence of the yose and by the second half of the nineteenth century, there were over 300 venues across Japan offering rakugo performances.[13]

Since its establishment, the presentation and style of rakugo performances have remained virtually unchanged. A rakugo performance is rather minimalistic and features a single storyteller dressed in a kimono, sitting in the *seiza* position (knees together, back straight, and buttocks resting on the ankles) on a *zabuton* (floor cushion) that is placed on a *koza* (an elevated stage or platform). The performer relies solely on a *sensu* (paper fan) and a *tenugui* (small hand towel) as props to help him or her convey the story to the audience. These items are given a great deal of versatility in the stories as they are used to represent a wide range of items. For instance, a fan can represent a writing brush, a pair of chopsticks, or a pipe. A hand towel can represent a wallet, a *tabako-ire* (Edo era tobacco pouch), or a book.

---

[13] "Sandai-Banashi: Impromptu Rakugo Based on Three Themes: Rakugo Special: Edo Tokyo Digital Museum - Historical Visit, New Wisdom." Tokyo Metropolitan Library.
https://www.library.metro.tokyo.lg.jp/portals/0/edo/tokyo_library/english/rakugo/page2-1.html.

Although some of the *koten rakugo* (classical rakugo) tales have been transcribed, the art of storytelling has traditionally been passed down by oral practice. A *zenza* (apprentice storyteller) learns by listening to his or her *shisho* (master) perform. The stories the master conveys are made up of three parts: the *makura* (prologue), the *hondai* (main story), and the *ochi* (the closing, or the punch line).

The stories are based on a range of topics, from comical to sentimental, and involve conversations between multiple characters. The storyteller switches seamlessly from one character to another, changing their voice, facial expression, mannerisms, and accent to fit the character who is speaking. A slight turn of the head and a change in pitch is used to indicate a switch from one character to another.

Rakugo performances follow the stylized conventions established long ago, but the storyteller's freedom to improvise and incorporate modern vernacular and references to recent events has enabled the art form to survive for hundreds of years.

ii. Panels from Shunshoku Sandaibanashi illustrated by Ikkeisai Yoshiiku (Tokyo Metropolitan Library)

iii. Sandaibanashi (impromptu rakugo stories) were introduced by Sanshotei Karaku I (1773-1833)

Kamigata Rakugo

The term, "Kamigata rakugo" first appeared in the journal *Kamigata* published on July 1, 1932.[14] Kamigata was the informal name of the region known today as Kansai. It encompasses the cities of Kyoto, Osaka, and Kobe.[15]

During the early 1670s, professional rakugo storytellers began to emerge from the streets, shrines, and temples of Kyoto and Osaka. Among them, Tsuyu no Gorobei I (1643–1703) from Kyoto and Yonezawa Hikohachi I (who died in 1714) from Osaka, are regarded as the forefathers of Kamigata rakugo.[16]

Gorobei was a former Nichiren sect Buddhist priest, who in 1691 compiled his narratives consisting of word games, episodes from the lives of famous authors, and plays on different dialects in a five-volume *hanashibon* titled *Karukuchi tsuyu ga hanashi* (*Tsuyu's Humorous Stories*).[17] A hanashibon, loosely translated as

---

[14] Yu, A. C. "Kamigata Rakugo (Comic Storytelling in Kyoto and Osaka) (上方落語)" - Japanese Wiki Corpus. https://www.japanese-wiki-corpus.org/culture/Kamigata%20Rakugo%20(Comic%20Storytelling%20in%20Kyoto%20and%20Osaka).html.
[15] "Kamigata," Wikipedia (Wikimedia Foundation, January 17, 2022), https://en.wikipedia.org/wiki/Kamigata.
[16] "Rakugo: Traditional Comic Story Telling," Rakugo: Learn Japanese - Japanese language and Culture, September 12, 2007, http://www.gaikoku.info/japanese/rakugo.htm.
[17] 露の五郎兵衛 (Tsuyu No Gorobei)," Wikipedia (Wikimedia Foundation, January 2, 2022), https://ja.wikipedia.org/wiki/%E9%9C%B2%E3%81%AE%E4%BA%94%E9%83%8E%E5%85%B5%E8%A1%9B. ; "Rakugo." Wikipedia. Wikimedia Foundation, August 22, 2020. https://en.wikipedia.org/wiki/Rakugo.; 小項目事典, "軽口露がはなしとは (Karukuchitsuyugahanashi to Wa)," ブリタニカ国際大百科事典 (Britannica International Encyclopedia) (コトバンク (Kotobank), accessed March 16, 2022, https://kotobank.jp/word/%E8%BB%BD%E5%8F%A3%E9%9C%B2%E3%81%8C%E3%81%AF%E3%81%AA%E3%81%97-47619.

"storybook," was a collection of jokes that became popular and was actively published during the Edo period.[18]

Gorobei was a masterful *tsuji-banashi* storyteller, and he shared his talent in various venues throughout Kyoto, including Shijo Kawara and Kitano Tenmangu Shrine.[19] Tsuji-banashi, which means storytelling at the crossroads, was the term used to describe the types of stories one can hear out on the street corners, temples, and shrines. Oftentimes, these types of stories were told by someone begging for money.[20]

In her book, *Rakugo: Performing Comedy and Cultural Heritage in Contemporary Tokyo*, Lorie Brau describes how rakugo storytellers were once perceived as *geinin* in Japanese society. During the Edo period, citizens were generally grouped into a cast system consisting of samurai, farmers, artisans, and merchants. The geinin did not fit into these groups; therefore, they were considered outcasts. The professional rakugo storytellers and other performers including kabuki actors were clustered into the same

---

[18] "咄本とは (Hanashibon to Wa)." ブリタニカ国際大百科事典 小項目事典 (Britannica International Encyclopedia Small Item Encyclopedia). コトバンク (Kotobank). Accessed March 16, 2022. https://kotobank.jp/word/%E5%92%84%E6%9C%AC-115641#E3.83.96.E3.83.AA.E3.82.BF.E3.83.8B.E3.82.AB.E5.9B.BD.E9.9A.9B.E5.A4.A7.E7.99.BE.E7.A7.91.E4.BA.8B.E5.85.B8.20.E5.B0.8F.E9.A0.85.E7.9B.AE.E4.BA.8B.E5.85.B8.

[19] "露の五郎兵衞とは (Tsuyunogorobee to Wa)," 日本大百科全書(ニッポニカ) (Encyclopedia Nipponica (Nipponica))/ 朝日日本歴史人物事典 (コトバンク (Kotobank), accessed March 16, 2022, https://kotobank.jp/word/%E9%9C%B2%E3%81%AE%E4%BA%94%E9%83%8E%E5%85%B5%E8%A1%9B-572694#%E5%88%9D%E4%BB%A3.

[20] "Meaning of 辻噺, つじばなし, Tsujibanashi: Japanese Dictionary," JLearn.net, accessed March 16, 2022, https://jlearn.net/dictionary/%E8%BE%BB%E5%99%BA.

category as beggars and other citizens outside of respectable society.[21]

Hikohachi gained a reputation while telling stories in Osaka's Ikukunitama Shrine. At the time, it was common for various entertainers to gather at the precincts of the shrine to perform. They performed in performance stalls in an atmosphere closely resembling that of a flea market. He often found himself competing with other performers such as *biwa hoshi* (lute priests) who earned their income by reciting vocal literature to the accompaniment of *biwa* (Japanese short-necked lute) music.[22] For this reason, Hikohachi incorporated impersonations into his act to attract spectators. He dared to impersonate samurai and daimyo at an age when Japanese society adhered to a rigid feudal system, and doing so would most certainly have gotten him in deep trouble. Indeed, Hikohachi's performances were being monitored and on one occasion an official was dispatched to arrest him. Hikohachi swiftly escaped by slipping into the audience before the official could seize him.[23]

---

[21] Brau, Lorie. Rakugo: Performing Comedy and Cultural Heritage in Contemporary Tokyo. Lanham, MD: Lexington Books, 2008. Page 78.

[22] Masaki Kinoshita, "What Kind of Person Is Hikohachi Yonezawa, the Founder of Kamigata Rakugo?," 神戸っ子 | 神戸・芦屋・西宮の上質で厳選した情報をお届けするサイト, September 2018, https://kobecco.hpg.co.jp/34133/. ;"Biwa Hōshi," Wikipedia (Wikimedia Foundation, December 25, 2021), https://en.wikipedia.org/wiki/Biwa_h%C5%8Dshi.

[23] Masaki Kinoshita, "What Kind of Person Is Hikohachi Yonezawa, the Founder of Kamigata Rakugo?."

According to Kinoshita Masaki, the author of *Tenkaichi no karukuchi otoko* (*The Funniest Man in the World*), "[Hikohachi] made people laugh up until the final curtain was brought down by showing people how he died." [24] He was asked by a prominent local merchant to perform in the city of Nagoya. The merchant, banking on Hikohachi's popularity, spent a great deal of money advertising the performance and expected a large crowd to gather; however, Hikohachi suddenly passed away in Nagoya just before the performance.[25]

Osaka's pioneer professional storyteller had a deep passion for comic storytelling, and he was renowned for his versions of "Jugemu," a story about a boy with an extremely long name, and "Kagekiyo," based on Kagekiyo Shichibei, a military commander of the Heike clan.[26] He is highly revered by modern rakugoka who gather at the Ikukunitama Shrine annually on the first weekend in September to pay homage to him. The event is known as the *Hikohachi Matsuri* (Hikohachi Festival).

Kamigata rakugo uses the Kansai dialect, which may sound peculiar to those who are not familiar with it. For this reason, Kamigata rakugo did not appeal to the Tokyo audiences prior to

---

[24] Masaki Kinoshita, "What Kind of Person Is Hikohachi Yonezawa, the Founder of Kamigata Rakugo?."
[25] Masaki Kinoshita, "What Kind of Person Is Hikohachi Yonezawa, the Founder of Kamigata Rakugo?."
[26] Masaki Kinoshita, "What Kind of Person Is Hikohachi Yonezawa, the Founder of Kamigata Rakugo?." ; "Kagekiyo," 能・演目事典：景清：あらすじ・みどころ, 2022, https://www.the-noh.com/jp/plays/data/program_066.html.

World War II. After the war, however, the Osaka dialect was introduced to Tokyo through mass media and Kamigata rakugo became widely available.

As Japan initiated its rebuilding process after the war, numerous theaters began to crop up in Osaka. These newly established theaters offered a mixed repertoire of rakugo storytelling and manzai comedy. While rakugo utilizes a single storyteller, manzai comedy usually involves two performers; a straight man (*tsukkomi*); and a funny man (*boke*), who rapidly exchange jokes with one another. In the years during the military occupation of Japan, certain aspects of American culture became part of the post-war Japanese landscape. American music and films were common and younger audiences demanded more appealing modern forms of entertainment. The popularity of rakugo, with its age-old traditions, began to decline rapidly. Yoshimoto Kogyo Co., Ltd., one of Japan's most influential talent agencies employing most of the country's popular comedic talent, regarded rakugo as having no commercial value.[27]

Kamigata rakugo did not have a home in post-war Japan until 1947, when Shirai Matsujiro, the founding member and president of Shochiku Co., Ltd. converted an existing movie theater in Osaka into a vaudeville type theater known as the Ebisubashi Shochiku.

---

[27] Yu, A. C. "Kamigata Rakugo (上方落語)."

It was the only seki in Osaka immediately after the end of the Pacific War, drawing rakugo performers such as Shofukutei Shokaku VI, Katsura Beicho III, Katsura Bunshi V, and Katsura Harudanji III, who later came to be known as Kamigata rakugo's *shitenno,* or big four (上方落語四天王). This triggered the subsequent revival of Kamigata rakugo.[28]

Shokaku, Beicho, Bunshi, and Harudanji united to form the *Saezurikai* (the Twitters). Together, they garnered the interest of the flourishing commercial broadcasting companies, and they vigorously recruited apprentices through their workshops. In turn, these young apprentices soared to fame against the backdrop of the booming television industry in the mid 1960s.[29]

Around this time, there was a surge in the number of radio programs featuring Kamigata rakugo. Programs such as "Onward Rakugo Selection" and "Kamigata FM Yose" appealed to younger listeners, notably college students. As Kamigata rakugo's popularity increased, groups of amateur rakugo storytellers were formed. The most active among these groups were the rakugo societies established by young college students. Many talented

---

[28] "戎橋松竹 (Ebisubashishōchiku)," Wikipedia (Wikimedia Foundation), accessed March 16, 2022, https://ja.wikipedia.org/wiki/%E6%88%8E%E6%A9%8B%E6%9D%BE%E7%AB%B9#%E8%90%BD%E8%AA%9E.
[29] Yu, A. C. "Kamigata Rakugo (上方落語)."

students eventually became professional storytellers, providing the backbone of today's Kamigata rakugo industry. [30]

Although Kamigata rakugo no longer employs the *shinuchi* (master storyteller) hierarchical system, a ranking system known as *koban* still exists. Katsura Sanshi (later known as Katsura Bunshi VI), who was the president of the Kamigata Rakugo Association from 2003-2018, had planned to reinstate the shinuchi hierarchical system, but he was forced to give it up due to overwhelming opposition.[31]

Edo Rakugo

Unlike noh, an art form that was intended to be enjoyed exclusively by royalty and nobles during special ceremonies, rakugo's target audience, regardless of the style of performance, has always been the common people. In feudal Japan, commoners were often less educated, understood literature mostly by oral tradition, and enjoyed art forms that reflected daily lives. However, being an *Edokko* (Edo native) carried with it a certain sense of aesthetics. The term *iki* which means chic or stylish was a trait shared among many who were born and raised in Edo. As such, the style of rakugo which developed in Edo was more refined than its Kamigata counterpart. The storytellers placed

---

[30] "Rakugo." Wikipedia, August 22, 2020.
[31] Yu, A. C. "Kamigata Rakugo (上方落語)."

greater emphasis on their storytelling technique and less on simply pleasing their audience. Since Edo rakugo developed indoors, its storytellers do not rely on the various outdoor props used in Kamigata rakugo, such as the kendai and kobyoshi. As a result, Edo rakugo is quieter and sounds more somber than the Kamigata version.

As with Kamigata rakugo, Edo rakugo also had a pioneer storyteller. He was Kamigata-native Shikano Buzaemon (1649-1699). Buzaemon performed for the samurai and merchants of Edo, and he rose to fame as a storyteller. But eventually, he was banished due to an incident arising from one of his popular stories.

The story was about a horse who had the ability to communicate with humans. In 1693, two men devised a plan to deceive people using Buzaemon's story idea. They spread a rumor throughout Edo about a horse that had predicted the city would be devastated by a plague. They attempted to play on people's fears and profit by selling medicine that would protect them from the disease. The men were eventually captured and one of them was beheaded, and the other was exiled. For no wrongdoing of his own, Buzaemon was also exiled to the uninhabited island of Izu Oshima. Following this incident, the popularity of rakugo in Edo began to wane, and for the next 100 years, humorous stories were available only in written format. [32]

Then, toward the end of the eighteenth century, Utei Enba (1743-1822), a carpenter turned storyteller and author, founded two exclusive artistic groups. One group was called *Hanashi no kai*. It was a gathering of literati who presented their own original stories, and storytelling enthusiasts who displayed their skills. The other group was called *Mimasuren*.

Enba, who often referred to himself as Tatekawa Danshuro (a reference to the Tatekawa River near where he lived and to one of the most famous kabuki actors of all time, Ichikawa Danjuro V), based the name of the second group on Danjuro's acting family crest. The crest featured three squares nested inside one another and was called *mimasu*.

The stories that originated from the artistic groups Enba founded were eventually published, and they inspired a surge in humorous storytelling in Edo. This led to the emergence of countless professional rakugo performers throughout the city. [33] Among them, several outstanding figures appeared, launching the rakugo tradition we know today. These figures included Sanyutei Ensho

---

[32] 落語「通」検定粋に楽しむ落語: Yahoo!インターネット検定公式テキスト. Japan: インプレスジャパン, 2006. Page 11.
[33] "Rakugo Special," Tokyo Metropolitan Library. Page 1.

iv. Ichikawa Danjuro V in the play Shibaraku (Los Angeles County Museum of Art)

(1766-1838), Asanebo Muraku (1776-1831), Hayashiya Shozo (1781-1842), and Senyutei Senkyo (d. 1829).

Ensho originated *shibaibanashi* (kabuki stories) while Muraku adapted ninjobanashi from *kodan* (another style of traditional Japanese storytelling that focuses on prominent historical figures).

Shozo specialized in kaidanbanashi and Senkyo was known as the creator of *ongyokubanashi* (musical stories).

In 1845, another prominent rakugoka surfaced and his most notable works included kaidanbanashi. His name was Sanyutei Encho (1839-1900). Encho was instrumental in elevating rakugo, which had always been considered a low art, to the rank of a high art with refined artistic rules. Under his influence, rakugo began centering more on ninjobanashi and drifting closer toward the serious kodan narration.[34]

It is highly probable that Edo rakugo would not have survived to the present day had it not been for rakugo performers such as Sanyutei Enyu and Yanagiya Kosan II. Their stories stressed popular humor, wit, and they enabled rakugo to once again capture the interest of the common folk.[35]

---

[34] Heinz Morioka and Miyoko Sasaki. Rakugo, the Popular Narrative Art of Japan (Cambridge, MA: Council on East Asian Studies, Harvard University, 1990), Page 419.
[35] Heinz Morioka and Miyoko Sasaki. Rakugo, the Popular Narrative Art of Japan. Page 419.

Both Encho and Enyu left artistic legacies that survive to this day in the famous Sanyutei, Hayashiya, Yanagiya, and Katsura artistic houses.[36]

---

[36] Heinz Morioka and Miyoko Sasaki. Rakugo, the Popular Narrative Art of Japan. Page 419.

2. The Early Performers

> "*Rakugo isn't something you can do alone.*"
> —*Sukeroku*
> *Showa Genroku Rakugo Shinju (English title, Descending Stories) Episode 12*

Sanyutei Encho

Sanyutei Encho, the son of renowned storyteller Tachibanaya Entaro (d.1872), was born in Edo in 1839.[37] As rakugoka who performed during the late Edo and early Meiji periods, he is considered to be the most exceptional among all the rakugo masters. As an author, he contributed over one hundred original stories to the art of rakugo.[38]

Encho entered the world of rakugo in 1845 at the age of six. Two years later, he became a disciple of his father's master, Sanyutei Ensho II. However, Ensho was envious of his young disciple and attempted to undermine him on the day when master and disciple were scheduled to perform together. He placed his apprentice in a

---

[37] Miller, J. Scott. "SANYUTEI ENCHO." Academic Dictionaries and Encyclopedias, 2009. https://japan_literature.enacademic.com/343/SAN%E2%80%99YUTEI_ENCHO.
[38] "San'yūtei Enchō." Wikipedia. Wikimedia Foundation, October 4, 2020. https://en.wikipedia.org/wiki/San%27y%C5%ABtei_Ench%C5%8D.

difficult position by performing a story Encho was planning to do. To overcome this problem in the future, Encho determined to write original stories and became quite prolific.[39]

He attained the second rank of *futatsume* at the age of ten, but he did not remain in rakugo for too long afterwards. In 1851, at age 12 and opposing his family's wishes, he became the live-in disciple of Utagawa Kuniyoshi, one of the last great masters of the Japanese *ukiyoe* style of woodblock prints and painting. But, Encho's life as a painter was short-lived and he returned to the rakugo stage just five years later at the age of seventeen. After achieving the final rank of shinuchi, he adopted the stage name Sanyutei Encho.

Encho, the master storyteller, opened up new possibilities for traditional Japanese storytelling and gained popularity for his original ghost stories and stories adapted from foreign literary works. Among the stories he adapted were "*Meijin Choji*" ("Master Choji"), borrowed from *Un Parricide* by Guy de Maupassant; "*Nishiki no maiginu*" ("The Silk Ball Gown"), styled after *La Tosca* by Victorien Sardou; "*Matsu no misao bijin no ikiume*" based on *Buried Alive*, a French novel translated into English; "*Koshobi: Oshu shosetsu*" from a French novel; and "*Eikoku koshi Joji Sumisu no den,*" *(The Life of George Smith, a Filial English Son)*. One of the most

---

[39] "三遊亭圓朝." Wikipedia. Wikimedia Foundation, November 28, 2020. https://ja.wikipedia.org/wiki/%E4%B8%89%E9%81%8A%E4%BA%AD%E5%9C%93%E6%9C%9D.

noteworthy of Encho's stories was "*Botan Doro*" ("The Peony Lantern"), which he adapted into rakugo in 1884.

The original "Botan Doro" appeared in a compilation of ghost stories called *Jiandeng Xinhua* (*New Tales Under the Lamplight*) by Chinese novelist Qu You. The story entered the Japanese literary culture in 1666 after it was translated into Japanese by the Buddhist monk and author Asai Ryoi (circa 1612-1691). Ryoi, regarded as one of the finest writers of *kanazoshi* (a form of popular literature written with little or no kanji making it accessible to common people), incorporated the story along with Qu You's other stories into his own vastly popular book called *Otogi Boko* (*Hand Puppets*).

In Ryoi's version, a beautiful woman named Otsuyu and a young girl holding a peony lantern stroll by the house of a widowed samurai on the first night of *Obon* (the Japanese Buddhist tradition of honoring the spirits of one's ancestors). The samurai is instantly smitten with the woman and vows his eternal love to her. From that night onward, the woman and the girl visit the samurai's house daily at dusk, always leaving before dawn.

An elderly neighbor grows suspicious about the mysterious visitors and spies through the bedroom door one evening. He almost faints when he discovers the samurai entwined in the arms of a skeleton. He reports the incident to a Buddhist priest, who convinces the samurai that he is in grave danger.

Afterwards, they place a protection charm on the house that prevents the woman and the girl from entering. The woman continues to come to the house each night and beckons her lover from outside. Unable to resist her charms, the samurai goes out to greet her and is led back to her house, a grave at a temple. When morning arrives, the samurai's dead body is found entwined with the woman's skeleton.

In the rakugo version, which was published as a stenographically transcribed story in 1886, a young man named Hagiwara Shinzaburo falls in love with the spirit of a beautiful young woman.[40] Encho's adaptation was particularly frightening because as he told the story, he used wooden clogs to imitate the footsteps of the beautiful ghost. The audience found this extremely disturbing because it was commonly believed that Japanese ghosts did not have legs. But by choosing to portray the ghost in this manner, Encho acknowledged that the source of the story was China and not Japan.

He also cooperated with Takusari Koki, the inventor of the Japanese shorthand system (*sokki*). While he recited his ghostly tales on stage, students from Takusari's stenography school sat backstage and used the new system of shorthand to transcribe Encho's stories, which were later made into a shorthand book and

---

[40] "Botan Dōrō," August 2, 2020. Wikipedia.
https://en.wikipedia.org/wiki/Botan_D%C5%8Dr%C5%8D.

serialized in newspapers.⁴¹ Some of his stories were even remade as kabuki plays.⁴²

Many of Encho's original stories are considered to be masterpieces and have been passed down to the present day. In particular, "Shinigami" ("God of Death"), another adaptation, has been performed by countless rakugo storytellers over the years.

It is likely that Encho based "Shinigami" on the fairytale by Jacob and Wilhelm Grimm called "Godfather Death." The Grimm brothers' story is about a poor man who struggles to feed his twelve children. When the thirteenth child arrives in the world, the man does not know what to do and runs out into the street, intending to ask the first man whom he met to be the child's godfather.

The father's first encounter is with God. When the man realizes he is speaking to God he says, "I do not wish to have you as a godfather. You give to the rich and let the poor starve." His second encounter is with the devil. Upon learning his identity, the man says "I do not wish to have you as a godfather. You deceive mankind and lead them astray."

---

⁴¹ "作家別作品リスト：No. 989." 作家別作品リスト：三遊亭 円朝. ("List of works by artist: No.989." List of works by artist: Sanyutei Encho.)
https://www.aozora.gr.jp/index_pages/person989.html.
⁴² Miller, J. Scott. "SANYUTEI ENCHO." Academic Dictionaries and Encyclopedias, 2009. https://japan_literature.enacademic.com/343/SAN%E2%80%99YUTEI_ENCHO.

Then, Death comes walking toward him and says, "Take me as your child's godfather."

The father asks, "Who are you?"

"I am Death, who makes everyone equal."

The father says, "You are the right one. You take away the rich as well as the poor without distinction. You shall be my child's godfather."

Death answers, "I will make your child rich and famous, for he who has me as a friend cannot fail."

After the boy comes of age, his godfather appears to him. He takes the boy out into the woods and shows him an herb growing there, saying, "Now you shall receive your godfather's present. I will turn you into a famous physician. Whenever you are called to help a sick person, I will appear before you. If I stand at the sick person's head, you may say with confidence that you can make him well again. Then give him some of this herb, and he will recover. But if I stand at the sick person's feet, he is mine. And you must say that he is beyond help and no physician in the world could save him. But beware of using this herb against my will, or something very bad will happen to you."[43]

---

[43] "Godfather Death." Grimm 044: Godfather Death. University of Pittsburgh, 2006. https://www.pitt.edu/~dash/grimm044.html.

Similarly, in the rakugo version, the God of Death appears to a poor man who is contemplating suicide. The man becomes rich by following the God of Death's advice to become a doctor, repeating the same scenario in the Grimm brothers' tale with only the slight variation of where the God of Death stands. In the rakugo story, if he stands at the foot of the sick person's bed, the person will recover. If he stands at his head, the sick person will die.

Later on, the man squanders his money and is left penniless. He once again attempts to earn money as a doctor, but the situation proves less favorable for him this time. He devises a plan to trick the God of Death and earn a substantial amount of money. His plan works, but the God of Death is displeased. He beckons the man to a place where the candles of life burn. The God of Death shows the man his candle, which is about to go out. He strikes a deal with the man that if he can transfer the flame of his candle to a new candle, he can live.

There are several endings to the story based on Encho's original version and the adaptions made by modern rakugo performers. In the original story, the man attempts to transfer the flame of his nearly extinguished candle to a new candle, but he fails and dies. Sanyutei Ensho VI loved this story the most, and he faithfully performed it as it was originally written. This story became Ensho's signature act, and no other rakugoka dared to perform it while he was alive. Following his death, other rakugo performers began performing the story of "Shinigami" and changed the ending to suit themselves.

In Yanagiya Kosanji's version, the man attempting to light the candle has a cold. He succeeds in transferring the flame to a new candle, but inadvertently sneezes and blows the candle out. In Tatekawa Shinosuke's version, the man successfully lights the new candle and turns toward the exit of the cave. The God of Death tells him to blow out the candle since it is bright outside, and the man heeds his advice and dies. In Tatekawa Shiraku's version, the man successfully transfers the flame of his almost extinguished candle to a new candle, but winds up blowing the candle out after the God of Death sings "Happy Birthday" to him.

The story "Shinigami" is a classic representation of the tragicomic ninjobanashi. The many variations of the ending demonstrate that one can listen to the same rakugo story performed by different storytellers and walk away with a unique experience each time. This is the beauty and appeal of rakugo.

Encho, renowned for his ghostly tales, was an avid collector of paintings and artwork featuring ghosts and supernatural beings. After his death, the collection was brought to Zenshoan Temple in Yanaka, where his grave is located. Every August, the month in which Encho passed away, the collection is put on display for the public.

Wakayagi Enjo (born 1870)

While it is true that rakugo is an art form established and dominated by men for hundreds of years, the fact that there was a female rakugoka active during the Meiji period cannot be overlooked. Her name was Wakayagi Enjo and she was the disciple of the famous rakugo master Danshuro Enshi (1837-1900), an apprentice of Shunputei Ryushi, and a contemporary of Sanyutei Encho.

Like Tatekawa Danshuro (Utei Enba), who adored the famous kabuki actor Ichikawa Danjuro V, Enshi adopted the name Danshuro in 1885 in honor of Ichikawa Danjuro IX, one of the most celebrated kabuki actors of the Meiji period. Fittingly, Enshi's rakugo stories mostly revolved around the theater.[44]

Wakayagi Enjo, whose real name was Aso Tama, was born in Shiba, Tokyo in 1870. She was the daughter of a Tango Province swordsman named Aso Yaatsu. (The old Tango Province once comprised the area currently known as northern Kyoto Prefecture.) With the decline of the *bakufu* government (the military government of Japan between 1192 and 1868), Yaatsu gave up swordsmanship and became a rice trader in Nihonbashi. He earned a substantial living as a rice trader and was able to send

---

[44] "Danjuro Dictionary - D-F." NARITAYA, 2009.
http://www.naritaya.jp/english/compendium/dictionary_02.html.

his daughter to the Shin'ei Girls' School in the Tsukiji neighborhood.[45]

Fujiu Teiko, Tama's older sister, was an English language scholar, and Tama had hopes of following a similar career path. However, Yaatsu was a poor businessman, who eventually wound up losing his entire fortune. This forced Tama to drop out of school and pursue a teaching certificate instead of following in her older sister's footsteps. She succeeded in earning her certificate and found work as a kindergarten teacher at the Morioka Normal School in 1889. Just three years later, the kindergarten shut down and Tama found herself seeking another source of income.[46]

The details of Tama's life after this point are sketchy and it is not known why she turned to storytelling in 1898. But she managed to join the *Yanagiha* (the Yanagiya school of rakugo) in 1901 and gained popularity as a performer in the Kyoto-Osaka area. She was performing at the yose in the Ushigome Ward in Tokyo in 1903 when the Japanese novelist, Ozaki Koyo, encountered her for the first time and recorded his impressions in his diary.[47]

In addition to her rakugo performances, Enjo also appeared on stage with Kawakami Otojiro's theater troupe in 1905. She met and

---

[45] "若柳燕嬢." Wikipedia. Wikimedia Foundation, September 21, 2020.
https://ja.wikipedia.org/wiki/%E8%8B%A5%E6%9F%B3%E7%87%95%E5%AC%A2.
[46] 明治～平成 新撰 芸能人物事典. "若柳 燕嬢とは." コトバンク.
https://kotobank.jp/word/%E8%8B%A5%E6%9F%B3%20%E7%87%95%E5%AC%A2-1674783.
[47] "若柳燕嬢."

married a student actor named Chiba Shuho, who later became a newspaper reporter. Enjo persevered and gave all of her earnings to her husband, but the marriage ended in 1906 due to Shuho's infidelity.

Enjo eventually opened an acting school for girls in Tokyo and married an actor named Shizuma Saburo. The name Wakayagi Enjo appeared on radio broadcast appearance records until 1945, but what became of the female storyteller afterwards is unknown.[48]

---

[48] "若柳燕嬢." Wikipedia. Wikimedia Foundation, September 21, 2020. https://ja.wikipedia.org/wiki/%E8%8B%A5%E6%9F%B3%E7%87%95%E5%AC%A2.

v. Sanyutei Encho

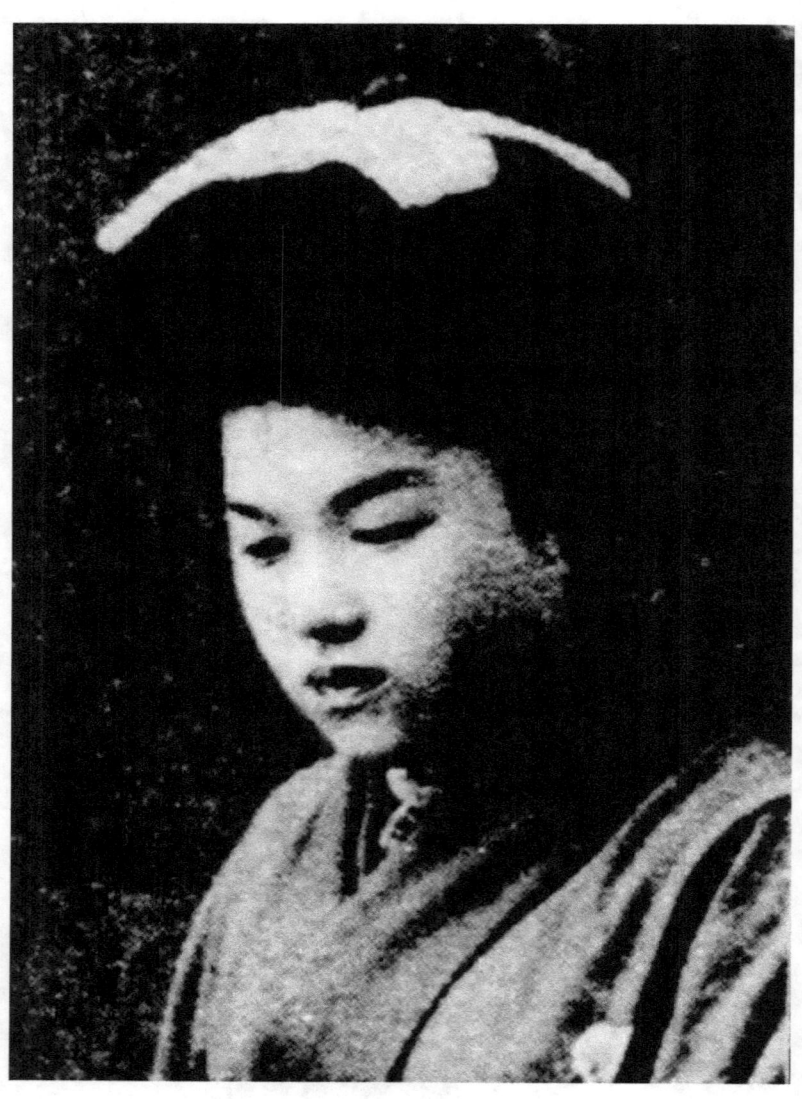

vi. Wakayagi Enjo

Living National Treasures

Ningen kokuho (Living National Treasure) is a Japanese term for those individuals certified as "Preservers of Important Intangible Cultural Properties."[49] Over the years, three rakugo performers have earned this designation from the Minister of Education, Culture, Sports, Science and Technology in the category of Drama /Classical Rakugo. They are Yanagiya Kosan V (1915-2002), designated in 1995; Katsura Beicho III (1925-2015), designated in 1996; and Yanagiya Kosanji X (1939-2021), designated in 2014.[50]

Yanagiya Kosan, the first rakugoka recognized as a living national treasure, was born in Nagano Prefecture in central Honshu. His father was a Tokyo-born farmer who left his home and moved to Nagano as there was no possibility that he would inherit the family's farm, which traditionally went to the eldest son. After suffering two major business failures, he uprooted his family from Nagano and settled them in Tokyo's Asakusa district where Kosan was raised from the age of three.

Kosan became an accomplished practitioner of the Kendo martial art and won the Tokyo City Kendo Tournament while still in high school. After graduation, he enrolled in evening classes at the Tokyo Municipal Commercial School, but he dropped out a short

---

[49] "Living National Treasure (Japan)." Wikipedia. Wikimedia Foundation, April 11, 2020. https://en.wikipedia.org/wiki/Living_National_Treasure_(Japan).
[50] "List of Living National Treasures of Japan (Performing Arts)," June 28, 2020. https://en.wikipedia.org/wiki/List_of_Living_National_Treasures_of_Japan_(performing_arts).

time later to pursue rakugo. He was working as a clerk in a law firm in 1933 and began studying rakugo under Yanagiya Kosan IV.

As luck would have it, Kosan was forced to temporarily pause his rakugo training after being drafted into the Third Regiment of The Imperial Japanese Army and he unwittingly took part in what is now known as the *Ni Ni-Roku Jiken* (the 2-26 Incident). The incident, which began on February 26, 1936, involved an attempted coup d'état organized by a group of young Imperial Japanese Army officers. These young men believed that the problems facing the nation were the result of Japan straying away from the essence of *kokutai* (the system of government involving the proper relationship between the Emperor, the people, and the state).

The insurrectionists called themselves the "Righteous Army" and adopted the slogan "Revere the Emperor, Destroy the Traitors." By leading a general uprising, they hoped to instigate a "Showa Restoration" (named after the Meiji Restoration of 1868) that would enable the Emperor to reclaim his authority and purge Japan of Western ideas and those who exploited the Japanese people.

During the siege, the Righteous Army assassinated several leading officials, including two former prime ministers. They managed to occupy the government center of Tokyo, but they failed to assassinate Prime Minister Keisuke Okada and secure control of the Imperial Palace. Facing overwhelming opposition as the army moved against them, the rebels surrendered on February 29. After a series of closed trials, 19 of the uprising's leaders were executed for mutiny and another 40 were imprisoned.

During the incident, Kosan was dispatched to occupy the Metropolitan Police Department with a machine gun in hand. He was following orders and unaware that a coup was planned. While staying at the rebel unit's camp, he performed the rakugo story, "Kohome" ("Complimenting a Child") to help raise the soldiers' morale. But tension at the camp was high and Kosan failed to make his audience laugh. He resumed his rakugo studies following his discharge in March 1939.

When his master, Kosan IV, suddenly passed away in 1947, he became the disciple of Katsura Bunraku VIII. He attained the final level of shinuchi in September 1950.

Two things set Kosan V apart as a rakugo performer, his cheerful performances and affable appearance. He was particularly adept at convincingly portraying traditional craftsmen in simple everyday scenarios such as eating soba noodles or drinking sake.[51] Once, while eating at a soba restaurant, he attracted the attention of the other patrons, who recognized him and watched in

---

[51] "'Rakugo' Storytelling Master Kosan Dies." The Japan Times, May 17, 2002.
https://www.japantimes.co.jp/news/2002/05/17/national/rakugo-storytelling-master-kosan-dies/.

anticipation as he ate his soba noodles. They wanted to see if he would eat his noodles in the same manner he did on stage. Not wanting to disappoint those who were watching him, Kosan attempted to duplicate his actions on stage. After he finished eating, he quietly confessed that he was unable to enjoy his noodles because he had been too focused on the manner in which he ate them.

Even as a cheerful performer, he was occasionally prone to sudden outbursts. In one instance, he was performing a story called, "Toki Soba" ("Time Noodles") at a yose and messed up his lines. During the part where the noodle salesman was supposed to tell the customer the time, Kosan mistakenly said nine instead of four. A surprised audience waited eagerly to see how he would recover from such a mistake. Highly embarrassed, he told the audience that this sort of thing had the potential to happen, repeated the punchline, and promptly marched off the stage.

He was also the master of telling stories which involved animals such as *tanuki* (racoon dogs) and foxes. One day, one of his disciples approached him and asked if he had any advice to give with regard to portraying a tanuki. Kosan simply responded, "Think and act just as a tanuki does."[52]

---

[52] Kanariya Eiraku. Email interview with author, September 17, 2020.

With the advent of television, Kosan's popularity skyrocketed after he appeared in a series of dramas and commercials. He also acted in a total of seventeen films between 1963 and 2013. In later years, his grandson, Yanagiya Karoku, appeared in commercials for the same tombstone company his grandfather had helped advertise on television, Sudo Sekizai.[53]

Karoku displayed a brilliance for the art of rakugo early in life and began his career at the age of fifteen. He attained shinuchi status when he was only twenty-two, becoming the youngest master rakugoka at the time. As he began to accept disciples, he questioned whether he should bother at such a young age. He approached his grandfather for advice and Kosan offered these words of wisdom, "Take on disciples because to teach is to learn." [54] Encouraged by his grandfather's words, Karoku continued to receive apprentices.

As president of the *Rakugo Kyokai* (The Rakugo Association) between 1972 and 1996, Kosan played a major role in promoting rakugo in postwar Tokyo and worked hard to modernize the organization.

Sadly, a brilliant career came to an end in February 2002. Kosan contracted influenza and was undergoing medical treatment at

---

[53] "Master Kosan Dies." Japan Times.
[54] "Rakugoka's Daily Life Verification Site Learned by Teaching 'Disciple Is a Master' ⇒ Rakugoka, Karoku Yanagiya." ダイヤモンド・オンライン, August 18, 2015. https://diamond.jp/articles/-/76841?page=4.

home when he passed away in his sleep. He was 87 years old. The rakugo world suffered two major blows with Kosan's passing. In October 2001, they said farewell to another prominent rakugo performer, Kokontei Shincho III, who died of liver cancer.[55]

Only one year after Kosan's designation as a national living treasure, Katsura Beicho became the second rakugo artist to receive the honor. Beicho's most significant achievement was reviving and refining the art of Kamigata style storytelling through his performances of long-forgotten classical stories, which he adapted for modern times.

He was also the first rakugoka to receive the *Bunka Kunsho* (Order of Culture) award in 2009. The award is conferred by the Emperor of Japan on Culture Day (November 3). It is given to people who have made contributions to further Japan's art, literature, science, and technology.

Beicho's birthplace was Dalian, Manchuria. He came from a long line of priests belonging to the Kusho Goryo-ten Shrine (also known as the Kamiya Tenjin Shrine) in the city of Himeji. When Beicho was five, his grandfather passed away, forcing his parents to return to Japan so his father could take his grandfather's position as priest at the shrine. Beicho himself trained for the

---

[55] Master Kosan Dies." Japan Times.

priesthood and briefly served at the shrine prior to relocating to Tokyo.

After graduating from high school in 1943, Beicho moved to Tokyo to study at the *Daito Bunka Gakuin* (Daito Cultural Academy). While still a student, he attended a rakugo event hosted by Masaoka Iruru, a novelist who studied rakugo under Sanyutei Enba III. Through Iruru, Beicho met Shofukutei Shokaku V and Katsura Yonenosuke III, the son of an Osaka movie theater owner.

Unfortunately, Beicho's enthusiasm for rakugo had to be put on hold when he was drafted into the military in February 1945. The next month, he was hospitalized with acute pyelonephritis (kidney infection) and was later transferred to a sanatorium to recuperate. It was around this time when he met rakugoka Tachibanano Ento, who happened to be visiting the hospital to console the patients. By the time Beicho was discharged on August 12, the Pacific War had already ended and he returned to his parents' home in Himeji. Rather than returning to the university, he found a job as an office worker in Kobe City and focused on hosting amateur and regular rakugo performances.

In September 1947, his friend, Yonenosuke, introduced him to Katsura Yonedanji IV. Yonedanji agreed to take him on as an apprentice, but Beicho's decision to go into rakugo was met with harsh criticism from his family. In order to appease them Beicho took a job at the Himeji Post Office, but he quit within a year to pursue rakugo full time.

After his debut and subsequent success as a rakugoka, Beicho became a diligent researcher, excavating long-forgotten stories such as "Tengu Sabaki" ("The Judgement of Tengu") and "Jigoku Bakkei Moja no Tawamure" ("Playful Guys in Hell"), and conducting extensive interviews with his predecessors in the rakugo world. [56]

Beicho was a skillful rakugoka and his makura, in particular, were perfectly masterful. The following short story, which involves a man browsing in a department store, was one he liked to tell before breaking into a tale about an antique shop, for instance.

―――

A man browsing in a department store came across a small pot priced higher than a larger-sized version and decided to ask the sales clerk about it.

"Why is the small pot more expensive than the big one?" he asked.

"The value of the pot does not depend on its size," the clerk explained, "it depends on the design. Look at the design of the

---

[56] "桂米朝 (3代目)." Wikipedia. Wikimedia Foundation, November 22, 2020. https://ja.wikipedia.org/wiki/%E6%A1%82%E7%B1%B3%E6%9C%9D_(3%E4%BB%A3%E7%9B%AE)#%E6%99%A9%E5%B9%B4.

small pot," the clerk continued. "It is much more profound, and you will be drawn to the design while you are looking at the pot."

"Is that right?" asked the man. "Let me see. Yes, you're right. If I look at it closely, it is as though I am drawn to the design."

"See? That's how it works," the clerk happily continued on. "The size does not matter. Now you know more about pots."

Just then, another clerk rushed in and said, "Sorry, I switched the price tags by mistake. The price for the small pot is affixed to the large one, and the price for the large pot is on the small one."[57]

In addition to working tirelessly to revive Kamigata rakugo, Beicho trained twenty-two rakugo disciples in his lifetime, including Katsura Shijaku II. He established his own production company, Beicho Office, in 1974, and authored or co-authored thirty-six books, appeared in various television and radio programs, and acted in six films between 1957 and 2009. Since both his father and his rakugo master passed away at the age of 55, Beicho was determined to leave his rakugo for future generations in as many books and records as possible before his 55th birthday. His original rakugo story, "Ichimon Bue" ("One Mon [Old

---

[57] Kanariya Eiraku. Email interview with author, September 17, 2020.

Japanese currency in circulation from 1336 until 1870.] Flute"), is highly valued and performed by other rakugo performers including those in Tokyo.

Always looking for an opportunity to make people laugh, Beicho often joked that since the kanji for his name could be translated to "U.S.-North Korea," he was startled every time he saw his name in the news. It was also highly unusual that his disciples affectionately referred to him by his nickname, "Chaachan." When Beicho's son (now Katsura Yonedanji) was small, he was unable to pronounce *otochan* (dad) and instead called his father *chaachan*. Over the years, the name stuck and became the nickname by which Beicho's disciples referred to him.

Unlike Kosan, he refused to appear in commercials and made only one exception, in 1983, when he recorded a public service announcement for a cornea donation center. Beicho made his last stage appearance in January 2013. His regular radio program ended in August that year, the same time he was admitted to a hospital suffering from pneumonia.[58] He passed away on March 19, 2015, from its complications. Upon learning of his passing,

---

[58] "'Rakugo' Classic Comic Storyteller Beicho Dies at 89." The Japan Times, March 20, 2015. https://www.japantimes.co.jp/news/2015/03/20/national/rakugo-classic-comic-storyteller-beicho-dies-89/.

fellow rakugo performer Katsura Utamaru lamented, "We lost the encyclopedia of the rakugo world!"[59]

After Beicho's designation as a national living treasure, eighteen years passed before another rakugoka was given the honor. He was Yanagiya Kosanji, the disciple of Yanagiya Kosan, the first rakugoka to be designated.

Kosanji was born in Shinjuku, Tokyo in 1939, to a family of teachers and educators. Having four sisters and being the only boy, he endured a strict upbringing. Less than perfect test scores were not tolerated. In defiance, he turned to rakugo.

While still in high school, he participated in and was judged the winner fifteen consecutive times on Tokyo Radio's *Shiroto Yose* (*Amateur Yose*). *Shiroto Yose*, which began in 1955, was a program where listeners actively competed and whose skill levels were evaluated by judges.

After graduating from high school, Kosanji failed to gain entry to the Tokyo Gakugei University and abandoned his studies in education all together. He turned to rakugo full time and apprenticed under Yanagiya Kosan V.

He rose to the second level of futatsume in 1963 and attained the final level of shinuchi three years later. He is regarded as the

---

[59] Kanariya Eiraku. Email interview with author, September 17, 2020.

master of the makura for his outstanding and highly interesting introductions to his stories.[60]

Kosanji was also an avid bowler. During his futatsume years, he was scheduled to give a performance in Numazu City, Shizuoka. He decided to bowl a game before his performance and was approached by a young woman. She pleaded with him to please stop fussing with television programs and focus more on rakugo. Kosanji was quite taken aback by this statement for he too had been thinking about doing less television work and focusing more on rakugo. He later learned that the young woman's name was Emiko and she worked at an inn called Umenoya.

Three years later when Kosanji was promoted to shinuchi, he sent Emiko his tenugui towel and sensu fan as gifts, but there was no response. He eventually learned that Emiko had passed away. The revelation deeply saddened Kosanji and he decided to pay tribute to her by immortalizing her name in a rakugo story. That story is called "Unagi no Taiko" ("Eels and the Male Geisha"). [61]

At times, it appears that the stories which surround rakugo storytellers are just as interesting as the ones they tell on stage. Kosanji's, of course, are no exception to this.

---

[60] 桂米朝（3代目）."（"Yanagiya Kosanji"). Wikipedia. Wikimedia Foundation, November 22, 2020. https://ja.wikipedia.org/wiki/%E6%A1%82%E7%B1%B3%E6%9C%9D_(3%E4%BB%A3%E7%9B%AE)#%E6%99%A9%E5%B9%B4.

[61] 桂米朝（3代目）."（"Yanagiya Kosanji"). Wikipedia.

Kosanji died of heart failure at his home in Tokyo on October 7, 2021. He was 81.

vii. Yanagiya Kosan V

viii. Katsura Beicho III

ix. Yanagiya Kosanji X

3. Kairakutei Black

> "Today's rakugoka do not teach, and instead [train] apprentices merely by making them clean the house before finally letting them give a zenza in a yose. It doesn't serve the apprentices any purpose, and there is no hope that rakugo will progress."
> —Kairakutei Black
> *Yomiuri Shimbun, 1896*

Since its beginning, rakugo had been performed strictly by Japanese storytellers. However, that tradition was finally broken in the early 1890s, when Henry James Black (1858–1923), performing under the name Kairakutei Black (快楽亭ブラック), became Japan's first foreign-born rakugoka.[62]

Henry was the eldest son of John Reddie Black, a Scottish publisher, journalist, photographer, and soloist. John hailed from a long line of Royal Navy officers, but he elected to pass up a career in the navy and relocated to Australia with his wife Elizabeth Charlotte in 1851.[63] Henry was born in Adelaide, Australia on

---

[62] "Kairakutei Black I." Wikipedia. Wikimedia Foundation, May 4, 2020. https://en.wikipedia.org/wiki/Kairakutei_Black_I.
[63] "J. R. Black," Wikipedia (Wikimedia Foundation, December 1, 2021), https://en.wikipedia.org/wiki/J._R._Black.；"明治時代に活躍した'元祖 快楽亭ブラックの人生 (Meiji Jidai Ni Katsuyaku Shita Ganzo Kairakuteiburakku No Jinsei)," Yokohama History Salon, March 26, 2018, https://yokohamasalon.link/wp-content/uploads/2018/06/tokushu201803.pdf.

December 22, 1858.⁶⁴ After several business failures, John embarked on a singing career, touring the Indo-Pacific region.⁶⁵ But earning a living as a soloist proved to be difficult and he resolved to return to England. He left Australia in 1861 and made a brief stopover in Nagasaki, Japan. It was the end of the Edo period and Japan was on the verge of modernization. John became captivated by Japan's readiness to learn from the West and decided to prolong his stay.⁶⁶

In 1864, he received an offer from Albert Hansard, the owner of the *Japan Herald* (one of the first English-language newspapers in Japan), to join his auction business in Yokohama. The following year, Hansard offered him a partnership in the newspaper. With a steady job in hand, John summoned his wife and son to join him in Yokohama.⁶⁷ Henry was only seven years old at the time. Just two years later, following Hansard's death, the partnership of Hansard and Black declared bankruptcy. Undeterred, John founded his own newspaper, the *Japan Gazette*, that same year.⁶⁸ Henry's younger brother, John Reddie Black Jr., was born in

---

⁶⁴ "Kairakutei Black I." Wikipedia.
⁶⁵ "J. R. Black," Wikipedia.
⁶⁶ Heinz Morioka and Miyoko Sasaki. Rakugo, the Popular Narrative Art of Japan. Page 256.
⁶⁷ "J. R. Black," Wikipedia.
⁶⁸ John Reddie Black (Biglobe), accessed March 14, 2022, http://www2s.biglobe.ne.jp/matu-emk/black.html.

Yokohama in 1867. Their younger sister, Elizabeth Pauline, was born in 1869.[69]

The Blacks left the foreign enclave in Yokohama in 1872 and settled in Tokyo.[70] That same year, John founded a Japanese-language newspaper, the *Nisshin Shinjishi* (日新真事誌). It was the first Japanese-language newspaper established by a foreigner. The first issue was published on April 23, 1872.[71] Fourteen-year-old Henry helped his father gather news and other materials for the paper by traveling back and forth between Tokyo and Yokohama on horseback. [72] Driven to provide a high quality newspaper published in Japanese, John obtained permission to publish government meeting notes and reports on policies. However, his open support of freedom of speech and social equality provoked the Meiji government to maneuver to silence him.[73]

The Japanese government relied on the cooperation of foreigners to help modernize and build a new Japan both before and after the Meiji Restoration. These foreigners were known as *oyatoi gaikokujin* (hired foreigners). By 1874, there were 520 such persons employed by the Japanese government for their specialized knowledge and

---

[69] Heinz, Morioka, and Sasaki Miyoko. "The Blue-Eyed Storyteller: Henry Black and His Rakugo Career." Page 134.
[70] Asakura-Ward, Toshiki. "A Bridge to the Near North: The 1980s Resurrection of Henry Black (1858-1923)," Western Sydney University, 2017. Page 23.
[71] "J. R. Black," Wikipedia.
[72] Heinz, Morioka, and Sasaki Miyoko. "The Blue-Eyed Storyteller: Henry Black and His Rakugo Career." Page 135.
[73] Asakura-Ward, Toshiki. "A Bridge to the Near North: The 1980s Resurrection of Henry Black. Page 21.

skills.⁷⁴ Most of these advisors were dismissed as soon as the Japanese authorities deemed that their services were no longer required.⁷⁵

In 1874, John was offered a position as an oyatoi gaikokujin by the Japanese government on the condition that he resign from the *Nisshin Shinjishi*. He accepted the proposal and became the foreign advisor to the Administrative Section of the *Sa-in* (the Left Government), a chamber of the *Daijo-kan* (also known as the Great Council of State, it was the highest organ of Japan's premodern Imperial government). A year later, new laws were introduced forbidding criticism of the government and excluding foreigners from editing Japanese-language newspapers (*Shinbunshi Jorei*). One week after the laws were implemented, John was transferred to a lesser position in the translation bureau, and soon thereafter he was dismissed.⁷⁶

John attempted to launch another newspaper, but he was unsuccessful under the new press regulations. Frustrated, he departed Japan in 1876 and settled in Shanghai, where he launched the *Shanghai Mercury* on April 17, 1879. John was suffering from stomach cancer when he rejoined his family in Japan later that

---

[74] "Foreign Government Advisors in Meiji Japan," Wikipedia (Wikimedia Foundation, March 2, 2022), https://en.wikipedia.org/wiki/Foreign_government_advisors_in_Meiji_Japan.
[75] Heinz, Morioka, and Sasaki Miyoko. "The Blue-Eyed Storyteller: Henry Black and His Rakugo Career." Page 135.
[76] "J. R. Black," Wikipedia.

year. [77] John Reddie Black passed away from a cerebral hemorrhage on June 11, 1880. His body was buried in the Yokohama Foreign Cemetery.[78]

Henry's mother was an English teacher and a devout Anglican. It is said that she engaged in missionary work in the Ogasawara Islands. She was also an accomplished piano player and often provided musical accompaniment for her husband during his recitals in Yokohama.[79] Henry apparently inherited his penchant for the stage from his parents, but his public performances drew the ire of his brother and sister.

Following his father's departure from Japan, Henry took to the stage and made his debut as a conjurer at the Yoshikawa Theater in Asakusa on July 16, 1876. It is likely that even though John had given musical recitals and participated in amateur dramatics in Yokohama, he would not have approved of Henry performing on stage. As a newspaper editor, John had denounced the yose performances which he regarded as "low entertainment."[80]

Soon thereafter, Henry was invited to make a political speech at the Yuraku Hall in Yurakucho. The man who extended the

---

[77] Heinz, Morioka, and Sasaki Miyoko. "The Blue-Eyed Storyteller: Henry Black and His Rakugo Career." Page 138.
[78] John Reddie Black (Biglobe).
[79] "明治時代に活躍した '元祖 快楽亭ブラックの人生 (Meiji Jidai Ni Katsuyaku Shita Ganzo Kairakuteiburakku No Jinsei)," Yokohama History Salon.
[80] Heinz, Morioka, and Sasaki Miyoko. "The Blue-Eyed Storyteller: Henry Black and His Rakugo Career."Page 138.

invitation was a retired naval officer named Hori Ryuta, a friend of his father.[81] While engaged in political speechmaking, Henry met and befriended Shorin Hakuen II (1832-1905), a prominent kodan storyteller who was highly regarded for his *gundan* (historic and political tales).[82] The roles of speech-making and storytelling were vital in those days as nearly eighty percent of Tokyo's residents were illiterate. They relied on the storytellers to disperse relevant news and knowledge.[83]

Kodan storytelling, like Kamigata rakugo, is usually performed kneeling behind a small wooden table, using a wooden clapper or a special fan called *hari-ohgi* to mark the rhythm of the recitation.[84] An illustration of Kairakutei Black published in *Au Japon Les Raconteurs Publics* in 1899 depicts him sitting behind a large table.

After receiving coaching from Hakuen, Henry made his next stage appearance at Yokohama's Kiyotake yose theater in January 1879, where he delivered a talk in the kodan style about Joan of Arc and Charles I. Kodan storytelling was actually more popular than

---

[81] Heinz, Morioka, and Sasaki Miyoko. "The Blue-Eyed Storyteller: Henry Black and His Rakugo Career.". Page 138.
[82] Heinz, Morioka and Sasaki, Miyoko. Rakugo, the Popular Narrative Art of Japan. Page 256. ; "Hakuen Shorin." prabook.com. https://prabook.com/web/hakuen.shorin/3747055.
[83] Asakura-Ward, Toshiki. "A Bridge to the Near North: The 1980s Resurrection of Henry Black. Page 29.
[84] "Kōdan." Wikipedia. Wikimedia Foundation, October 12, 2018. https://en.wikipedia.org/wiki/K%C5%8Ddan.

rakugo during the early Meiji era. With Hakuen's help, Henry soon became a novelty in Tokyo.[85]

In the spring of 1880, Henry delivered a series of political speeches at various train stations along the Tokaido line.[86] Until 1899, foreigners living in Japan were prohibited from traveling beyond thirty miles of the treaty ports, unless they were contracted by the government. Any expedition outside of this boundary required special permission and a passport.[87] Treaty ports were port cities opened to foreign trade by the unequal treaties forced upon Japan by the Western powers. Henry later managed to bypass this restriction by becoming a naturalized Japanese citizen.

At the end of April, however, Henry was forced to give up his public speechmaking after the *Shukai jorei* (Law Regulating Assemblies) was adopted.[88] Hakuen and the other *kodanshi* (kodan performers) circumvented the government's public assembly laws by disguising their political speeches as gundan and delivering them at yose theaters. In 1883, Henry joined a gundan group headed by storyteller Hogyusha Torin and gave performances in Osaka.[89]

---

[85] Heinz, Morioka and Sasaki, Miyoko. Rakugo, the Popular Narrative Art of Japan. Page 256.
[86] Heinz, Morioka, and Sasaki Miyoko. "The Blue-Eyed Storyteller: Henry Black and His Rakugo Career." Page 138.
[87] Martha Chaiklin, "Treaty Ports," Treaty Ports | Japan Module (University of Pittsburgh), accessed March 21, 2022, https://www.japanpitt.pitt.edu/essays-and-articles/history/treaty-ports.
[88] Heinz, Morioka, and Sasaki Miyoko. "The Blue-Eyed Storyteller: Henry Black and His Rakugo Career." Page 139.
[89] Heinz, Morioka, and Sasaki Miyoko. "The Blue-Eyed Storyteller: Henry Black and His Rakugo Career." Page 139.

Henry's family and other members of the foreign community did not support his public activities for they feared that his association with actors and storytellers would tarnish his family's reputation. Wanting to appease them, Henry temporarily put aside his public speaking activities and opened up an English-language school in Kyobashi.[90] He also published a 100-page English-Japanese conversation guide. Henry's mother and sister were very pleased with his latest venture and they both volunteered to help teach English at the school.[91] However, around 1886, Japan's efforts to renegotiate the unequal treaties and end extraterritoriality were delayed, giving rise to anti-foreign sentiment. As a result, the popularity of learning English declined and Henry's school was bankrupted. Left without a source of income, he once again turned to the stage.[92]

In early 1890, Henry became popular on the kabuki stage portraying female characters mainly.[93] In September of the same year, he joined the *Sanyuha* (the Sanyutei school of rakugo).[94] According to Henry's own account, a *gorin* (a manager for rakugo performers) named Ennosuke extended the invitation and the

---

[90] Heinz, Morioka, and Sasaki Miyoko. "The Blue-Eyed Storyteller: Henry Black and His Rakugo Career." Page 139.
[91] 明治時代に活躍した'元祖 快楽亭ブラックの人生 (Meiji Jidai Ni Katsuyaku Shita Ganzo Kairakuteiburakku No Jinsei)," Yokohama History Salon.
[92] Heinz, Morioka, and Sasaki Miyoko. "The Blue-Eyed Storyteller: Henry Black and His Rakugo Career." Page 139.
[93] "Kairakutei Black I." Wikipedia.
[94] Japan Today, "Henry Black (1859-1923): Japan's First Gaijin Talent," Japan Today, September 13, 2011, https://japantoday.com/category/features/opinions/henry-black-1859-1923-japan%25e2%2580%2599s-first-gaijin-talent.

school's leaders, Sanyutei Encho and Sanyutei Ensho IV, willingly gave their consent. Six months after joining the Sanyuha, Henry adopted the stage name Kairakutei (Pleasure) Black and enjoyed a thriving career on stage alternating between rakugo, kodan, and kabuki performances.[95] Japanese audiences were astounded by the fact that Henry was not only fluent in Japanese, but also articulate enough to make them laugh.[96]

Several of his narratives were published including his version of the humorous English story "Biiru no Kakenomi" ("The Beer Drinking Bet") which appeared in the March 1891 edition of the yose magazine, *Hyakkaen*.[97] The story is about a man who accepts a challenge to drink fifteen bottles of beer in one sitting. However, he stops by a pub on the way in order to confirm that he can actually pull off the challenge. This story, now known as "Tameshi Zake" ("Test Sake"), is still being performed by rakugoka today.[98] You will find the script at the end of this book.

In June 1892, "Iwade Ginko Chishio no Tegata" ("Bloodstained Handprint at the Iwade Bank") was printed in the kodan-rakugo journal *Azuma Nishiki*. The story caused quite a sensation at the time because it was the first detective tale to use forensic

---

[95] Heinz, Morioka, and Sasaki Miyoko. "The Blue-Eyed Storyteller: Henry Black and His Rakugo Career." Page 141.
[96] "Kairakutei Black I." Wikipedia.
[97] Heinz, Morioka, and Sasaki Miyoko. "The Blue-Eyed Storyteller: Henry Black and His Rakugo Career." Page 142.
[98] "Kairakutei Black I." Wikipedia.

fingerprinting. [99] The first person to advocate the usage of fingerprinting for identification purposes was British physician Dr. Henry Faulds. Faulds was working at the Tsukiji Hospital in Tokyo in 1878, when he noticed traces of fingerprints preserved in clay pottery unearthed during an excavation. His research was published in the October 1880 issue of the English scientific journal *Nature*.[100] In Henry's narrative, the president of Iwade Bank takes in a street urchin, enrolls him in school, and later hires him as an employee at the bank. The president's daughter falls in love with the young man and wishes to marry him. The president opposes the marriage and fires the young man after he shows no signs of relinquishing his love. Several days later, the president is found murdered in his office. A sheet of white paper stained presumably with the murderer's bloody handprint was left on a table at the crime scene. The president's younger brother, who happens to be an attorney, enters the scene and is shown the bloody print. Upon seeing it, he responds, "Perhaps this won't seem like evidence to you, but in my opinion it is without a doubt the most important evidence we've got. We know the criminal with this."[101]

As Henry's popularity rose, his family grew increasingly more hostile toward him. During a performance in 1895, Henry's

---

[99] Heinz, Morioka, and Sasaki Miyoko. "The Blue-Eyed Storyteller: Henry Black and His Rakugo Career." Page 144.
[100] Seth Jacobowitz and Ranpo Edogawa, in The Edogawa Rampo Reader (Fukuoka: Kurodahan Press, 2008), p. 24.
[101] Seth Jacobowitz and Ranpo Edogawa, in The Edogawa Rampo Reader (Fukuoka: Kurodahan Press, 2008), p. 24.

brother, John, unexpectedly burst in and succeeded in bringing the show to an early end by loudly yelling out insults and calling him an embarrassment to the family. Henry stood up before the shocked audience, left the stage, and announced that his career was on hiatus.[102]

In 1892, Henry was adopted as a *mukoyoshi* (son-in-law adopted as an heir) by a *wagashiya* (confectionary shop) owner named Ishii Mine. It is common practice even today for Japanese families to adopt an adult man as a daughter's husband and give him the family's surname. Henry married Ishii's daughter Aka and became a naturalized Japanese citizen. He then legally changed his name to Ishii Black.[103] When the Ishii family registered the adoption in Tokyo Prefecture, the Ministry of Home Affairs was obliged to conduct a behavioral investigation of Henry. The Metropolitan Police Department responded to the request and reported that even though Henry was married to Aka, he was living with a younger man named Takamatsu Motosuke. The police concluded the report by stating, "there is no evidence of misbehavior."[104] Henry and Aka were divorced shortly thereafter. Due to his

---

[102] "Kairakutei Black I." Wikipedia. ; Japan Today, "Henry Black (1859-1923): Japan's First Gaijin Talent."; "明治時代に活躍した'元祖 快楽亭ブラックの人生 (Meiji Jidai Ni Katsuyaku Shita Ganzo Kairakuteiburakku No Jinsei)," Yokohama History Salon.
[103] "Kairakutei Black I." Wikipedia. ; Japan Today, "Henry Black (1859-1923): Japan's First Gaijin Talent."; Heinz, Morioka, and Sasaki Miyoko. "The Blue-Eyed Storyteller: Henry Black and His Rakugo Career." Page 141.
[104] "快楽亭ブラック (初代) (Kairakutei Black (1st Generation))," Wikipedia (Wikimedia Foundation, October 30, 2021),
https://ja.wikipedia.org/wiki/%E5%BF%AB%E6%A5%BD%E4%BA%AD%E3%83%96%E3%83%A9%E3%83%83%E3%82%AF_(%E5%88%9D%E4%BB%A3).

lifestyle, Henry was childless and he adopted a full-blooded Japanese boy named Seikichi (known also by his stage name Hosuko). The boy eventually became one of Henry's disciples.[105] A rare rakugo catalog dating back to 1916 lists six of Henry's disciples including Hosuko, Hare, Rakumatsu, Kairaku, Kairyu, and Rakusho.[106]

On August 11, 1900, Henry's friend and greatest supporter Sanyutei Encho passed away. By this time, Henry's career had already begun to spiral downward. He did not have much support from the younger members of the Sanyuha who could not accept having such a highly critical foreigner among their ranks. They did not openly criticize Henry, but they began to ignore him as much as possible.[107]

In 1903, Frederick William Gaisberg (1873–1951), a recording engineer for the Gramophone Company in the United Kingdom, came to Japan. His assignment was to make recordings of traditional Japanese instruments, *nagauta* (traditional Japanese music played on the shamisen and used in kabuki theater), and *minyo* (Japanese folk songs) from various areas of Japan. Henry was tasked with helping to coordinate the project. Gaisberg was

---

[105] 明治時代に活躍した'元祖 快楽亭ブラックの人生 (Meiji Jidai Ni Katsuyaku Shita Ganzo Kairakuteiburakku No Jinsei)," Yokohama History Salon.
[106] Heinz, Morioka, and Sasaki Miyoko. "The Blue-Eyed Storyteller: Henry Black and His Rakugo Career." Page 141.
[107] Heinz, Morioka, and Sasaki Miyoko. "The Blue-Eyed Storyteller: Henry Black and His Rakugo Career." Page 146.

delighted to be paired with an individual who was fluent in both English and Japanese. Ultimately, Henry helped Gaisberg produce 273 records and released nine recordings of his own.[108]

One of the stories Henry recorded was "A Laugh at a Soba Noodle Restaurant," an account of his visit to a noodle restaurant when he was very hungry. In the story, Henry visits a soba noodle restaurant and orders three bowls of tempura noodles and four bowls of meat noodles. He waits a long time for his order to arrive, but it never does. He becomes agitated when he notices that customers who arrived at the restaurant after he did are being served. He assumes that he is being discriminated against because he is a foreigner, and he confronts the waitress. The waitress tells him that she was simply waiting for his friends to arrive before serving his order. He responds by telling the waitress that he had planned to eat all seven bowls by himself. After seeing the shocked look on the waitress' face, he runs away embarrassed.

In his later years, Henry's creativity was diminished by depression and psychological problems. He drifted away from rakugo and increasingly performed as a conjurer, hypnotist, and narrator of short stories.[109] He even tried his hand as a *benshi* (a performer who

---

[108] "快楽亭ブラック (初代) (Kairakutei Black (1st Generation))," Wikipedia.
[109] Heinz, Morioka, and Sasaki Miyoko. "The Blue-Eyed Storyteller: Henry Black and His Rakugo Career." Page 149.

provided live narration for silent films).[110] On September 25, 1908, the *Yamato Shimbun* reported that he had attempted suicide by ingesting arsenic. The incident had taken place during a tour of the Kansai region. Henry's colleagues found him writhing in pain backstage at the Ebisu Theater after a performance.[111]

Henry was largely ignored by the press after this incident, but his name was still included among the Sanyuha members in 1911, 1913, and 1917. Between 1916 and 1917, he traveled to Shanghai and Hong Kong, where he performed on stage with his adopted son Hosuko and his daughter-in-law, Rosa.[112] Henry officially retired from show business in the summer of 1920, and withdrew to a house in Meguro. Although his mother and sister lived nearby in Shirokane, there was never any contact between them. When their mother passed away in 1922, his sister never bothered to inform him. Henry was overwhelmed with grief and burst into tears when he eventually learned of his mother's passing.[113]

On September 1, 1923, what became known as The Great Kanto Earthquake struck the Yokohama and Tokyo areas. The initial jolt was followed a few minutes later by a 40-foot-high tsunami. The

---

[110] Heinz, Morioka and Sasaki, Miyoko. Rakugo, the Popular Narrative Art of Japan. Page 258.;"Benshi," Wikipedia (Wikimedia Foundation, November 22, 2021), https://en.wikipedia.org/wiki/Benshi.
[111] Heinz, Morioka, and Sasaki Miyoko. "The Blue-Eyed Storyteller: Henry Black and His Rakugo Career." Page 149.
[112] Heinz, Morioka, and Sasaki Miyoko. "The Blue-Eyed Storyteller: Henry Black and His Rakugo Career." Page 150.
[113] Heinz, Morioka, and Sasaki Miyoko. "The Blue-Eyed Storyteller: Henry Black and His Rakugo Career." Page 151.

ensuing fires burned everything in their path. The death toll was a staggering 140,000.[114] Henry managed to survive the earthquake, but he passed away eighteen days later from a cerebral hemorrhage just as his father had done 43 years earlier.[115] His sister had his body buried next to their parents in the Yokohama Foreign Cemetery.[116]

Due to the calamity and chaos caused by the earthquake, Henry's death passed unnoticed in the rakugo community.[117] Six months later, Sekine Mokuan, a kodan and rakugo expert, published a survey of rakugo and kodan, past and present. In it, he mentioned Kairakutei Black, listing him both as a narrator of Western stories and as a conjurer. At the end of the short report, he wrote, "In recent years, Black has appeared as an interpreter of silent movies. But nowadays foreigners are no longer such an attraction as before. Black has withdrawn his shingle. He is still alive and is spending the rest of his days without worries somewhere in a remote village." [118] According to Toshiki Asakura-Ward, the author of "A Bridge to the Near North: The 1980s Resurrection of Henry Black," a fire destroyed the publishing house and Sekine

---

[114] Joshua Hammer, "The Great Japan Earthquake of 1923," Smithsonian.com (Smithsonian Institution, May 1, 2011), https://www.smithsonianmag.com/history/the-great-japan-earthquake-of-1923-1764539/.
[115] 明治時代に活躍した '元祖 快楽亭ブラックの人生 (Meiji Jidai Ni Katsuyaku Shita Ganzo Kairakuteiburakku No Jinsei)," Yokohama History Salon.
[116] Heinz, Morioka, and Sasaki Miyoko. "The Blue-Eyed Storyteller: Henry Black and His Rakugo Career." Page 151.
[117] Asakura-Ward, Toshiki. "A Bridge to the Near North: The 1980s Resurrection of Henry Black. Page 45.
[118] Heinz, Morioka, and Sasaki Miyoko. "The Blue-Eyed Storyteller: Henry Black and His Rakugo Career." Page 151.

Mokuan passed away two months later. Consequently, the publisher did not have the means to confirm whether Henry was alive or dead.[119]

These days, Henry Black may be obscure, but he is not entirely forgotten. Henry's distant relative, Sudo Haruko, and others gather at his grave every year on the anniversary of his death and hold a small memorial service for rakugo's first foreign-born son.

---

[119] Asakura-Ward, Toshiki. "A Bridge to the Near North: The 1980s Resurrection of Henry Black. Page 46.

x. *Kairakutei Black depicted in Au Japon Les Raconteurs Publics (Hasegawa Takejiro, 1899)*

xi. *Grave of Kairakutei Black in Yokohama (Kanariya Eiraku)*

The Transformation of Rakugo

4. Rakugo During the War Years

> "Listen to rakugo. It is filled with wisdom on how to survive this world."
> —Katsura Beicho (1925-2015)

As Japan inched closer toward political totalitarianism and ultra-nationalism during the war years, countless institutions — including rakugo — were affected. The playful wit and unpretentious humor that typically characterized the art form gave way to stories which glorified the feats of the Imperial Japanese forces. These tales, which were collectively called *kokusaku rakugo* (national policy rakugo), were penned by contemporary rakugo performers such as Hayashiya Shozo VII at the request of the military.

Given rakugo's mass appeal, the military seized the opportunity to capitalize on it and the rakugo community sheepishly obliged. New narratives such as "Shussei Iwai" ("Celebrating Soldiers Departing to the Front"), "Boku Enshu" ("Air-Raid Drill"), and "Shimero Jugo" ("Bolster the Home Front") served to encourage support for the military and Japan's war efforts.

However, the new wartime stories lacked the one element which appealed most to rakugo fans, the aspect in which common folk ridiculed authority. As a result, these stories failed to attract an extensive audience and were abandoned after the war.

This was also the time when rakugo performers in Tokyo were forced to refrain from performing 53 classical stories, including "Takao" ("Takao, the Oiran") and "Kowakare" ("Separation from a Child"), which had been labeled as *kin-en rakugo* (prohibited rakugo). [120]

Although *ken-etsu* (censorship) had existed in Japan since the Edo period, censors exercised a particularly heavy hand during the war years from the Japanese invasion of Manchuria in 1931 to the end of World War II in 1945. Naturally, anything deemed detrimental to the war effort was banned and the ban was extended to include rakugo.

Wartime censors shared a belief that rakugo stories about love and stories that seemed effeminate would weaken the fighting spirit of the people. Therefore, of the various popular texts used by the rakugoka, they disallowed fifty-three stories. These stories were about the pleasure quarters, alcohol, and mistresses, all of which were deemed demoralizing and degenerate by the censors. Stories such as "Akegarasu" ("The Rooster Crows"), "Gonin mawashi"

---

[120] "VOX POPULI: 'Rakugo' in Wartime Japan Still Serves as a Cautionary Tale." The Asahi Shimbun, August 15, 2020. http://www.asahi.com/ajw/articles/13638016.

("Making the Rounds"), and "Miiratori" ("Hunting Mummies"), which had been considered masterpieces of Edo literature, were all prohibited.

"Akegarasu" was one of several stories that were banned due to their settings. It is a story about a father who asks his servants to trick his son, Tokijiro, into going to the pleasure quarter under the pretense of taking him to a temple for seclusion. When they arrive and Tokijiro discovers the plot, the servants convince him not to leave by telling him that the guards at the entrance won't allow him to leave without the group he arrived with. He reluctantly stays and drinks with them, but refuses to see the oiran. Afterwards, he is led to bed drunk and has a good time. When morning comes, he refuses to leave.

The story "Gonin mawashi" also takes place in the pleasure quarter. Seikichi, an employee at the pleasure quarter, gets accosted by four customers who are waiting for the oiran, Kisegawa. Seikichi searches for Kisegawa and finds her with her favorite client. Kisegawa tricks her client, so he antes up the money to pay the refunds to the four men waiting for her and his own refund. She then commands him to leave.[121]

---

[121] "Fallen Words." Wikipedia. Wikimedia Foundation, November 30, 2020. https://en.wikipedia.org/wiki/Fallen_Words.

"Miiratori" centers around a father who tries to coax his son back home after a long period of wantonness in the pleasure quarter. Every single person he sends to retrieve him ends up becoming corrupted and remains in the pleasure quarter. So, rather than bringing back the mummy, they all become mummies themselves.[122]

The censorship of these stories deeply impacted the rakugoka who enjoyed telling them and relied on them as a means for earning a living. Then, a famous rakugo critic named Nomura Mumeian made an off-the-cuff suggestion that they erect a tomb for the banned stories on the grounds of Honpo-ji, a temple in Tokyo's Asakusa district.

The storytellers jumped at the suggestion, and in 1941 they erected a stone monument called *Hanashi Zuka* at Honpo-ji Temple. They inscribed the words "Mourning the buried masterpieces" on it and placed the texts of the forbidden stories and their own sensu beneath it. [123]

After Tokyo and Honpo-ji were significantly damaged by the Allied bombing campaigns during World War II, the rakugoka came together once again and proposed rebuilding the temple. Two hundred storytellers contributed one stone block each to build a fence around the temple. They managed to erect a fence

---
[122] Brau, *Raguko*. Page 11.
[123] "VOX POPULI: 'Rakugo.

measuring approximately seven feet high and almost thirty feet long. Each stone block bears the name of its contributor.

When the war ended, so did the ban on the stories. A revival festival was held in September 1946, and the previously prohibited stories were once again shared with the people gathered in front of the Hanashi Zuka monument. Today, rakugo storytellers still visit the monument and offer their prayers for the unfortunate stories. There is also an annual rakugo show held at the temple called *Kin-en rakugo wo kiku kai* (*A Show to Listen to Banned Stories*). It is one way to remind their audiences of what happened during the war.

Annually, on August 31st, the *Rakugo Geijutsu Kyokai* (the Rakugo Arts Association) also presents a performance of the banned stories at the Asakusa Engei Hall. It is customary for everyone to travel to the Honpo-ji temple at the conclusion of the program and pray.[124]

The censorship of rakugo stories during the war years was not limited to the performers in Tokyo. In September 1945, ten entertainers belonging to the Yoshimoto Kogyo agency established what was known as the *Engei Jishuku Doshi Kai* (the Self-Restraint

---

[124] Yu, A. C. "Kamigata Rakugo. (上方落語)."

xii. Hanashi Zuka monument in Tokyo (Kanariya Eiraku)

Hanashi Zuka

This mound was built during the Pacific war in 1941, at that time, comic storytellers were forced to eliminate some of comic stories from their program in theaters. They selected 53 comic stories about the pleasure quarters, sake, a mistress, etc. and announced that they would not play these subjects of comic stories anymore, thereby showing their attitude toward to wartime to the government. Some of comic stories abolished were "Akegarasu(A crow in the morning)", "Gonin mawashi(Rolling by five persons)" and "Miiratori (Mummy hunting)" which were said to be the masterpieces of Edo literature, however these stories have never been played thereafter.

This mound was built in remembrance and memory of these masterpieces of comic stories and the deceased storytellers by the Rakugo association and all comic storytellers, etc. and scripts of the comic stories abolished were stored in the mound.

After the war, the revival festival of abolished plays was held in front of the mound in September 1946. Scripts of comic stories played in wartime are stored in the mound now instead of what was stored before.

xiii. Storytellers' Wall (Kanariya Eiraku)

Committee of Entertainment). Of the ten, only one was a rakugo storyteller. Following the example set in Tokyo, the group devoted two months to reviewing and selecting various scripts that were not in line with the national policy at the time. They focused mainly on comedy scripts, and rakugo was included among the stories that were scrutinized. In the end, the committee selected 140 rakugo stories to be banned, which was significantly higher than the number of stories selected in Tokyo. Naturally, these stories were about drinking, burglars, mistresses, and gamblers. Among them were "Yoriai-zake" ("Drinking Together"), "Kama-doro" ("Burglar of a Pot"), "Go-doro" ("Go Game and a Burglar"), and "Goke-goroshi" ("Killing a Widow").

Katsura Mikisuke II (1884-1943), the only rakugoka on the committee, was primarily responsible for selecting the stories to be banned. He included a broader range of topics in the selection process than those that were considered by the censors in Tokyo. Mikisuke later remarked that since the Kamigata rakugo repertoire consisted of 400 stories, it took him a considerable amount of time to narrow down the list to the 140 stories to be excluded.[125]

The war's profound impact also touched the many yose operating in Tokyo and Osaka at the time. Intense bombing operations over Tokyo and the resulting fires caused some of the yose to burn to

---

[125] Gomi, Makoto. 『藝能懇話』第二十一号 特集 上方落語史考―橋本礼一論文集 (2016(平成28)年 大阪藝能懇話会/ "Gei Nō Konwa" Dai Nijūichigō Tokushū Kamigata Rakugo-Shi Kō — Hashimoto Reiichi Ronbun-Shū., Page 213. August 2021.

the ground. The Ningyocho Suehiro managed to survive the raids, but the Suzumoto Engeijo and Suehiro-tei in Shinjuku were completely destroyed. The intensification of the war also caused the yose in Osaka to be shuttered. Later, an air raid on March 13, 1945, reduced them all to ashes. Without a place to perform, many rakugoka held storytelling sessions in rural areas and in the cities of Kobe and Kyoto, where there were relatively few air raids. Other rakugoka traveled to Manchuria to entertain the Japanese troops.

Some of these storytellers joined groups of entertainers known as the *Warawashi-tai* (Funny Corps) and entertained the soldiers on the battlefields of China during World War II. The Warawashi-tai was made up of stand-up comedians, musicians, magicians, and rakugo and kodan storytellers. These entertainers received a warm welcome from the Japanese soldiers who were hungry for entertainment and something to take their weary minds off the war.[126]

For the performers, conditions on the battlegrounds were both dangerous and taxing. They had difficulty adjusting to such things as the modest meals they were served, oftentimes leaving the scarce food uneaten. One rakugoka, however, was an exception. His name was Yanagiya Kingoro. Kingoro had previously served

---

[126] Yu, A. C. "Kamigata Rakugo."

in the military and was fully aware of what it was like to be out on the battlefield; he never complained or left food uneaten.

Not all rakugo storytellers who travelled abroad to entertain the troops belonged to the Warawashi-tai. Kokontei Shinsho V and Sanyutei Ensho VI both journeyed to Manchuria in 1945, and they remained there for two years before returning to Japan. Their story was eventually brought to the stage as a musical drama, "Ensho to Shinsho" ("Ensho and Shinsho") [127] by a leading Japanese playwright, Inoue Hisashi.

Kokontei Shinsho, one of the leading post-war rakugo performers, had a career which spanned the late Meiji period through the Showa period.

Born in Tokyo's Kanda Ward, Shinsho was the fifth son of Minobe Moriyuki, a descendant of a high-ranking samurai who served the Tokugawa shogunate of feudal Japan. After the Meiji Restoration, however, the samurai class became obsolete and their source of income dissipated, thrusting Shinsho's family into poverty.

In 1901, at the age of eleven, Shinsho was expelled from elementary school and became an indentured servant. He was sent to work in a printing company in what is now Seoul, Korea, but he

---

[127] "Hakone Gora Hotel Playhouse." Hakone Gora Hotel, 2005. https://www.nntt.jac.go.jp/english/season/s265e/s265e.html.

managed to escape. By 1904, he was back in Japan, living in Tokyo's Asakusa Ward.

Shinsho traveled to Manchuria with fellow rakugoka Sanyutei Ensho and a manzai comedian named Sakano Hiroshi. When the war ended, Shinsho and Ensho were stranded in Manchuria, unable to return to Japan. For about two years, the two rakugo entertainers endured a life and death existence while waiting for the rescue ship from Japan to arrive. Shincho finally set foot on Japanese soil on January 12, 1947.

His return was reported in the newspapers, giving his career the much-needed momentum to boost his popularity as a rakugoka and a talent featured on various radio programs. In June 1956, he published his autobiography; but since he was unable to read and write well due to his lack of education, the book was written by his disciple, Kingentei Umanosuke.[128]

Sanyutei Ensho VI is considered to be one of the top masters of the Showa era rakugo world. He abandoned his ambition to become a dancer in order to help his family financially after his stepfather, Sanyutei Ensho V, passed away in 1941. In 1945, he inherited the

---

[128] "古今亭志ん生（5代目）(Kokontei Shinsho (5th Generation))." Wikipedia. Wikimedia Foundation, November 28, 2020.
https://ja.wikipedia.org/wiki/%E5%8F%A4%E4%BB%8A%E4%BA%AD%E5%BF%97%E3%82%93%E7%94%9F_(5%E4%BB%A3%E7%9B%AE).

name Sanyutei Ensho VI, which was recommended by Ichiryusai Teizan VI, the chairman of the Rakugo Association.

Ensho became Kokontei Imasuke V's replacement on the Manchuria trip, when Imasuke's mother suddenly passed away preventing him from joining Shinsho. In 1947, while still stranded in Manchuria, he married a local Japanese woman, ignoring the fact that he already had a wife and family in Japan. This caused Shinsho to feel abandoned and he grew to resent Ensho. He later told Japanese arts critic, Koyama Kan'o (Koyama Akimoto), "I thought I'd kill such a ruthless guy, but he apologized to me at the yose, so I stopped killing him."[129]

Ensho eventually returned to Japan, and those who saw him perform at the yose said that he had become a better performer. Ensho himself claimed that the hardships he experienced in Manchuria lived in his art. He spent the rest of his career searching for stories containing laughter and tears instead of trying to make the audience laugh without cause.[130]

After World War II, the rakugoka who were still alive returned to their cities. Still, many who had been performing in Tokyo and Osaka before the war had been evacuated and their whereabouts

---

[129] "三遊亭圓生（6代目）(Sanyutei Ensho VI)." Wikipedia. Wikimedia Foundation, December 21, 2020.
https://ja.wikipedia.org/wiki/%E4%B8%89%E9%81%8A%E4%BA%AD%E5%9C%93%E7%94%9F_(6%E4%BB%A3%E7%9B%AE).
[130] "三遊亭圓生（6代目）(Sanyutei Ensho VI)." Wikipedia.

were unknown. The entertainment district in Osaka wasted no time in rebuilding, but the yose were replaced with movie theaters, which still left the storytellers without a place to perform.

In the fall of 1946, Shofukutei Shokaku V gathered all the rakugo performers he could locate and they began giving free performances. Their first show was held in the charred remains of an elementary school. To attract an audience, they hung a sign on the front gate stating that the show was free and open to all.

In time, the number of rakugo storytellers began to increase and rakugo once again gained popularity among the common people.[131]

---

[131] Ogita, Kiyoshi, and Sadao Osada. "Intabyu: Shitenno Wagashi o Kataru." Kamigata geino 93 (November 1986): 24.

xiv. Kokontei Shinsho V

xv. Sanyutei Ensho VI

5. Rakugo Beyond the Yose

> "We rakugoka make you happy by telling stories.
> The most important thing is to help the audience visualize the
> story by painting the scene and delivering it."
> —Katsura Utamaru (1936-2018)

Although the popularity of rakugo had been declining after World War II, it did have a surprising resurgence in the 1950s and 60s thanks in part to a thriving working class and the technological advances of radio and television.

Japan was one of the first countries in the world to have an experimental television service in 1939. With the start of the Pacific War, the experimentation was halted and regular television broadcasts did not take place until 1951.[132] Then, the commercial broadcasting explosion occurred, starting with the re-establishment of the Japan Broadcasting Corporation (NHK) under the terms of the Broadcast Law on June 1, 1950. On December 27, 1950, the New Japan Broadcasting Company was founded. The company commenced radio broadcasting from the Hankyu Department Store on September 1, 1951. On December 1,

---

[132] "Television in Japan," Academic Dictionaries and Encyclopedias, accessed March 13, 2022, https://en-academic.com/dic.nsf/enwiki/11643185.

1956, NJB founded Osaka Television Co., Ltd. NJB was renamed Mainichi Broadcasting System, Inc. on June 1, 1958.[133]

Eager to improve their programming, the newly established TV stations turned to rakugo for program content and rakugo storytellers evolved into television personalities. These stations hosted rakugo shows linked to their programs and signed exclusive contracts with the storytellers. NHK organized the Kamigata Rakugo Society, which was linked to its program *TV Engei-kai*. Asahi Broadcasting Corporation (ABC) followed suit, and started the ABC Society for Kamigata Rakugo. Later, it included a segment called "Midnight Yose" within the program *ABC Young Request* that broadcasted routines performed by the ABC Society for Kamigata Rakugo. As a result, numerous rakugo performers including Katsura Beicho and Morino Fukuro were able to jump on board and ride the wave to success.[134]

Shoten

Shoten, the show which currently holds the Guinness World Record as the longest-running television entertainment variety program in Japan and worldwide, first aired on May 15,

---

[133] "Mainichi Broadcasting System," Wikipedia (Wikimedia Foundation, February 14, 2022), https://en.wikipedia.org/wiki/Mainichi_Broadcasting_System.
[134] Yu, "Kamigata Rakugo"（上方落語）.

1966. Hosted by the prominent rakugo storyteller Tatekawa Danshi V, the show was based on the ogiri format of rakugo.

Danshi was one of the original *Edo Rakugo Wakate Shitenno* (Edo Rakugo's Four Young Major Performers), which also included Sanyutei Enraku V, Kokontei Shincho III, and Shunputei Ryucho. Ryucho passed away at an early age, so another extraordinary rakugoka named Tachibanaya Enzo took his place.

The word *ogiri* means "the last" and refers to an item that is presented at the end of the day's performance. It is rather common in the classical Japanese performing arts. In kabuki, for instance, many performances end with a lively dance finale (*ogiri shosagoto*) featuring the entire cast.[135]

In rakugo, ogiri was originally performed as a bonus for the audience. It was a sideshow act in which all of the performers came on the stage and competed with one another based on a topic given by the audience.

These days, the word ogiri is most often associated with *Shoten*. The format of the show involves six rakugo performers who appear on stage together and are asked to respond to the host's questions or suggestions with funny or witty comebacks. Should the resultant response be funny or witty, the storyteller will receive

---

[135] Larsen, Brooke. "What Is Kabuki? 6 Things to Know About Kabuki Theater." Japan Objects. Japan Objects, February 1, 2021. https://japanobjects.com/features/kabuki/#elements.

one or more floor cushions with the number increasing according to the audience response and the host's own amusement or admiration. If, on the other hand, a storyteller's answer falls flat with the audience, is excessively distasteful, or is construed as insulting to the host or fellow storytellers, the rakugoka will lose one or more floor cushions. On certain occasions, the host may confiscate more than one storyteller's floor cushion if he deems that they conspired together. Should a storyteller acquire a total of ten floor cushions, he will be entitled to that day's special prize.[136]

Since its inception, *Shoten* has had six hosts: Tatekawa Danshi V (1966-1969), Maeda Takehiko (1969-1970), Minami Shinsuke (1970-1983), Sanyutei Enraku V (1983 – 2006), Katsura Utamaru (2006 - 2016), and Shunputei Shota (2016-current).[137]

Although Maeda Takehiko was not a rakugo storyteller, he was asked to step in as the host on *Shoten* after Danshi stepped down on November 9, 1969. Danshi, who also hosted a program called *Yoru no shotaiseki*, was familiar with Maeda's comedic talent and recommended him for the host position on the program. Maeda originally accepted the role short term, but as the ratings were holding steady while he was the host, he agreed to stay on for one

---

[136] Yu, A. C. "Ogiri (Professional rakugo storytellers play on words.) (大喜利)." Japanese Wiki Corpus. https://japanese-wiki-corpus.github.io/culture/Ogiri%20(Professional%20rakugo%20storytellers%20play%20on%20words.).html.
[137] "笑点 web (Shoten)." 日本テレビ. https://www.ntv.co.jp/sho-ten/encyclopedia/index.html.

year. He was responsible for writing the lyrics for the show's second theme song composed by Nakamura Hachidai, a composer and jazz pianist who composed Kyu Sakamoto's 1961 hit song, "*Ue o Muite Arukou*" (English title, "Sukiyaki").[138]

Because Maeda was not a rakugoka, the show became more diverse and the storytellers began to wear colorful kimonos. However, there was a dissimilarity between Maeda's way of thinking and that of the show's regulars that lead to his dismissal as the host after just one year.[139]

Katsura Utamaru, who first appeared on the program when it began in 1966 and continued on the show for five decades, became the host in 2006 after Sanyutei Enraku V officially retired due to health reasons.

Utamaru, who was born into a family that ran a *yukaku* (licensed brothel) in Yokohama, became interested in rakugo after listening to it on the radio when he was just an elementary school student. In 1951, at the age of 15, he was taken under the wing of Kokontei Imasuke V and given the stage name Kokontei Imaji. But Utamaru was eventually dismissed by his master due to their dissimilarities in performance style. Imasuke preferred modern rakugo, while his disciple favored classical rakugo. Following his dismissal,

---

[138] Canuck, J. "Hachidai Nakamura -- Theme from Shoten" (笑点) , January 1, 1970. http://kayokyokuplus.blogspot.com/2012/12/hachidai-nakamura-theme-from-shoten.html.
[139] "前田武彦 (Maeda Takehiko)." Wikipedia. Wikimedia Foundation, December 31, 2020. https://ja.wikipedia.org/wiki/%E5%89%8D%E7%94%B0%E6%AD%A6%E5%BD%A6.

Utamaru abandoned the world of rakugo for a period of two and a half years. He returned in 1961 and apprenticed with Katsura Yonemaru IV, under the stage name Katsura Yonebo. He changed his stage name to Katsura Utamaru in 1964 and became a full-fledged rakugo storyteller four years later.[140]

His promotion to shinuchi was celebrated on *Shoten* with his first master, Imasuke, in attendance. As the host of the show, Utamaru became the first to order a complete confiscation of the entire cast's floor cushions in 2006 after Sanyutei Enraku VI (then known as Sanyutei Rakutaro), in concert with the other storytellers, compared the elderly host to a talking corpse. Enraku was particularly notorious during Utamaru's tenure as host for frequently insulting him with his characteristically merciless wit and accuracy, often resulting in the confiscation of all of his floor cushions.[141]

In 2004, Utamaru became chairman of the Rakugo Geijutsu Kyokai and he was awarded the Order of the Rising Sun from the Japanese government in 2007.

Although he suffered from chronic back pain and emphysema, he continued as the host of *Shoten* until May 2016, when the program

---

[140] "Rakugo Storyteller, TV Personality Katsura Utamaru Dies at 81." The Mainichi, July 4, 2018. https://mainichi.jp/english/articles/20180702/p2a/00m/0na/008000c.
[141] "Shōten." Wikipedia. Wikimedia Foundation, December 11, 2020. https://en.wikipedia.org/wiki/Sh%C5%8Dten.

marked its 50th anniversary. He passed away from chronic obstructive pulmonary disease in Yokohama on July 2, 2018 at the age of 81.[142]

---

[142] "Rakugo Storyteller Katsura Utamaru Dies at 81." Manila STV, July 2, 2018. https://manila-stv.ph/lifestyle/rakugo-storyteller-katsura-utamaru-dies-at-81.html.

xvi. Katsura Utamaru hosting Shoten

A Classic Art Form in Popular Culture

Once rakugo transitioned from the yose to radio and television, it was only a matter of time before it was featured in films and other media in popular culture.

In August 1975, a compelling film called *Oni no Uta* (*Song of the Demon*), directed by Murano Tetsutaro, was released. Featuring rakugo performers Katsura Fukudanji and Tsuyu no Gorobei II, the story is based in part on the life of the rakugo artist Katsura Beikyo II (1860-1904) and the pursuit for ultimate artistry. The film is an adaptation of the award-winning novel by Fujimoto Giichi (Yoshikazu), a screenwriter turned novelist.

In the story, Bakyo, portrayed by Fukudanji, is a talented but unsuccessful rakugo artist. In contrast, his contemporary Rokyu, portrayed by Gorobei, is very successful. He wants to take Bakyo under his wing, but Bakyo refuses owing to the fact that Rokyu's rakugo is tainted by elements of kabuki. However, Bakyo later has a change of heart and resolves to learn (or steal) Rokyu's craft and make it his own.

He becomes obsessed with copying every detail of Rokyu's performance; he even imitates his lifestyle.

One night, while Bakyo is watching Rokyu perform, Bakyo's pregnant wife has an accident. When Bakyo returns home, he finds her dying in a pool of blood. Overwhelmed by the shock of losing his wife, he behaves very strangely during her funeral.

After a long absence, he returns to the yose with a new story he created. He impersonates a female psychic who will eat anything offered by the audience—even horse manure. The story becomes a huge success, but Bakyo contracts smallpox after eating the horse manure. His face becomes horrifically disfigured from the disease, but Bakyo uses his deformity to both shock and captivate his audience.[143]

Six years later, a film called *No yohna mono* (*Something Like It*) also featured rakugo as its central theme. Directed by Morita Yoshimitsu, the story focuses on a 23-year-old rakugoka named Defunetei Shintoto, who meets a girl named Elizabeth when he visits a soapland (a bathhouse where sexual services can be performed) on his birthday. She is not interested in rakugo, but the two begin to date, nonetheless. Later, he is forced to teach at a girls' high school rakugo study group and falls in love with a girl named Yumi. Soon, a three-way relationship ensues.[144]

In 2015, a sequel to *No yohna mono* was released under the title *No Yona Mono No Yona Mono* (*Something Like, Something Like It*). The story follows Defunetei Shinden in his quest to locate the former

---

[143] "Song of the Devil (1975)." Song of the Devil (1975) directed by Tetsutaro Murano. • Letterboxed. Fans of Auckland. https://letterboxd.com/film/song-of-the-devil/.
[144] "Something Like It." MyDramaList. https://mydramalist.com/51563-something-like-it.

rakugoka, Defunetei Shintoto. Shintoto, now fifty-five, abandoned the world of rakugo after his master's passing. Shinden wishes Shintoto to appear in a special rakugo show to commemorate the 13th anniversary of his master's death.[145]

In 2007, Sato Takako's novel, *Shaberedomo Shaberedomo* (*Talk, Talk, Talk*), was made into a movie with the same name. Starring actor Kokubun Taichi and directed by Hirayama Hideyuki, the film centers around a struggling but determined rakugo storyteller named Mitsuba. Everyone but Mitsuba himself agrees that he's not very talented, yet he stubbornly insists on performing only the classical stories written by his master, who seems to have given up on him altogether.

Then, through a strange twist of fate, he winds up with three misfits who want him to teach them how to become better conversationalists. A failed communicator himself, Mitsuba ends up teaching them the only thing he knows; rakugo routines. The camaraderie and good-natured squabbles during these rakugo classes serve as catalysts for each of the characters, including Mitsuba himself, to grow as individuals and to face the problems they have in their personal lives.[146]

The following year, the film *Rakugo Musume* (*Daughter of Rakugo*) was released. It tells the story of a girl named Kazumi Nakamura

---

[145] "Something Like, Something Like It." AsianWiki. https://asianwiki.com/Something_Like,_Something_Like_It.
[146] Hotes, Cathy Munroe. "Talk Talk Talk （しゃべれどもしゃべれども, 2007)." Nishikata Film Review, 2009. https://www.nishikata-eiga.com/2009/05/talk-talk-talk-2007.html.

who becomes fascinated by the art of rakugo after her uncle takes her to a live performance. Following her graduation from university, Kazumi becomes the apprentice of the rakugo master she had seen perform years ago. She devotes five long years to training as a rakugo performer, always being looked down upon by her fellow male apprentices and without any real chance of becoming a master rakugo performer. After failing her promotion examination, she accepts an invitation from another rakugo master to join his school.[147]

In 2013, directors Endo Mikihiro, Sakashita Yuichiro, and Matsui Issey presented filmgoers with modern adaptations of three rakugo tales in the form of three short films. *Rakugo Eiga* (*The Rakugo Movie*) is an anthology film based on three classical rakugo tales: "Before After," based on "Nezumi," ("Mouse"); "Life Rate," based on the "Shinigami" ("The God of Death"); and "Sarugoke wa Tsuraiyo," based on "Sarugoke" ("Monkey Widow").[148]

In 2014, Hayashiya Taihei, a regular on the television show *Shoten*, created a heartwarming film called *Mo Ichido* (English title, *His Master's Voice*).

---

[147] K, Anthony. "Rakugo Musume." AsianWiki. Accessed February 7, 2021. https://asianwiki.com/Rakugo_Musume.
[148] "Japan Foundation Los Angeles: Japanema Rakugo Eiga." Japan Foundation Los Angeles | Japanema Rakugo Eiga, 2017. https://www.jflalc.org/ac-japanema-110817.

Its story is about a nineteenth century rakugo apprentice who has lost hope of ever becoming a master storyteller. In his despair, he takes up residence at a *nagaya* (rowhouse) in Tokyo's Fukagawa district, where he meets an emotionally detached boy named Sadakichi. Eventually, he teaches the boy rakugo.[149]

Turning to television, in 2005, Tokyo Broadcasting System (TBS) aired a twelve-episode drama called *Tiger & Dragon*. The story develops around the relationships Toraji and Ryuji have with the offbeat and comical characters around them. Toraji is a stereotypical *yakuza* (gangster) with aspirations of becoming a rakugo storyteller. Ryuji is a designer with terrible taste. The series is a collection of one-off stories blending the modern with the traditional by basing each episode on a classical rakugo storyline.[150]

In 2015, TBS aired another rakugo-themed drama called *Akamedaka (Red Medaka)*, based on the life of rakugoka Tatekawa Danshun. The program is an adaptation of Danshun's 2008 book with the same title. Starring Ninomiya Kazunari, the drama tells the story of a 17-year-old Danshun on his journey to becoming a rakugo storyteller under the tutelage of the legendary Tatekawa Danshi V.[151]

---

[149] "HIS MASTER'S VOICE." Japanese Film Database, 2014. https://jfdb.jp/en/title/4304.
[150] "Tiger and Dragon." AsianWiki, 2005. https://asianwiki.com/Tiger_and_Dragon.
[151] "Aka Medaka." MyDramaList. TBS, 2015. https://mydramalist.com/15936-aka-medaka.

In 2019, NHK aired its 58th *taiga drama* (Japanese historical drama series) *Idaten-Tokyo Olympic Story*. The series focuses on the lives of two twentieth century Japanese Olympians, the marathon runner Shiso Kanakuri and swimming coach Masaji Tabata. Although the story is not directly about rakugo, it is narrated by rakugoka Kokontei Shinsho V, portrayed by actor and comedian Kitano Takeshi.[152]

Notwithstanding all of the films and television shows, one medium certainly stands out for having introduced the art of rakugo to a younger generation outside Japan. It is the popular manga *Showa Genroku Rakugo Shinju* (English title, *Descending Stories*), first serialized in Kodansha's ITAN magazine in 2010.

Written and illustrated by Kumota Haruko, the story is based on a former prisoner who becomes the apprentice of a famous rakugoka, Yutakutei Yakumo. The tale, which focuses on the backstories of the rakugoka and their struggles to gain popularity, was later adapted into an anime television series that initially aired between January 9, 2016, and April 2, 2016. A live-action series adaptation starring Okada Masaki as Yurakutei Yakumo was aired on NHK between October 12, 2018, and December 14, 2018.[153]

---

[152] "Idaten (TV Series)." Wikipedia. Wikimedia Foundation, January 17, 2021. https://en.wikipedia.org/wiki/Idaten_(TV_series).
[153] "Descending Stories: Showa Genroku Rakugo Shinju." Wikipedia. Wikimedia Foundation, January 23, 2021. https://en.wikipedia.org/wiki/Descending_Stories:_Showa_Genroku_Rakugo_Shinju.

By no means is this an all-inclusive list, but it does help illustrate rakugo's power to transcend the barriers of time and remain relevant in the modern age. The art of storytelling itself offers infinite possibilities for story ideas and it continues to delight and appeal to audiences of all ages and backgrounds.

6. Tatekawa Danshi V

> "The person who is hated by ten people is a villain. The person who is liked by ten people is a hypocrite. The person who is hated by five and liked by five people is the real star."
> —*Tatekawa Danshi V (1936-2011)*

Tatekawa Danshi was a young storyteller who rose to fame with the television boom in the 1960s. Born in Tokyo's Koishikawa district on January 2, 1936, he dropped out of high school at the age of 16 to become the disciple of master storyteller Yanagiya Kosan V.

Danshi worked hard and performed stand-up comedy in tandem with his rakugo performances at the yose. He attained the level of shinuchi in 1963, but his promotion came late and caused him a great deal of humiliation. Two other prominent rakugoka, Kokentei Shincho III and Sanyutei Enraku V, who had entered the world of rakugo a few years after Danshi, were promoted to shinuchi a year earlier.

On May 5, 1966, Danshi became the television host of what was to become a highly popular and long enduring program called *Shoten*. The show was broadcast every Sunday evening, and it became a vehicle by which he could convey his dark sense of humor through his witty dialogue. Unfortunately, the audience did not appreciate Danshi's humor and the initial ratings proved to be sluggish. Ultimately, the ratings coupled with his eroding relationship with the first group of performers proved to be his undoing. He was forced to resign as host.

Following his departure from *Shoten*, Danshi entered politics. He ran for a seat in the House of Representatives in the 1969 general election. Of the nine candidates, Danshi ranked sixth after the votes were counted. Undaunted, he made another attempt in 1971. With the blessing of his master, Kosan, he joined the Liberal Democratic Party (LDP) and was elected to the House of Councilors. Although he won a seat in government, there were 50 candidates nationwide and Danshi ranked 50th for the number of votes collected.

On December 26, 1975, Danshi was appointed Deputy Secretary of State for the Development of Okinawa. In his first duty as the deputy, he attended the press conference at the Okinawa Ocean Expo with a hangover. Consequently, he faced significant backlash from within the LDP and resigned his position after just 36 days. Ishihara Shintaro, a fellow LDP member and close friend, attempted to persuade him to apologize, but Danshi refused. He considered running for a second term, but withdrew in due course, ending his six-year political run. He later remarked, "I'm the only one who had an inimical career as a politician." [154]

Danshi's turbulent mood did not end after he left politics and returned to rakugo. In 1983, he confronted the Rakugo Kyokai's chairman over the implementation of the shinuchi promotion test. The two men reached an impasse and Danshi left the organization to found his own association known as the Tatekawa-ryu. [155]

He was known to be quite temperamental with his disciples as well. On one occasion, Danshi decided to perform a rakugo story about a sumo wrestler. His first disciple, Katsura Mojisuke IV, who was very knowledgeable about sumo was listening to his master's performance and pointed out his mistakes afterwards. This angered Danshi and he responded by saying, "I see. I will never perform sumo stories ever again. But, from now on, you will only perform sumo stories." Mojisuke left the Tatekawa-ryu in 2015.

Ultimately, however, cancer became the maverick rakugoka's most formidable adversary. In 1997, he underwent surgery for esophageal cancer. A heavy smoker for most of his life, he remained defiant despite the diagnosis, and continued to smoke cigarettes.

---

[154] "立川談志." Wikipedia. Wikimedia Foundation, November 4, 2020.
https://ja.m.wikipedia.org/wiki/%E7%AB%8B%E5%B7%9D%E8%AB%87%E5%BF%97.
[155] 立川談志." Wikipedia.

The disease did little to soften his disposition. In 1999, during a performance in Iida City, Nagano Prefecture, he abruptly ordered an audience member to leave. The gentleman had fallen asleep and was snoring audibly during the performance. The ejected audience member later filed a civil suit against the organizer of the show, but the claim was dismissed.

Then, in May of 2008, the discovery of a suspicious polyp forced Danshi to be admitted to the hospital once again. Not long after being admitted, he walked out to attend a rakugo party and the taping of a television program, ignoring his doctor's orders.

On October 14, it was revealed that Danshi was suffering from cancer of the larynx and the only solution was the removal of his vocal cords. All of his scheduled appearances were cancelled on August 26, 2009, and a public announcement was issued stating that Danshi's physical strength had decreased and he was undergoing treatment for diabetes.

He still managed to attend the promotion ceremony of Sanyutei Enraku VI on March 2, 2010. Katsura Utamaru, who was also at the party, commented that he was happy to see Danshi once again. There were no hard feelings between the two men even after Danshi, while hosting *Shoten*, had boldly stated that Utamaru should quit rakugo.

Danshi returned to the stage after an eight-month hiatus. But in November, it was revealed that his glottic cancer had returned. Determined to continue performing, he refused to have a cordectomy.

On March 6, 2011, the Tatekawa *ichimon* (group) held a meeting at the Aso Cultural Center in Kawasaki City. Danshi delivered two classical stories, "Nagaya no Hanami" ("Cherry Blossom Viewing by the Row House Tenants") and "Kumo Kago" ("Spider Palanquin") while coughing incessantly. Among the stories that Danshi performed throughout his career, "Shiba Hama" ("Shiba Beach") and "Gonbei Danuki" ("Gonbei and the Racoon Dog") were his favorites. "Shiba Hama" is a story about a fishmonger who finds a wallet stuffed with gold on the seashore. Believing he is rich and never has to work again, he calls his friends over to celebrate. After he gets drunk and falls asleep, his wife hides the wallet and tells him it was all a dream. Disappointed, he gives up drinking and works very hard to become successful. Once successful, his wife confesses to him about the wallet. "Gonbei and the Racoon Dog" is at the end of this book.

Sadly, Danshi's performance on March 6th was to be his last. He was hospitalized fifteen days later and underwent a tracheostomy. Since he had lost his voice, he canceled all future engagements and retreated to his home to recuperate. On September 12, he was readmitted to the hospital and fell into a coma on October 27, never to regain consciousness. Tatekawa Danshi passed away at 2:24 p.m. on November 21, 2011, at the age of 75.

Danshi's death was not disclosed for another two days, even to his disciples. A secret farewell service was held, attended only by his family, and he was cremated at the Ochiai Funeral Home on November 23. On that day, his agency issued a press release confirming his death. His disciples learned of their master's passing by watching the news. It was said that a plush lion named Raibo, which Danshi had adored, was cremated along with him. However, the following day (on the 24th) it was revealed that it was another plush animal that was cremated and that Raibo was safe.

Throughout his life, Danshi was often criticized for his temperament and straightforward personality, but he was also admired for his ambitious efforts to inject classical rakugo with modern values and sensibilities.[156] He loved his art and motivated and influenced future rakugo artists and fans alike through his work both on and off stage.

In his first and highly influential book, *Gendai Rakugo Ron* (*Modern Theory of Rakugo*), published in 1965, Danshi expressed deep concern for the future of rakugo. He explained that the art form

---

[156] "立川談志." Wikipedia.

would likely become obsolete unless more rakugo performers attempt to infuse the stories with modern values.

From Danshi's perspective, rakugo was both the acceptance of human nature (*rakugo to wa go no koteidearu*) and an illusion. The first is a rather esoteric concept and conveys the genius of Danshi. It basically means that rakugo, unlike kodan, which is mostly based on historical heroes, is filled with human imperfections. It is a world where characters like Hachigoro, Kumagoro, and Yotaro exist. These characters are all flawed in some way and yet they endure in the world of rakugo. In this way, it is easy to understand why rakugo appeals to the common people.

The second concept is based on the idea that reality, ideas, and even ego are illusions for humans. The theory was developed by Japanese psychologist Kishida Shu, whom Danshi respected. In fact, he once said, "The only book you will ever need is the one written by Kishida Shu!"[157]

According to Kishida, human beings are animals whose instincts are broken, so rather than having a code of conduct regulated by instincts, they have invented culture as a substitute for instinct. Danshi explained that common sense derives from this culture and human beings must possess it in order to live. It is educated into

---

[157] Kishida, Shigeru. "『唯幻論＜岸田秀＞』(Tada Maboroshi-Ron Taizen) 可い長の寝床ブログ (Kai-chō no nedoko burogu). Ameba, January 11, 2010. https://ameblo.jp/hansyouteikaichou/entry-10430657203.html.

every individual and incorporated into society, but everyone does not adopt it. It is an illusion which serves as a basis for rakugo.

Danshi believed that most rakugoka were unaware of this essential meaning of rakugo and that they were part of the common sense side of the world. "What is common sense?" he asked. "Common sense is fiction, isn't it?"[158]

Finally, Danshi's ultimate contribution to the world of rakugo was Tatekawa-ryu. He proved to be a great mentor and had many disciples, some of whom attained superstar status including Tatekawa Shinosuke, Tatekawa Danshun, and Tatekawa Shiraku.

Having achieved stratospheric success in his own life, Danshi's words and teachings still resonate throughout the world of rakugo and beyond, a full decade since his passing.

---

[158] Kishida, Shigeru. 『唯幻論＜岸田秀＞』 (Tada Maboroshi-Ron Taizen).

xvii. *Tatekawa Danshi V in 1986 (Kanariya Eiraku)*

7. *Sanyutei Enraku V*

> *"It's amazing how rakugo can make even the people with somber faces who were robbed of everything during the war laugh."*
> —*Sanyutei Enraku V (1932-2009)*

Sanyutei Enraku, whose rakugo career spanned several decades, was best known for being the longest-serving host of the popular television program *Shoten*.[159]

Born at Sukeroku-dera, a temple originally located in Tokyo's Asakusa Ward, on December 29, 1932, Enraku was the son of a Buddhist monk, and he was one of nine brothers born to the Yoshikawa family. Later in his life, Enraku researched the history of this temple, which was relocated to the Adachi Ward of Tokyo, and wrote a story called "Sukeroku-den" ("A History of Sukeroku"). Enraku's story is not to be confused with the popular kabuki play known as "Sukeroku," which is based on a tragic incident involving a courtesan named Koito.

As a youngster, he was given the nickname "The Little Prince" for his tidy appearance, and perhaps rightfully so because the

---

[159] "San'yūtei Enraku V." Wikipedia. Wikimedia Foundation, October 4, 2020. https://en.wikipedia.org/wiki/San%27y%C5%ABtei_Enraku_V.

Yoshikawa family were descendants of Kikkawa Tsuneie (1547-1581), a prominent samurai during Japan's Sengoku period.

Owing to the postwar food shortages, Enraku initially decided to take up farming. However, since Tokyo was not a suitable place to learn about agriculture, he enrolled in and graduated from the Saitama Prefectural Sugito Agricultural School (currently the Sugito Agricultural High School) in the neighboring prefecture.

Then, the inevitable happened. He saw a rakugo performance at the Suzumoto Entertainment Hall in Ueno. Enraku was amazed by the way rakugo made people laugh, even those individuals who had lost everything in the war and had nothing to laugh about. It was at that moment when he decided to become a rakugoka.

Although Sanyutei Ensho VI was not his first choice to study with, he gained an introduction to the master in February 1955. He initially considered becoming the apprentice of either Kokontei Shinsho or Katsura Bunraku, but both masters were well over 60 years old and Enraku was not sure how long they would be able to mentor him. Enraku was 23 years old at the time, and set a goal for himself: if he did not get promoted to shinuchi by the time he was 30, he would quit rakugo altogether.

He was promoted to futatsume in March 1958 and attained the shinuchi level in October 1962, just three months shy of his 30th birthday.

In 1965, together with Katsura Utamaru and Hayashiya Kompei, he appeared on a television program called *Kinyo yoru seki* (the precursor to *Shoten*), hosted by Tatekawa Danshi. He moved over to *Shoten* when it aired in 1966, but left the program in 1968 due to a conflict with Danshi and the other members of the show. He would later rejoin and depart from the show several times before becoming its host.

In 1978, at the age of 78, his master Ensho withdrew from the Rakugo Kyokai over a disagreement about the shinuchi promotional requirements, and his disciples followed. At the time, he told Enraku, "After I retire, you will protect your disciples as the president of the Sanyu faction," implying that Enraku would generationally inherit his master's name and position as head of the Sanyutei rakugo family.[160] Although Enraku disagreed with his master about the promotion system, he could not contradict him. Obediently, he helped his master establish the Rakugo Sanyu Association.

When Ensho passed away on September 3, 1979, some of his disciples rejoined the Rakugo Kyokai. Enraku and the other disciples did not, and he established the Dai Nippon Rakugo

---

[160] " 三遊亭圓楽（5代目）." Wikipedia. Wikimedia Foundation, November 12, 2020. https://ja.wikipedia.org/wiki/%E4%B8%89%E9%81%8A%E4%BA%AD%E5%9C%93%E6%A5%BD_%285%E4%BB%A3%E7%9B%AE%29.

Sumirekai on February 1, 1980. The organization was renamed the *Enraku Ichimonkai* (Enraku Association) in 1990.

Unable to perform at the yose after leaving the Rakugo Kyokai, Enraku established his own yose theater, *Wakatake* (Young Bamboo), in the old suburb of Toyocho in the Koto Ward in March 1985. He chose this location because Toyocho means "the town of the rising sun in the east." Enraku dreamed that his young disciples would grow swiftly like bamboo under the sun.

However, with all good intensions aside, it was clear that Enraku was not a businessman. He exercised poor judgement when he established the theater in the business district. Further, he accumulated a lot of debt through the mismanagement of Wakatake, forcing its closure on November 25, 1989.

In order to pay down his debts, Enraku embarked on a lecture tour that took him all over Japan. He returned to *Shoten* in January 1983 after its host, Minami Shinsuke, suddenly passed away in December.

Once he became the host, Enraku intentionally strayed away from the show's established format in an effort to breathe new air into the program. In 1984, he appointed Yamada Takao to replace Matsuzaki Makoto as the *zabuton hakobi* (floor cushion carrier). This changed the dynamics of the show giving both the respondents and the floor cushion carrier an active role in the flow of the program. He also invited Sanyutei Koraku to join the cast in 1988. Once Koraku joined the program, the cast remained intact for sixteen continuous years. The lineup changed only when Hayashiya Taihei joined the group.

Enraku firmly believed that all of the members of *Shoten* formed one cohesive family, a concept which enabled him to serve as the show's host for twenty-three years. Utamaru even said, "There is no one in the rakugo world who would go against Mr. Enraku."[161] Enraku was not only respected by his disciples, Koraku and Rakutaro (currently Sanyutei Enraku VI), but also by other rakugo artists.

Initially, he struggled with audience ratings after becoming the show's host and was criticized on occasion for laughing too much. Eventually the changes he made paid off, and *Shoten* regained its status as one of the most popular programs on television.

Enraku was in his 18th year as the host of the program when his failing health began to interfere with his performance. As a child, he had suffered from pneumonia and tuberculosis, which impacted his long-term health. In 1999, he experienced kidney failure and required dialysis three times a week. He was found to

---

[161] "三遊亭圓楽（5代目）." Wikipedia.

have stomach cancer in November 2007 and underwent surgery for lung cancer in April 2008.

During the February 11, 2001 broadcast, he made the mistake of ending the program after only asking two questions rather than the program's usual three. Then on June 12, 2005, he could not remember Taihei's name during the broadcast. When Taihei raised his hand to respond to the question, Enraku turned to others in the lineup and asked, "Who is he?"[162]

It was clear that Enraku had suffered a stroke, but the symptoms were not severe enough to require hospitalization until October 13, 2005. *Shoten*, which was taped ahead of time, was temporarily halted following the broadcast on October 16.

He returned to taping the program on March 26, but he was still in poor physical condition and could not manage the job as the host of the show. On May 14, a special broadcast celebrating the 40th anniversary of *Shoten* was aired. It was on that program that Enraku officially announced his retirement as host and handed over the reins to Utamaru.

Not wanting to give up rakugo entirely, Enraku attempted to return to the stage on February 25, 2007. He practiced for half a year before the actual performance, but he was not satisfied with

---

[162] " 三遊亭圓楽（5代目）." Wikipedia.

the result. At a press conference following the show, he announced his retirement from rakugo entirely. His disciple, Enraku VI, tried to persuade him not to retire as the show to commemorate his retirement had not been scheduled yet. However, for Enraku, who had been known for the stories, "Hamano Noriyuki" ("Hamano Noriyuki, the Sculptor") and "Nozarashi" ("Bone Fishing"), the story "Shiba hama" that he presented on that fateful day in February was to be his last.

His lung cancer returned in May 2009. To make matters worse, he suffered another stroke, which left him paralyzed. He was admitted to the Keio University Hospital in September, but was discharged on October 23 to undergo treatment at home. He was receiving medical treatment at his eldest son's home when he passed away on October 29. The cause was attributed to metastatic lung cancer. Enraku was 76 years old.

In 2019, on the 10th anniversary of his death, a television drama called *BS Shoten Dorama Supesharu - Godaime Sanyutei Enraku* (*BS Shoten Drama Special - 5th Generation Sanyutei Enraku*) starring Tanihara Shosuke was broadcast. The program depicts Enraku's life from the point when he entered the rakugo world until his inauguration as the host of *Shoten*.[163]

---

[163] " 三遊亭圓楽（5代目）." Wikipedia.

xviii. Sanyutei Enraku V

8. Kokontei Shincho III

> "*Kabuki actors cannot transcend the limits to stardom unless they are descendants of a great acting family, but rakugoka can become great with only a single fan.*"
> —*Kokontei Shinsho V (1890-1973)*

It isn't uncommon for the offspring of rakugo storytellers to follow in their parents' footsteps. Born in the Bunkyo Ward of Tokyo on March 10, 1938, Kokontei Shincho was the second son of a prominent rakugoka named Kokontei Shinsho V. Highly regarded both by rakugo fans and his fellow performers alike, he once earned the praise of Tatekawa Danshi V, who stated, "Only Shincho is worth paying money to listen to."[164] During the years he was actively performing, it was said that Shincho is to the East what Katsura Shijaku is to the West.

In the beginning, however, Shincho showed no interest in becoming a rakugo performer. As a high school student, he studiously learned German expressly to fulfil his dream of becoming a diplomat. He never lost his love for the country; and

---

[164] "古今亭志ん朝." ("Kokontei Shincho.") Wikipedia. Wikimedia Foundation, November 14, 2020. https://ja.m.wikipedia.org/wiki/%E5%8F%A4%E4%BB%8A%E4%BA%AD%E5%BF%97%E3%82%93%E6%9C%9D.

as a rakugo performer, he traveled to his beloved Germany with his disciples every year.

After graduating from high school, he aspired to become a kabuki actor until his father warned him, "Kabuki actors cannot transcend the limits to stardom unless they are descendants of a great acting family, but rakugoka can become great with only a single fan." With those words, he entered the world of rakugo. And with his father as his master, he earned his promotion to shinuchi after only five years of training. His older brother, who took the stage name Kingentei Basho, was also mentored by their father.

It was Shinsho V's wish to have his second son succeed his rakugo stage name. Shincho's life-long rival, Tatekawa Danshi V, also supported the succession, but he cautioned the young man, "To succeed Shinsho, you need to be an even better rakugoka." [165] Shincho asked Danshi if he would be willing to speak at the succession ceremony, which he agreed to do. However, their dreams went unrealized when Shincho suddenly passed away at an early age.[166]

Although Shincho admired and respected his father, he felt that he could not imitate his art because his father's lifestyle and experiences were completely different from his own. Shincho

---

[165] Minobe, Mitsuko. *Sanninbanashi: Shinshō basho shinchō.* Tōkyō: Fusōsha, 2002.
[166] Minobe, *Sanninbanashi.*

focused instead on Katsura Bunraku VIII, and carefully developed his own art by watching and imitating the master storyteller.

He also had great admiration for Sanyutei Ensho VI, and during the big turmoil within the Rakugo Kyokai in May 1978, Shincho followed Ensho's lead and announced that he would leave the association. However, he realized that if he left, he would no longer be permitted to perform in the yose. For young rakugo performers, performing at the yose is critical for refining their skills. After thinking the matter over more seriously, Shincho decided to remain with the association. Thereafter, he stayed relatively far away from the political affairs of the Rakugo Kyokai, yet he still served as its vice president for five years from 1996 until his death in 2001.

Like other rakugo performers of his generation, he often appeared on television and worked as a comedy actor during his early years as a storyteller. But, as he grew older, rakugo became his primary focus. Ultimately, he became so popular that tickets for his solo performances sold out quickly. Popularity led to fame and fortune, and he became the first rakugoka to drive a luxury foreign car and build a mansion. That drew a lot of criticism. One weekly magazine reporter commented, "He does nothing and builds a mansion while Hayashiya Shozo VIII still lives in a tenement house."[167]

Shincho's frequent interactions with the rakugoka from Osaka made him unique as an Edo storyteller. He was fascinated with Kamigata storyteller Shofukutei Shokaku VI, and Shokaku in turn had great admiration for Shincho. This connection enabled him to perform frequently in Osaka. He was initially rejected, but later welcomed, by the Kamigata fans. These interactions proved to be highly beneficial for Shincho and enabled him to refine his art.

Although he had stated earlier that he could not imitate his father's art because his father's lifestyle and experiences were completely different than his own, the stories he enjoyed performing the most were the ones his father liked to perform. These included "Kaen Daiko" ("Flaming Drum"), a classical rakugo story about a dusty drum that turns out to be a valuable art piece worth a fortune, and "Daiku Shirabe" ("The Trial of the Carpenter") about a carpenter who is behind on his rent.

He resembled his father in one more regard; they were both heavy drinkers. Although it can't be said with certainty whether his love of alcohol contributed to his poor health, he did suffer from diabetes for many years and was occasionally hospitalized.

---

[167] Minobe, *Sanninbanashi*.

Shincho was a versatile performer, and he mastered a traditional dance called *Sumiyoshi Odori* that he learned from fellow rakugoka Kaminarimon Sukeroku VIII. Beginning in 1978, he and other rakugo storytellers performed the dance at the Asakusa Engei Hall, and the event became an ongoing attraction during the summer months. Shincho never missed a performance, even when he was struggling with cancer in 2001. He left the hospital every day between August 11 and August 20 and went to the theater. He passed away from liver cancer just twelve days later, at the age of 63.

More than 2,500 people, including fans, attended his funeral on October 6. It was reported that the German dictionary that Shincho cherished was placed in his casket during the funeral.[168]

A year after his death, Shincho's sister Minobe Mitsuko released a book titled *Sannin banashi, Shinsho, Basho, Shincho* (*Stories of Three People: Shinsho, Basho, Shincho*). In it, she relates an interesting story about how her brother had given up eating his favorite dish after becoming a rakugoka at the age of nineteen. Shincho was very fond of eel dishes; however, he gave up eating eel after learning that it was the messenger of his protective deity. In Japan, people are assigned their own protective deity corresponding to their zodiac sign and each deity has its own messenger. This act

---

[168] Minobe, Sanninbanashi.

demonstrated Shincho's commitment to his art and his drive to succeed.

Shortly after Shincho passed away, Mitsuko's friends took her to a well-known restaurant serving eel. Although there were only three people in their party, they ordered four boxes of eel. The fourth box was for her brother.

Mitsuko placed one box of eel and a cup of sake on the table and said, "Kyoji (his real name), here is your favorite food. You haven't eaten eel for a very long time and devoted yourself to rakugo. I admire you."[169]

---

[169] Minobe, Sanninbanashi.

xix. Kokontei Shincho III

9. Tachibanaya Enzo VIII

> "It's impossible to teach artistic skills.
> You must steal them like a thief."
> —Tachibanaya Enzo (1934-2015)

With his signature thick, black-rimmed glasses, which he wore to correct his severe myopia, Tachibanaya Enzo rounded out the four-member group of extraordinary rakugo performers known as the Edo Rakugo Wakate Shitenno. He replaced Shunputei Ryucho, one of the original four, after Ryucho passed away from stomach cancer on Feb 7, 1991 at the age of 61.

Born in 1934, Enzo spent his entire life in the Hirai neighborhood of the Edogawa Ward in Tokyo and was often referred to as *Hirai no shisho* (Hirai's master). His father once worked as a *taikomochi* (a male geisha) and later as a *kamishibai* storyteller. A "male geisha" in Japan is the equivalent of a *jester*, the court entertainer in Europe during the medieval and Renaissance eras. Kamishibai is a form of Japanese street theater and storytelling that was popular during the 1930s and the post-war years. With the advent of television in the 1950s, however, its popularity declined drastically.[170]

xx. Kamishibai storyteller in Asakusa (Kanariya Eiraku)

The art of kamishibai originated during the Meiji era, and its purpose was to attract children and sell a snack called *mizu-ame*. *Mizu-ame*, which literally translates to "water candy," was a sticky

---

[170] "橘家圓蔵（8代目）" ("Tachibanaya Enzo VIII.") Wikipedia. Wikimedia Foundation, January 24, 2021.

sugar reduction with the viscosity of very thick honey. It was usually sold on a stick.

The kamishibai narrator generally performed on street corners with a set of illustrated boards that he placed in a miniature stage-like device. As he narrated the story, he changed the images in the device to correspond to a particular segment of the story.[171]

Enzo obviously inherited his father's passion for entertaining. His first exposure to storytelling came about as a result of helping his father during his kamishibai performances. From there, he gravitated toward rakugo, officially becoming an apprentice in 1952.

During his zenza years, he was known as Tachibanaya Takezo. He adopted the stage name Tachibanaya Masuzo after his promotion to futatsume in 1955, and changed it to Tsukinoya Enkyo III after he was promoted to shinuchi in March 1965.

From the mid-1960s through the 1980s, he built a dual career as a rakugoka and a radio/television personality. His face was a familiar sight in many Japanese living rooms at the time and his voice could be heard almost daily over the radio. Of the various radio shows he hosted, the longest running program was *Niji no*

---

[171] "Kamishibai." Wikipedia. Wikimedia Foundation, December 29, 2020. https://en.wikipedia.org/wiki/Kamishibai.

Otoko (*2:00 P.M. Man*). It ran on the Nippon Cultural Broadcasting station from 1966 to 1981.

He also engaged in quite a bit of commercial work, promoting everything from the International Electric Industry to yakiniku sauce. His catchphrase, "My wife Setsuko," was easily recognized by everyone.[172]

Enzo made film appearances in 1967 and 1969. The first was a comedy directed by Sugie Toshio called *Rakugo yaro dai bakusho*. It featured a long list of rakugo performers in a tale that involved a kidnapping from one of Edo's nagaya. The second film, *Yotaro senki*, was an adaptation of Shunputei Ryusho's story with the same title. The plot centered around a man named Yotaro and his misadventures in the military.[173]

As a rakugo artist, Enzo was known for his comedic talent even though he concentrated mostly on mystery stories. One of his favorite stories was "Shichimendo," about a burglar who sneaks into the Shichimendo Temple to steal an incense burner and a wooden gong. Naturally, things do not go as planned and he gets caught. The news of the robbery spreads all over town. Upon hearing the news, the townspeople go to the temple in scores to worship. The temple flourishes and within ten years has over 3,000

---

[172] "橘家圓蔵（8代目）"("Tachibanaya Enzo VIII"). Wikipedia.
[173] "橘家圓蔵（8代目）"("Tachibanaya Enzo VIII"). Wikiwand. https://www.wikiwand.com/ja/%E6%A9%98%E5%AE%B6%E5%9C%93%E8%94%B5_(8%E4%BB%A3%E7%9B%AE).

ryo (a gold currency unit during the Edo period) in its coffers. After learning about the temple's prosperity, the burglar demands that they give the 3,000 ryo to him, claiming that his robbery attempt ten years earlier was what brought good fortune to the temple. During the argument, a temple boy enters and tells the burglar to stop being such a *shichimendo*. (The word also means "nuisance.")

Another tale Enzo loved to tell was "Neko to Kingyo" ("Cat and Goldfish"). In this story, the master's goldfish are eaten by the cat next door, so the master tells the head clerk, Banto, to keep an eye on the cat. What he doesn't know is that Banto was born in the Year of the Mouse and is deathly afraid of cats.

Enzo's love of mystery stories enabled him to share a long-term friendship with author Hanmura Ryo, who churned out an extraordinary number of radio scripts during a very prolific period in his life. Enzo also shared a special bond with Tatekawa Danshi, whom he regarded as his big brother.

Danshi and Enzo had a very popular radio program together on the Nippon Broadcasting System from 1969 to 1973, called *Danshi/Enkyo Kayo Gassen* (*Danshi/Enkyo Song Competition*). One broadcast in particular, in which Danshi and Enzo performed a gag of conversing nonsensically, became extremely popular and was later released on CD. Enzo was also a welcome guest on

Shoten, where he amazed the audience with his quick and witty responses to the host's questions.

Indeed, his swiftness was what set him apart as a storyteller. He was known for his ability to transition between characters at an unprecedented speed. With a quick twist of the head, he effortlessly and seamlessly moved from one character to another in the story, which is a talent that has yet to be duplicated by any other rakugo artist.

When the Rakugo Kyokai descended into turmoil in 1978, Enzo and his master Tachibanaya Enzo VII withdrew from the association. Although he was allowed to return to the Rakugo Kyokai after his master passed away in 1980, there were a series of complications he had to overcome. Therefore, it was with hesitation that he inherited the name Tachibanaya Enzo VIII in October 1982. The Enzo name had been tarnished by the chaos created in 1978, and it became the successor's responsibility to establish a positive relationship with the association once again.

But that wasn't the end; there was still one more hurdle Enzo had to conquer after the succession. It became known that his master had borrowed the name Enzo from Sanyutei Ensho VI with the promise that no one else would inherit the name afterwards. When his master died, Enzo was faced with a dilemma. He decided to approach the widow of the late Ensho and officially obtain her consent to inherit the name of Enzo.

Enzo eventually achieved good standing with the Rakugo Kyokai and was appointed as a consultant for the association in 2006. In 2012, he received the Edogawa Culture Award in recognition of his many contributions and efforts to cultivate the rakugo culture in Edogawa.

After Enzo passed away on October 7, 2015, the Edogawa Ward purchased his Hirai residence and preserved it as a memorial hall. It was later made accessible to the public as the "Hirai Enzo-tei" and currently hosts many rakugo-related events, including workshops and performances by both professional and amateur rakugo performers. To date, Enzo and Hayashiya Sanpei are the only two rakugoka to have memorial halls dedicated to them.[174]

---

[174] "橘家圓蔵（8代目）"("Tachibanaya Enzo VIII"). Wikipedia.

xxi. Tachibanaya Enzo VIII

10. Hayashiya Sanpei

>
> *"There are three superstars in the Showa period: me, Misora Hibari, and Hayashiya Sanpei."*
> —Ishihara Yujiro, actor (1934-1987)

Born in Tokyo's Taito Ward on November 30, 1925, Hayashiya Sanpei grew up to become a vastly popular and dominant force in the worlds of rakugo and television during the Showa era, earning the title "the Showa King of Laughter."[175]

He was introduced to rakugo by his father, Hayashiya Shozo VII, who also served as his master until his death in 1949. Following his father's passing, the twenty-four-year-old began training with his father's disciple, Tachibanaya Enzo VII.

Despite his greatness, Sanpei chose not to succeed to the name Shozo, and excused himself from the nomination for succession to the names Kosanji and Enkyo. He maintained the name Sanpei, his father's zenza stage name, throughout his entire rakugo career.

---

[175] "Negishi Sanpei-Do." *Hello Japan* - Japan Travel Guide. http://www.hellojapan.asia/en/travel-guide/negishi-sanpeido.html.

However, rakugo was not his early ambition; he enrolled at Meiji University with the purpose of pursuing a medical career. But Japan was in the grips of war, and in March 1945 he was drafted into the army, where he was engaged in civil engineering work on the mainland. Fortunately, his military service was curtailed after Japan surrendered in August. He was demobilized two months later and entered the world of rakugo in February 1946.

In the fall of 1947, he was promoted to futatsume, but after his father's death on October 29, 1949, he had to start all over again as a zenza when he became the apprentice of his father's disciple, Enkyo. Enkyo, who had been treated rather coldly by his master, Shozo, refused to acknowledge his new disciple's prior training and subsequent promotion at the Toho Meijinkai, and he decided to make him redo everything at the Rakugo Kyokai.

Like his father, Sanpei concentrated mostly on classical rakugo stories. One of the stories he enjoyed performing was "Seisho Muhitsu" ("Unable to Write"), about an illiterate father and his school-age son. One day, the son arrives home from school with an assignment to create a poster for fire prevention week. He asks his illiterate father for help. In turn, the man approaches his wife for advice, and she tells him that as there are plenty of posters outside, so simply steal one. The man follows his wife's advice and shows the stolen poster to his son the next day. The poster reads, "Dancers Wanted!"

Sanpei also incorporated his father's original stories such as "Genpei Seisuiki" ("The Rise and Fall of the Genji and Heike Clans") into his repertoire. This historic story about the battle between the two clans was adapted from kodan with contemporary news items infused into the rakugo version.

Despite his story selections, his unconventional storytelling style and the fatal mistakes he made in the beginning left some people in the audience wondering whether he was suited for rakugo. Oftentimes, he forgot the words in the middle of a story, or he could not remember the names of the characters.

He also had a highly unusual storytelling style, and presented a series of jokes without a solid story to fall back on. When he wanted the audience to laugh, he would cue them by placing his right hand on his forehead. There were even times when he stood up on the zabuton cushion and sang songs. Notwithstanding these unconventional practices, Sanyutei Kinba III (1894-1964), who had apprenticed under Sanyutei Enka, recognized his talent and predicted that he would develop into a great rakugoka someday.

Although 1951 saw him promoted to futatsume for the second time in his career, the following year would prove to be one of mixed fortunes for Sanpei. He wed essayist Ebina Kayoko, but he fell ill shortly thereafter and required hospitalization for a month. The medical crisis put him in dire straits financially, and he was forced to sell off much of the land he had inherited from his father.

Then, in 1955, he became the host of the television program *Shinjin Rakugokai* (*Rakugo's Newcomers Show*), which helped launch his transformation from an economically downcast rakugo performer to the darling of the television world. One of Sanpei's big career achievements was developing a common ground between rakugo and television variety shows.

He attained the level of shinuchi in October 1958, and because he was a TV celebrity, his promotion ceremony was carried live on television.

Outside of his rakugo circle, Sanpei shared a very close relationship with popular actor Ishihara Yujiro, who was called the Japanese Elvis Presley at the time. The bond established by Sanpei and Yujiro extended to include their families and lasted long after both men passed away. Yujiro's company, Ishihara Promotion, covered the full costs of Sanpei's sons' promotion parties when they were promoted to shinuchi. No expenses were spared for either event.

Both boys initially apprenticed under their father. The older son recalled that his father was a very kind parent, but his attitude changed completely and became extremely harsh when his sons became his disciples.

Sanpei became the director of the Rakugo Kyokai in 1968, a position which he held for the remainder of his life. When the association was undergoing a massive shakeup in May 1978 and his master Enzo joined a new group (Rakugo Sanyu Association), Sanpei elected to remain behind.

Sanpei's career almost came to an abrupt end in early 1979, when he suffered a cerebral hemorrhage and was rushed to the Tokyo Teishin Hospital, where he lay in a coma for one week. When he regained consciousness, he found that the right side of his body had been paralyzed and he suffered from a speech disorder. Fortunately, he was able to recover with extensive rehabilitation work and returned to the rakugo stage in October that year.

However, Sanpei delivered what was to become his last rakugo performance at the Ueno Suzumoto Entertainment Hall on September 7, 1980. He passed away from liver cancer just thirteen days later at the age of 54. A consummate performer, he was working, trying to find interesting stories and information from newspapers and weekly magazines, up until a few hours before his death.[176]

Fifteen years after his death, a memorial museum called the Negishi Sanpei-do was established. The museum exhibits his

---

[176] "林家三平（初代）" ("Hayashiya Sanpei I"). Wikipedia. Wikimedia Foundation, January 20, 2021. https://ja.wikipedia.org/wiki/%E6%9E%97%E5%AE%B6%E4%B8%89%E5%B9%B3_(%E5%88%9D%E4%BB%A3).

various belongings and memorabilia, and hosts a rakugo meetup (*Sanpei-do rakugokai*) on the third Saturday of each month.[177]

---

[177] "Negishi Sanpei-Do." *Hello Japan.*

xxii. Hayashiya Sanpei

11. Mainstream Comedians Who Trained as Rakugoka

> "Don't become number one. Try to be number two."
> —*Yanagiya Kingoro (1901–1972)*

Akashiya Sanma (July 1, 1955-)

Easily recognized by his protruding front teeth, Akashiya Sanma is regarded as one of the "Big Three" comedians of Japan, together with Beat Takeshi (Kitano Takeshi) and Tamori (Morita Kazuyoshi). Sanma, whose real name is Sugimoto Takafumi, is represented by the Yoshimoto Kogyo agency, the organization which played a significant role in promoting manzai comedy in Osaka.

Sanma's interest in rakugo was sparked after hearing one of Shofukutei Matsunosuke's original rakugo stories, after which he grew determined to study rakugo under the tutelage of the master storyteller. In February 1974, when he was in his third year of high school, Sanma was accepted as an apprentice by Matsunosuke. He officially began his training after graduating in March and took up residence with his master in his home in Nishinomiya City, Hyogo Prefecture. He was bestowed the stage name of Shofukutei Sanma because his parents were engaged in the fish processing industry in Nara. Sanma is the Japanese name for Pacific Saury, a fish that becomes available in autumn.

Sanma's apprenticeship was not very strict, yet after only six months he threw everything away and ran off to Tokyo with a woman he had been dating. Matsunosuke did not react harshly to his apprentice's elopement to Tokyo and simply allowed him to do as he pleased.

Life in Tokyo did not go as planned for Sanma, and he returned to Osaka temporarily. He had no intention of resuming his rakugo training at this point, but he paid a visit to his master nonetheless, under the pretense of wanting to return a book he had borrowed from him. Expecting to be scolded, Sanma was rather surprised when Matsunosuke offered his support and encouragement.

Finally, when the woman Sanma was dating got married to someone else, he decided to recommence his rakugo training. He met his master in the dressing room of the theater where he was performing. Upon seeing his emaciated figure, Matsunosuke said to him, "Don't say a word," and took him to a ramen shop for dinner.[178]

---

[178] "明石家さんま," ("Akashiya Sanma"). Wikipedia. Wikimedia Foundation, January 9, 2021. https://ja.wikipedia.org/wiki/%E6%98%8E%E7%9F%B3%E5%AE%B6%E3%81%95%E3%82%93%E3%81%BE.

In January 1976, Sanma made his television debut on a rakugo coming of age program, which was broadcast live on Yomiuri Television (YTV). The show gathered a number of 20-year-old storytellers in the studio to talk; rakugoka and television personality Katsura Koeda (a regular on the *Knight Scoop* television program airing on the Asahi Broadcasting Corporation channel) was one of them. Rather than using the stage name he had been given, Sanma appeared on the program under the name Akashiya Sanma. Akashi was Matsunosuke's real name and many of his apprentices were calling themselves Akashiya at that time. Matsunosuke had watched the show and offered exceeding praise to his disciple afterwards.

After seeing Sanma's performance on television, Sashiki Takashi, an employee of Yoshimoto Kogyo, described him as a shy individual with not a lot to say, but someone who lights up and changes his demeanor when he is performing. Takashi later approached Matsunosuke and said, "I want Sanma to rise up from the floor cushion," meaning he wanted him to discontinue his rakugo and develop as a comedian and television personality.

Conveniently, Matsunosuke soon abandoned rakugo and became a television personality himself. Sanma officially changed his stage name to Akashiya Sanma, the name he had used when he made his television debut in 1976, and eventually caught the eye of Katsura Bunshi. He began to make appearances on the popular

Mainichi Broadcasting program called *Yangu Oh! Oh!* and became a regular on the show in 1978.

Sanma eventually moved from Osaka to Tokyo with his first Tokyo television appearance on the 1978 Fuji TV New Year special, "Hatsumode Saegusa no Bakusho Hittoparedo" ("Saegusa's New Year's Laughter Hit Parade"). This initial encounter with producer Yokozawa Takeshi brought many opportunities for Sanma to work on projects that Yokozawa was involved in.

Billing himself as an Osaka entertainer in Tokyo, Sanma was extremely busy in the 1980s, commuting to jobs in the two cities. On August 12, 1985, he was scheduled to take the ill-fated Japan Airlines Flight 123, which crashed in the area of Mount Takamagahara and killed 520 passengers. Sanma escaped the disaster by changing to an ANA flight that day. Badly shaken from the incident, he started to use the *shinkansen* (bullet train) to travel between Osaka and Tokyo.

Sanma's master, Matsunoske, passed away on February 22, 2019. The next day, Sanma made an appearance at Cool Japan Park Osaka during the unveiling of the new theater, where he presented a program featuring his master's stories. He attended his master's funeral on the following day.[179]

Shofukutei Tsurube II (December 23, 1951-)

Shofukutei Tsurube, whose real name is Suruga Manabu, is a popular rakugoka, actor, and television personality. He was born in Osaka, the youngest of five siblings, and grew up living in a *nagaya,* a common setting for Kamigata rakugo stories.

As a junior high school student, he became fascinated by the classical rakugo story "Hori no Uchi" as told by Katsura Shinji II (Katsura Bunji X). The story involves a very mixed-up character named Kumagoro and a series of mishaps during his journey to the Hori no Uchi Myohoji Temple, including mistaking a pillow wrapped in his wife's obi sash for his *bento* (lunch box), and returning home to yell at his wife only to learn that he was yelling in front of the neighbor's house instead.[180] Tsurube loved this story so much that he constructed a homemade koza at his school, where he performed his own version of the story in front of his classmates.

---

[179] "明石家さんま," ("Akashiya Sanma").
https://ja.wikipedia.org/wiki/%E6%98%8E%E7%9F%B3%E5%AE%B6%E3%81%95%E3%82%93%E3%81%BE.
[180] "堀の内（落語）." ("Horinouchi (rakugo)"). Wikipedia. Wikimedia Foundation, December 2, 2020.
https://ja.m.wikipedia.org/wiki/%E5%A0%80%E3%81%AE%E5%86%85_%28%E8%90%BD%E8%AA%9E%29.

When he reached high school, Tsurube joined a boxing club, but he ended up abandoning boxing after his eyes were damaged when an older student hit him. Near the end of his second year in high school, he organized a rakugo study group with two other students and gave himself the stage name *Dotei Mugaku* (Virgin Uneducated). It was around this time that he became interested in becoming a professional rakugoka, but naturally, his father objected to his career choice.

After graduating from high school, Tsurube chose to enroll at Kyoto Sangyo University simply because the tuition was significantly cheaper than other universities and a woman he had met earlier (who later became his wife) was a student there.

Unable to set aside his interest in rakugo, he joined the university's rakugo study group, where he performed using his real name instead of a stage name. Eventually, thoughts of quitting college and becoming a professional rakugoka pervaded his brain. He considered becoming a disciple of Shofukutei Nikaku III, but he changed his mind after seeing a performance by Shofukutei Shokaku VI in January 1971.

Tsurube waited for Shokaku at the entrance to his dressing room, but was disappointed when he did not see him. Afterwards, he decided to visit the rakugo master at his residence, but Shokaku pretended not to be at home. Subsequent visits followed, yet

Shokaku continued to decline Tsurube's requests to become an apprentice. In one final attempt to discourage him completely, Shokaku insisted that he needed to obtain his parents' consent before becoming an apprentice. Tsurube hatched a plan to ask his father to accompany him to Shokaku's home under the pretense that he needed to apologize for injuring a person in a fight. The plan worked, and Tsurube gained the introductory meeting he had been waiting for. In this way, he became the eleventh disciple of Shofukutei Shokaku on February 14, 1972.

But Tsurube rarely learned rakugo from his master, and his master claimed that Tsurube was "angry and untrainable." Eventually, he got into the habit of going to a bathhouse with his *ani-deshi* (older brother disciples), where he practiced and learned rakugo directly from them. Tsurube later said that he did not believe his master learned much from his own master, Shofukutei Shokaku V, and therefore he had a rather neglectful attitude when it came to practicing rakugo with his disciples. In place of lessons from Shokaku, Tsurube on occasion received *shamisen* (a traditional Japanese musical instrument with three strings) and rakugo lessons from Shokaku's wife, whom he called "Ah-chan."

On October 12, 1974, Tsurube married his girlfriend Reiko, the girl he had followed to Kyoto Sangyo University. The couple had plans to marry on December 23, 1980, ten years after the date they began dating, but Reiko became pregnant and the wedding date had to be moved up. It was an unusual wedding ceremony with no one from Reiko's side in attendance because Reiko had not received her family's consent to marry Tsurube.

Following their marriage, Tsurube managed to find work at local radio and television stations in Osaka, and in the mid-1970s he made an appearance on a television program in Tokyo. However, that appearance caused him to be banned from the station.

The program was a live broadcast on Tokyo Channel 12 (now TV Tokyo). In response to being arrogantly criticized by the producer for his performance on another program which aired on the same station in 1975, Tsurube exposed his crotch in front of the camera. He was forced to leave the studio after the incident.

Then, on March 26, 1977, during the final episode of the program, Tsurube made a special appearance at the station with a moderator named Yamashiro Shingo. Tsurube later claimed that Shingo encouraged him to do whatever he wanted since it was the show's final day.

Heeding Shingo's advice, Tsurube exposed his rear in front of the camera and tried to escape from the studio immediately afterwards. He jumped into a pond on the premises and ended up trampling the *Nishikigoi* (carp) valued at 7,000,000 yen. To make matters worse, the carp had been carefully raised by the president of the station, Nakagawa Sunao. This time, Tsurube was banned indefinitely. It wasn't until the station's name was changed to TV Tokyo, twenty-six years later, that the ban was finally lifted.

Fortunately for Tsurube, he still managed to become a successfully active rakugoka, actor, and TV personality in the 1990s. He created his own style of rakugo called "tsurubebanashi," in which he talks about everyday topics and daily occurrences in a humorous style. For this, he was awarded the *Kamigata Owarai Taisho* (the Kamigata Comedy Award) in 2000.

Tsurube became the director of the Kamigata Rakugo Association in May 2003. He served as the vice chairman starting in June 2008 until his retirement in 2018. Currently, he is a consultant for the association.[181]

Tsurube's master, Shokaku, passed away in 1986. Tsurube has continuously hosted a monthly live talk show called *Tezukayama Mugakunokai* from his late master's remodeled house in Tezukayama, Osaka ever since.

Shofukutei Shohei (November 7, 1956-)

While still a high school student, Shofukutei Shohei became enamored with acting. As an ambitious 16-year-old, he sent

---

[181] "笑福亭鶴瓶." ('Shofufutei Tsurube"). Wikipedia. Wikimedia Foundation, January 2, 2021. https://ja.wikipedia.org/wiki/%E7%AC%91%E7%A6%8F%E4%BA%AD%E9%B6%B4%E7%93%B6.

countless self-promotional postcards to Ishihara International Productions, pleading "Please let me appear in a drama."[182]

Later, he became fascinated by Shofukutei Tsurube after he heard him speak on the Mainichi Broadcasting System radio program *MBS Young Town*. He officially became Tsurube's apprentice in 1981, and was selected to appear as a regular on the television show *Totsuzen gabacho!* hosted by Tsurube and Nagae Kenji. The program had earlier served as a vehicle for Tsurube to cross over to Tokyo as an entertainer from Osaka.

When Shohei became an apprentice, Tsurube was active as an entertainer in Osaka and not performing as a rakugo storyteller. He told his apprentice that he rarely performed rakugo, to which Shohei responded, "I don't feel like doing rakugo either."[183]

Shohei was introduced to Tsurube's master, Shofukutei Shokaku VI, who asked him, "Do you like to make people laugh?" Without hesitation Shohei responded, "Yes, I do." Upon hearing this response, Shokaku told Tsurube, "This young man is a rakugoka too," and he advised Shohei to "emulate Tsurube's way of life."[184]

---

[182] "笑福亭笑瓶." ("Shohei Shofukutei"). Wikipedia. Wikimedia Foundation, November 30, 2020. https://ja.m.wikipedia.org/wiki/%E7%AC%91%E7%A6%8F%E4%BA%AD%E7%AC%91%E7%93%B6
[183] "笑福亭笑瓶." ("Shohei Shofukutei"). https://ja.m.wikipedia.org/wiki/%E7%AC%91%E7%A6%8F%E4%BA%AD%E7%AC%91%E7%93%B6
[184] "笑福亭笑瓶." ("Shohei Shofukutei"). https://ja.m.wikipedia.org/wiki/%E7%AC%91%E7%A6%8F%E4%BA%AD%E7%AC%91%E7%93%B6

Since the early 2000s, Tsurube has organized various rakugo events in which Shohei has taken the stage, both as a solo performer and with his disciple Shofukutei Shosuke in a master/disciple performance. His performances are characterized by the fact that he only presents new rakugo stories and avoids the classical Kamigata repertoire altogether.[185]

Showfukutei Showko (December 28, 1968-)

Showfukutei Showko (literally "Laughing Child,") is a female Japanese comedian, ventriloquist, and actor who also trained as a rakugo performer. [186] She completed a three-year rakugo apprenticeship with Shofukutei Kakusho; who like Shofukutei Tsurube, he was a disciple of Shokaku VI. (Based in London, Kakusho is a rather unique rakugo storyteller who incorporates elements of puppetry and slapstick comedy into his performances.)[187]

Prior to becoming a comedian, Showko worked for several notable radio stations in Osaka and Singapore. She was working in Singapore in 2003 when she encountered Kakusho's puppet rakugo for the first time. Having dabbled with ventriloquism on her own, she was intrigued by Kakusho's unique rakugo

---

[185] "笑福亭笑瓶." ("Shohei Shofukutei").
https://ja.m.wikipedia.org/wiki/%E7%AC%91%E7%A6%8F%E4%BA%AD%E7%AC%91%E7%93%B6
[186] Showko Showfukutei." Wikipedia. Wikimedia Foundation, July 28, 2020.
https://en.wikipedia.org/wiki/Showko_Showfukutei.
[187] "Shōfukutei Kakushō Kōshiki Saito." 【笑福亭鶴笑公式サイト】笑う門には福来る, 2009.
http://kakushow.jp/e-profile.htm.

performance. She invited him to appear as a guest on her radio show, and after the interview she made up her mind to study rakugo with the master storyteller. She traveled to London and officially became his apprentice in 2004.

After completing her apprenticeship in London, Showko performed on the international comedy and festival circuit, eventually becoming a finalist on *Australia's Got Talent.* Currently based in Melbourne, Australia, she is a familiar figure in television, radio, comedy clubs, and festivals, often appearing in her signature vivid-colored, sequined, and leopard print kimonos.

Having attended an English language school in Canada, she performs in both English and Japanese. She usually has two versions of a story and jokes to work for both English and Japanese-speaking audiences. Her rakugo performances are also unique as she invites audience members on stage to interact with her puppets. In traditional rakugo, audience members are not permitted on stage. As a matter of fact, when performers take their place on stage and kneel down on the zabuton, they place their paper fan in front of them to form a barrier between themself and the audience.[188]

Showko's puppets are an integral part of her performances and she shares a very special relationship with them. In an interview given

---

[188] "Showko Showfukutei." Wikipedia. Wikimedia Foundation.

to The Japan Foundation in Sydney in 2019, she explained that when she was young, she gave Valentine's Day chocolates to the boy she liked, and he threw them away. In Japan, it is customary for women to give chocolates to the men on Valentine's Day. The next day, she learned that her best friend and the boy had begun dating, and she was heartbroken.

The next time she decided to declare her love for a boy, instead of giving him chocolates she made a puppet and gave it to him. But the boy got scared and immediately threw it away! After the second heartbreak, puppets became her outlet. She would talk to them out loud and share her problems with them. Showko claims that she had a pretty tough family life, but she was able to overcome it with the aid of her puppets. "These puppet characters are a way of balancing the light and the dark," she said. "I feel like my story and my comedy [are] always trying to balance bitter and funny elements together."[189]

---

[189] Groves, Alison. "A Ventriloquist, a Rakugo Performer, and a Puppet Walk into a Bar...." Japan Art Directory in Australia, 2019. https://artdirectory.jpf.org.au/showko-showfukutei/.

12. Female Rakugoka

> *"The most important thing is for our audience to enjoy themselves. If our abilities are not recognized, we won't get another chance. The real game begins now."*
> —Kokontei Komako
> *Asahi Gunma, May 8, 2019*

In the highly disciplined world of rakugo, female rakugoka are still scarce even today. What's more, the art form was developed and successfully dominated by men until 1993, the year when not one, but two women, Kokontei Kikuchiyo and Sanyutei Karuta, were promoted to the shinuchi level. Twenty-five years later, Kikuchiyo's female apprentice, Kokontei Komako, became a shinuchi and the two women made history by becoming the first female master and disciple to attain the shinuchi status.

More recently, in May 2019, another female storyteller, Sanyutei Aiba, was promoted to the top rank of her craft after fifteen long years of dedication to the art of rakugo.[190] As of March 2021, of the nearly 600 rakugoka in Tokyo, there are only twelve female

---

[190] DeHaven, Shawn. "Sanyūtei Aiba: A Rising Female Voice in the Rakugo World." It's Funny in Japanese, 2019. http://www.itsfunnyinjapanese.com/interviews-sanyutei-aiba.

shinuchi. At the time of writing this book, eight of them are members of the Rakugo Kyokai and four are members of the Rakugo Geijutsu Kyokai.

When Kikuchiyo first expressed her interest in becoming a professional storyteller, she was told that rakugo masters would never accept a female apprentice. However, through her unwavering ambition and determination she was able to break down the centuries-old barrier and become the apprentice of Kokontei Engiku II at the age of twenty-seven.

Born in Tokyo's Itabashi Ward on July 24, 1956, Kikuchiyo attended Oberlin University in Tokyo, where she studied Chinese and Chinese Literature. After graduating in 1980, she enrolled in Tokyo Designer Gakuin to study design, but she abandoned her studies one year later in favor of joining the editorial department of an advertising agency. She officially entered the world of rakugo in 1984 and began her apprenticeship with Engiku.

Engiku, the disciple of the late rakugo phenom Kokontei Shinsho V (1890–1973), had earned a name for himself as a rather unconventional rakugo performer. During his performances, he had a way of moving his arms and twisting his body that drew criticism from conservative rakugo fans and performers. He was also the first storyteller to perform using sign language.

Author Lorie Brau, who apprenticed with Engiku while conducting research for her manuscript, relates a story that is very characteristic of the performer. She talks about how, following a performance at Nagasumitei in Asakusa one night, Engiku jumped up from his zabuton to plant kisses on the cheeks of some of the elderly women who were sitting in the front row.[191]

After apprenticing with Engiku for four years, Kikuchiyo was promoted to futatsume in September 1988, and she attained the level of shinuchi in March 1993. She has brought rakugo to audiences overseas, including those in North and South Korea, Argentina, and Brazil. When she was asked why she wanted to perform in North and South Korea, she responded by saying that she wanted to break down the cultural barriers by making people laugh.[192]

Komako became Kikuchiyo's apprentice in March 2004. Originally from the town of Kanra in Gunma Prefecture, she relocated to Tokyo to attend Komazawa Junior College. Although she had seen rakugo performed on television when she was in her early twenties, it wasn't until she attended a yose performance at the

---

[191] Brau, Lorie. Rakugo: Performing Comedy and Cultural Heritage in Contemporary Tokyo. Lanham, MD: Lexington Books, 2008. Page 14.
[192] "Female 'Rakugo' Narrator Packs Bags to Spread Mirth on Korean Peninsula." The Japan Times, June 28, 2001. https://www.japantimes.co.jp/news/2001/06/28/national/female-rakugo-narrator-packs-bags-to-spread-mirth-on-korean-peninsula/.

Ikebukuro Engeijo Theater that she understood the art's unique charm.

When she decided to pursue rakugo as a career, she selected Kikuchiyo as her master because she was the first woman to be promoted to the shinuchi level, and she exuded a certain gentleness and honesty.

Komako was promoted to futatsume in May 2007, and she attained the shinuchi designation on September 18, 2018, at the age of 46. She uses the song "Daydream Believer," as her *debayashi* (entrance music), and like her master, she enjoys performing overseas. Komako has given performances in China, Taiwan, and Thailand, and has stated that Japanese people living abroad often welcome opportunities to engage in Japanese culture. She also claimed that many Japanese people encounter rakugo for the first time while living outside of Japan and they seek out the yose when they return.[193]

Sanyutei Karuta earned her place as a pioneer in the world of rakugo in September 1981. Born in Minami-Senju, Tokyo, she encountered rakugo for the first time as a second-year high school student. Captivated by the vivid narratives of Tatekawa Danshi and Shunputei Koasa, she fell in love with the art of rakugo. After

---

[193] Hayashi, Tetsuya, and Mieko Nakajima. "Interview Series 'People': Rakugoka Kokontei Komako." Asahi Gunma, March 8, 2019.
https://www.asahigunma.com/%E8%90%BD%E8%AA%9E%E5%AE%B6-
%E5%8F%A4%E4%BB%8A%E4%BA%AD%E9%A7%92%E5%AD%90-%E3%81%95%E3%82%93/.

graduating from high school, she briefly enrolled at Kokugakuin University, but she dropped out to become the apprentice of Sanyutei Enka III. In May 1987, she was promoted to futatsume and in March 1993, she attained the level of shinuchi along with Kokontei Kikuchiyo. She was inaugurated as a director of the Rakugo Kyokai in July 2010.[194]

Sanyutei Aiba's first encounter with rakugo was at Asakusa Engei Hall as a 17-year-old high school student. She became fascinated with the art form and after graduating from high school, she discussed becoming a rakugo storyteller with her mother. At the time, there were only about eight female rakugo performers in Tokyo, and although Aiba wanted to pursue a future as a rakugoka, she felt insecure.

Her mother ran a beauty salon and advised her daughter to get a cosmetology license in order to have something to fall back on. Aiba followed her mother's advice, but she was not fully invested in becoming a beautician. She saw her fellow students pursuing their dreams, and she too wanted to go after her dream, the dream of becoming a rakugo storyteller.

She joined a group of amateur rakugo performers, and through one of the performers she learned about her future master,

---

[194] "人間的な成長が芸に磨きをかける。" Let's Enjoy Tokyo, 2020.
https://ranking.enjoytokyo.jp/fp/kizuna/1201.html?__ngt__=TT1119cd39a002ac1e4a5a19oFRghChYe hL50OLSwpIVIA.

Tachibanano Madoka III. He was one of the few veteran rakugoka who was willing to accept a female apprentice at that time.

Unlike other rakugo masters, he did not expect his disciples to help out at home, but Aiba did so willingly because she wanted to gain his affection and approval. For Aiba, her master's house was her home away from home.

At one point, Madoka explained to her, "Once we enter the dressing room, we are master and apprentice, but once we leave this environment, we are father and daughter." Aiba, who had been raised by a single mother, really did think of Madoka as her father.

She rose to the rank of futatsume in April 2009, with the stage name Tachibanano Futaba.[195] When her master passed away in May 2014, Aiba became the apprentice of Sanyutei Enba V. She was promoted to shinuchi in May 2019, and she currently belongs to an all-female group of rakugo performers known as Rakugo Girls, not to be confused with the 2009 manga series *Joshiraku* (*Rakugo Girls*). The 15-member group, founded in 2017, which also includes Kokontei Komako, bill themselves as "A group of young female rakugoka who transcend associations and schools."[196] And indeed they do, as the group includes female rakugo storytellers

---

[195] DeHaven, Shawn.
[196] "Rakugo Girls." rakugogirls. https://mgsdp835.wixsite.com/rakugogirls.

from the Hayashiya, Sanyutei, Tatekawa, Yanagiya, and Shunputei rakugo families.

xxiii. Kokontei Kikuchiyo

13. Amateur vs. Professional Rakugoka

> ❝
> *"Nowadays there are only a few hanashika who have really mastered it [ochi]. There are many who give good performances, but the conclusion falls flat."*
> — *Sanyutei Ensho VI*

Just as there are two styles of rakugo being performed today (Edo and Kamigata), there are also two classifications of rakugo performers, amateur and professional. *Tenguren* (amateur storytellers) date back to the Edo period and continue to flourish in the present day. They include students belonging to the *Rakugo Kenkyu-kai* (the rakugo study groups) at universities as well as performers hailing from all walks of life including teachers, office workers, housewives, and retirees, who enjoy performing rakugo. Like professional rakugoka, most have a teigo.

The term "tenguren" is a relatively new word in the rakugo world. A *tengu* is a legendary creature with a long nose found in Japanese folklore, and it is strongly associated with vanity and pride. The Japanese expression *tengu ni naru* (becoming a tengu) is used to describe a person with too much pride. Amateur performers are often proud of their performances; therefore, they came to be called *tenguren*.

A number of professional rakugo performers originated as tenguren including Katsura Shijaku, Shofukutei Enka, Shofukutei Nikaku, Hayashiya Somemaru, all from Kamigata rakugo, and Katsura Bunraku IV, Sanyutei Ensho III, Shunputei Ryucho III, Katsura Bunji IX, Tachibanano Enman, and Sanyutei Aiba from Edo Rakugo.[197] Even Swedish rakugoka, Sanyutei Koseinen, was an amateur rakugo performer appearing under the stage name Volvotei Ikeya until 2016.

Professional rakugoka came into existence during the seventeenth century and they continue to follow the rigid training system that was established during the end of the Edo period. They are ranked according to their experience and skill level. The ranking system in Edo rakugo consists of *minarai* (apprentice), *zenza* (first level), *futatsume* (second level), and *shinuchi* (final level). Up until the early twentieth century, a similar system of ranking was used in Kamigata rakugo, but today, Kamigata rakugoka are no longer officially ranked.

The minarai rank did not exist in the original ranking system of rakugo; but these days there are too many zenza, so they are placed on standby and called minarai at the beginning of their studies.

---

[197] "天狗連" (Tenguren). Wikipedia. October 4, 2020.
https://ja.wikipedia.org/wiki/%E5%A4%A9%E7%8B%97%E9%80%A3.

Unlike a zenza, a minarai is not given a stage name and cannot work at the yose. An apprentice rakugoka's tenure as a minarai can last anywhere from just a few months to a year. This is also the time when they are evaluated by their masters to determine whether they are suited to become professional rakugo performers.

Traditionally, both minarai and zenza engaged in doing the leg work and chores such as cleaning the master's house, cooking his meals, and assisting his family at home. In exchange, their shisho taught them rakugo. In more recent years, however, shisho have emerged who no longer require their apprentices to perform these tasks.

Originally, some of the apprentices lived in their master's house while others had their own residence. These days, the apprentices have their own residence and are supported financially (to a certain degree) by their respective masters.

While at the yose, the zenza perform odd jobs such as playing the drums and other musical instruments, carrying the *mekuri* (paper signage on which the performers' names are written), setting up the microphone and operating the sound equipment, serving tea, and managing the kimono. Sometimes the zenza are permitted to take the stage for the *kaiko ichiban* (first story) as part of their training. As such, their names are not included on the program and they do not receive a performance fee.

In Kamigata rakugo, this work is usually done by the *ochako* (part-time employees of the yose). Unlike the zenza, these women are not training to become rakugoka and will remain ochako for the duration of their employment at the yose.

After training as a zenza for three to five years, a disciple will be promoted to a futatsume. There are certain benefits associated with becoming a futatsume including no longer being required to do chores at their master's home or odd jobs at the yose. A futatsume is recognized as a full-fledged rakugoka and their name is listed on the program. A futatsume is allowed to have a *rakugokai* (rakugo show) on their own and to perform at shows that are not associated with their master. A futatsume will receive a *wari* (performance fee), but will have to find opportunities to perform on their own. Since futatsume no longer perform chores for their masters, they also stop receiving financial assistance from them.[198] This puts the futatsume at an economic disadvantage, and they have to be diligent about securing as many opportunities to perform rakugo as possible in order to support themselves.

After about ten years of training as a futatsume, a rakugoka finally reaches the shinuchi level. At this point, they are permitted to have

---

[198] Yu, "Rakugoka (Rakugo Storyteller) (落語家)."

disciples of their own. When a performer is promoted to this level, a special show and a recognition ceremony are held. The show is followed by a party which the newly-promoted shinuchi pays for out of their own pocket.[199]

When Tatekawa Shinoharu, a disciple of the illustrious rakugo performer, Tatekawa Shinosuke, was promoted to shinuchi in April 2020, his recognition ceremony was postponed for several months due to the coronavirus pandemic. Ironically, he was promoted to futatsume in 2011, the year the Great East Japan Earthquake struck, killing over 15,000 people and causing $360 billion in damage. His master, Shinosuke, joked that whenever his disciple got promoted, it triggered a devastating event.[200]

The life of a rakugoka is a difficult one. Yet in rakugo's 400-year history, countless rakugoka have devoted their souls to their art. Some rakugoka even jokingly confess that their rankings consist of zenza, futatsume, shinuchi, and *gorinju* (death).

Although the amateur rakugo performers do not go through the same long and arduous training that professional rakugo performers endure, their dedication and commitment to their art is still remarkable. Certain amateur performers show a high level of mastery that could rival some professionals. It is rather common

---

[199] Yu, "Rakugoka (Rakugo Storyteller)（落語家）."
[200] 東京かわら版 (Tokyo Kawara-ban). June 28, 2020. Page 14.

for some rakugo fans to begin their journey by listening to amateur performers first and later gravitating toward professional performers. Therefore, we cannot ignore the role of amateur rakugo performers in the development of the art form and its diffusion overseas.

Rakugo Kenkyu-kai or Ochiken

The term *Rakugo Kenkyu-kai*, which is often abbreviated as "ochiken," directly translates to "rakugo study group." These groups began to emerge during the 1940s and 50s at several universities as a form of extra-curricular activity. Tokyo University and Waseda University were the first to incorporate the ochiken into their extra-curricular offerings. Many of today's professional rakugo performers started out as ochiken members before becoming disciples of famous shinuchi.

Particularly notable are the ochiken of Nihon University and Meiji University, which have produced quite a number of professional rakugo performers over the years. For example, Tatekawa Shiraku, Yanagiya Kyotaro, Shuputei Ichinosuke, Yanagiya Wasabi, and Hayashiya Botan, a 41-year-old female rakugoka from Hamamatsu, Japan, all hail from Nihon University. Meiji University, on the other hand, has produced Tatekawa Shinosuke, Tatekawa Danko, Tatekawa Shirano, and Gokaido Kumosuke.

Kamigata rakugo also has its share of professional rakugo performers who were former ochiken members including Katsura Bunshi VI, Katsura Bunchin, Katsura Kichiya, Katsura Nanten, and Katsura Sansen.

In 2003, the first All Japan Student Rakugo Championship (Sakuden Grand Prize) was held. This nationwide rakugo competition for students is held annually in Gifu City, the birthplace of Anrakuan Sakuden. Both undergraduate and graduate students belonging to an ochiken are eligible to participate in a preliminary video competition for a chance to perform at the national championship. The contest takes place over the span of two days with the first day devoted to the qualifying round. The finals, consisting of eight student performers, are held on the second day. The finalists are judged by two judges and two professional rakugo performers. Katsura Fumie, a former ochiken member at Kansai University, and Tatekawa Shinosuke participate as judges every year. In addition to the Sakuden Grand Prize, the judges also hand out two special awards, the Judge's Special Award and the Encouragement Award to qualifying performers.

In its first year, the contest included 76 students from 29 universities all across Japan. In 2020, the competition's 17th year,

220 students from 51 universities and graduate schools participated.[201]

There are also several contests for adult amateur rakugo performers. One such competition is the All Japan Adult Rakugo Championship sponsored by the Rakugo Championship Executive Committee. The event began over thirty years ago and is open to all adults.

In 2009, Ikeda City in Osaka Prefecture began sponsoring a competition known as The Best Rakugoka in Japan to commemorate the city's 70th anniversary. The competition in Ikeda City is the only amateur rakugo contest to offer cash prizes. The first prize winner receives 300,000 yen (approximately US $2,800 as of this writing) while the second and third place winners receive 150,000 yen and 100,000 yen.

Two years later, in 2011, NPO Forever introduced an event in Chiba known as the International Rakugo Tournament in Chiba. Although the International Rakugo Tournament in Chiba has the word "international" in its title, the competition consists entirely of rakugo stories performed in Japanese.

Also, the first Chiritotechin Cup: National Women's Rakugo Tournament sponsored by Obama City in Fukui Prefecture was

---

[201] 全日本学生落語選手権・策伝大賞 (All Japan Student Rakugo Championship/Sakuden Grand Prize). Wikipedia. https://ja.m.wikipedia.org/wiki/全日本学生落語選手権・策伝大賞

held in 2008.[202] The tournament began in commemoration of, and gets its name from, the 2007-2008 television series *Chiritotechin* (English title, *Life's Like a Comedy*). The drama, which centers around a small-town girl who wants to become a rakugoka, is set in the city of Obama.

---

[202] "天狗連," (Tenguren). Wikipedia. October 4, 2020.

14. Rakugo on the Internet

> "Thank you for coming today. Of all the possible venues for entertainment, you picked the yose.
> You must be true fans of rakugo.
> But don't you have any place better to go?"
> —Kokontei Shingo (1949-2010)

Unlike other theater productions where the stage lights are turned up and the house lights are dimmed during the performance, rakugo is typically presented while both the stage and house lights remain on during the entire show. This is because rakugo has always been an interactive presentation. The storyteller relies on the visual and audible reactions from their audience in order to gauge their performance. Therefore, the audience's feedback is an essential element in rakugo performances.

More recently, a significant number of rakugoka have been turning to the Internet as an option for reaching a wider audience. The Internet played an important role in the rakugo world during the COVID-19 pandemic, as countless live performances had to be cancelled to help stop the spread of the virus. When performances resumed, the size of the audiences was restricted to comply with the safety measures imposed to limit the spread of the virus. This drastically impacted the revenue generated from these performances, and it impacted the performers' mindsets.

Although some rakugoka were initially opposed to performing in front of a camera without a live audience, many of them embraced the idea of streaming their performances over the Internet. Furthermore, by using particular streaming services, some performers were able to charge admission to their online performances, enabling them to recoup some of the revenue they lost during the main phase of the pandemic.

Since the majority of the world's population currently owns a computer, the Internet is a suitable medium by which a performer can reach an audience when live performances are not an option. Of course, there are both advantages and disadvantages to streaming performances over the Internet.

Obviously, the major advantage of utilizing the Internet is the opportunity to reach those who may not have the means to attend a live performance, including individuals who might experience mobility and logistical challenges. Internet connectivity has also enabled performers in Japan to reach audiences overseas and introduce them to the unfamiliar art of rakugo. And the Internet has been particularly impactful for entertainers who perform rakugo in English.

Many rakugo performers have also established YouTube channels where they are currently archiving their performances. This gives rakugo fans opportunities to watch their favorite performers over and over again without having to wait for a live performance to take place. While using services such as YouTube does not necessarily generate an income for a rakugo performer, it does simulate one of the essential purposes of a yose, which is to nurture the rakugoka. Even without venues in which they can give live performances, the rakugo artists can continue to perform for these video channels and continue to cultivate their art.

As stated before, rakugo's success is based on the collective efforts of the performer and the audience, which is where the disadvantage of using the Internet comes in. Without a live audience, the rakugo performer is prevented from receiving the instantaneous audience feedback they have grown accustomed to. When looking into a camera, a performer has no way of knowing whether a joke has succeeded immensely or failed miserably. The storyteller cannot hear the laughter from the audience or see their facial reactions. With the Internet, rakugo loses some of its spontaneity and makes the performance somewhat more challenging for the storyteller.

In some instances, rakugo performers have set aside time after an online performance to engage with their audience members. Although this type of interaction is not instantaneous, engaging in question and answer sessions and reviewing comments submitted by audience members before or after the show allows the performers to get some feedback about their performances.

The adaptability of rakugo has always been key to its survival, and the recent challenges of the pandemic are an affirmation of this time-tested fact. Overall, the Internet has been less of an impediment and more of a new avenue by which rakugo performers can flourish and perpetuate their art. Some YouTube channels for rakugo performances are listed next.

Rakugo Online:

The English Rakugo Channel (*Canary English Rakugo Company*)
https://www.youtube.com/channel/UCu2IzXUIB0r05D7ulCnnMlQ

Katsura Sunshine Rakugo Channel
https://www.youtube.com/channel/UCee2yrPm0CyXw7Oeyx9iMMA

Rakugo NZ Channel (*Kanariya Eishi*)
https://www.youtube.com/channel/UCwf1FhZwiasVAaIXSLPaMHg

Rakugo Short Stories in English (*Katsura Kaishi and Katsura Fukuryu*)
https://www.youtube.com/channel/UCtVVVU5QK6PGDpMzWaFcrpA

Sanyutei Koseinen's Channel
https://www.youtube.com/channel/UCBpMrzg_m6y6fMfuUcUUPOg

Shinoharu Rakugo (*Tatekawa Shinoharu*)
https://www.youtube.com/channel/UCaROWsReXkSJbb1qncPlhzA

Zabu Channel (*Yanagiya Tozaburo*)
https://www.youtube.com/channel/UCe3vHUcZDcSJws6x-tfk9qQ

15. Sign Language Rakugo

> *"Don't copy others. It is the only thing you should not do."*
> —*Sanyutei Enraku V (1939-2009)*

It is true that laughter is universal, people enjoy laughing in any language and sign language is no exception.

Kokontei Engiku II (1928-2012) was the first storyteller to perform rakugo using sign language. His disciple, Kokontei Kikuchiyo, also performs rakugo using sign language. Even rakugoka Katsura Fukudanji, known for his role in the film *Oni no Uta*, has performed using sign language.

Fukudanji conceived the idea of performing rakugo using sign language after he temporarily lost the use of his voice due to vocal polyps. As he began learning sign language, he became motivated to make his hearing-impaired friends smile by performing rakugo in sign language.[203]

Soon after, a disciple of Fukudanji became the first professional rakugo performer with a hearing disability. Nakayama Shinji, who

---

[203] "Implementation of 'AEON MALL Rakugo.'" AEON MALL/CSR, 2018. https://www.aeonmall.com/en/csr_2017/feature/feature1/page3.html.

is known by his stage name Rakufukutei Ippuku, began his apprenticeship with Fukudanji in 1979, after learning that the master storyteller had performed rakugo using sign language. Throughout the 1980s, sign language was becoming widespread in Japan and groups of people learning sign language were being established one after another all over the country. That being the case, sign language rakugo began to draw a lot of attention.

While he practiced performing rakugo, Ippuku noticed that simply interpreting a classical rakugo story into sign language did not appeal to a deaf audience. He realized that there was a difference between the laugh cultures of the deaf and others and stories needed to be arranged in a certain manner in order to elicit laughter from a deaf audience.

He began by altering stories to incorporate topics that were more familiar to deaf people. He also included a deaf person as a main character in his stories. Thus, he began to create his own rakugo to be performed in sign language.

When performing rakugo in sign language, the storyteller cannot rely on sign language that is usually used for daily conversation. These movements are too small and subtle to be seen easily by the audience. A rakugoka has to make the gestures much larger and clearer.

In addition, the performer must act out certain actions in the story by using a fan or a hand towel. This is especially true for classical rakugo where the traditional acting must not be changed. For example, there is a rule that the gesture for drinking sake must be expressed by using a fan. However, a storyteller using a fan cannot use sign language. Therefore, the rakugoka must strike a balance between using sign language and adhering to traditional acting practices.

Another challenge rakugo storytellers face when they perform using sign language is that some of the meanings of words used in classical rakugo are not always clear, or there is no suitable sign language for expressing certain words, since the words used are too archaic. In this case, if the meaning of the word is not clear, the performer must replace it with an easier word.

Also, modern sign language is quite different from the version that was used in the past. The older version had interesting expressions which can be very useful when it comes to conveying rakugo stories.

Understanding all of the mechanisms that come into play when performing rakugo in sign language is a great challenge and Ippuku's efforts have been recognized. He was promoted to shinuchi on September 6, 1992, and two years later, he changed his stage name to Fukudanjitei Ippuku. On February 8, 2001, he changed it once again, this time to Deaf Ippuku.

He was invited to perform overseas, and gave performances at the Congress and Festival of the Deaf in Italy, the United States, and the United Kingdom. During his first overseas presentation, he performed in front of a group of about 50 deaf people. He had concerns as to whether he could actually make them laugh, but when he began his performance and the audience burst into laughter, he realized that laughter is truly universal.

Presently, there are about 30 people who are actively performing sign language rakugo. Within that group, about 25 are actually deaf and five have difficulty hearing. Five of Ippuku's former apprentices still perform all over Japan. They mainly perform for the sign language learning circles. Ippuku himself is currently mentoring another disciple in sign language rakugo.[204]

---

[204] "Traditional Japanese Comedy Performed in Sign Language (March 2004)." Japanese Society for Rehabilitation of Persons with Disabilities.
https://www.dinf.ne.jp/doc/english/resource/rakugo.html.

Rakugo in Other Languages

16. Katsura Shijaku II

"Keep a smiling mask on, and someday the mask will be your own face."
—*Katsura Shijaku II (1939-1999)*

Just as Kairakutei Black's name was recorded in history as Japan's first foreign-born rakugoka who performed in Japanese, Katsura Shijaku II became the first Japanese-born rakugoka in history to perform his stories in English and to present them in front of foreign audiences overseas.

Shijaku, one of five children born to the Maeda family, was born in Kobe on August 13, 1939.[205] An employment opportunity forced the family to relocate to Itami City in 1946, where Shijaku and his younger brother Takeshi got their manzai stage name, the Itami Maeda Brothers. Shijaku was still in high school in 1957 when he and Takeshi participated in Asahi Broadcasting Corporation's (ABC Radio) *Manzai Classroom*.

The program featured three groups who competed and were judged by a professional manzai master. There were four stages of

---

[205] "Shijaku Katsura II." Wikipedia. Wikimedia Foundation, December 26, 2019. https://en.wikipedia.org/wiki/Shijaku_Katsura_II.

competition: Elementary (first week), Secondary (second week), Higher (third week), and Graduation Exam (fourth week). The contestants were awarded prize money after successfully completing each stage.

Although the brothers won the *Manzai Classroom* contest and several other amateur manzai competitions afterwards, Shijaku left manzai behind and turned to rakugo. In 1959, he received permission to become the disciple of the legendary rakugo performer Katsura Beicho III. Acting on his master's recommendation, he enrolled at Kobe University in 1960, where he studied the English language. However, after just one year as a university student he decided to drop out and pursue rakugo full time. [206] He officially became Beicho's *uchi deshi* (live-in apprentice) on April 10, 1961, and he was given the stage name Katsura Koyone.

He proved to be an enthusiastic pupil who often became so absorbed in learning a story that he grew oblivious to his surroundings. He continued practicing rakugo in this manner even after becoming a shinuchi.[207]

Shijaku learned koten rakugo from his master, but he focused more on the comedic element than mastering the classical aesthetics. His

---

[206] Morioka and Miyoko. *Rakugo*. Pages 282-3.
[207] 桂枝雀（2代目）(Katsura Shijaku II)." Wikipedia. Wikimedia Foundation, December 7, 2020. https://ja.wikipedia.org/wiki/%E6%A1%82%E6%9E%9D%E9%9B%80_(2%E4%BB%A3%E7%9B%AE).

unusual performance style, incorporating dramatic gestures and colorful language, made him a widely popular performer and he attracted fans from all over Japan.[208]

In October 1970, Shijaku married a shamisen musician named Shiyo, whom he had met a year earlier. The couple lived with Beicho at his house until 1971, when Shiyo discovered that she was pregnant with her first child. Shijaku and Shiyo moved to Toyonaka City in August of that year. According to Shiyo, their marriage was a strenuous affair, and she was surprised to learn that Shijaku was nothing like the person she knew while they were dating. In fact, he was a gloomy man who did not spend much time watching television and conversed rather infrequently.[209]

It was one thing to endure Shijaku's moods at home, but quite another when his mood swings began having an impact on his career. On February 1, 1973, he was scheduled to make an appearance in Dotonbori. Shiyo called for a taxi. But Shijaku refused to go, saying he was scared. In a state of panic, she contacted Beicho and later checked Shijaku into the hospital. After a medical evaluation, Shijaku was diagnosed with severe depression. The pressure from the responsibility of having a family and disciples coupled with his dissatisfaction with his own art had

---

[208] Morioka, and Miyoko. *Rakugo*.
[209] "桂枝雀（2代目）(Katsura Shijaku II)."

begun to take a toll. Following his release from the hospital, Shijaku confined himself to his room and refused to eat and bathe.

He remained in this state until he took the advice of a doctor at Osaka University Hospital, who told him that he didn't require medication. What he needed was to rest himself and rest his brain. The doctor also gave Shijaku his home telephone number and told him to call whenever he found himself struggling with anxiety.

This approach worked and Shijaku's mental health improved. He said to his wife, "I don't want to get sick again. I will put on a smiling face." In a later interview, Shijaku recalled that he was "thinking about fun things in an unpleasant manner." He said, "Keep a smiling mask on, and someday the mask will be your own face."[210]

Not long after he changed his stage named to Katsura Shijaku II, opportunities to perform began to pour in. Beginning in September 1979, he appeared on a television program on Asahi Television called *Shijaku's Yose*. In 1982, he was awarded the Japan Broadcasting Performing Arts Award, and he received the Newcomer Award for Fine Arts the following year. His rakugo performances were highly entertaining, and he even managed to

---

[210] "桂枝雀（2代目）(Katsura Shijaku II)."

earn the nickname "King of Laugher" during the height of the manzai boom.[211]

He gave a solo performance at the Kabukiza Theater (the principal theater in Tokyo for traditional Kabuki drama) on March 28, 1984. His was the first solo performance ever given by a Kamigata rakugo performer at this venue, and tickets sold out quickly. Applause from foreign audience members during the performance ignited Shijaku's interest in foreign languages once again.[212]

When he returned to Osaka, he enrolled at H.O.E. (Hiranomachi Office English) International, an adult English language school founded in 1970 to serve the business and corporate community. Its founder and director was Yamamoto Masaaki.

In the early 1980s, Yamamoto pioneered the idea of using simple English translations of familiar rakugo stories as a tool for teaching English. By 1984, several Osaka-based rakugoka had become involved with H.O.E, and together they organized English-language rakugo performances in and around Osaka.

Shijaku worked with Yamamoto to translate and polish several classical rakugo stories including "Toki Udon" ("Time Noodles"), "Manju Kowai" (English title, "My Favorite"), and "Dobutsuen" (English title, "The White Lion"). "The White Lion" was about an

---

[211] "桂枝雀（2代目）(Katsura Shijaku II)."
[212] Morioka, and Miyoko. *Rakugo*

unemployed man who takes a job at a zoo, only to learn that the job is to become a tiger to replace the one that had recently died. In time, it became one of Shijaku's signature stories. [213]

On June 2, 1986, Shijaku presented two stories in English, "Sagi Tori"("The Bird Hunter") and "Kaze Udon" ("Udon Vendor"), to an international audience at the Keio Plaza Hotel in Tokyo. He was surprised to see that the audience members who laughed the most were Japanese. They simply enjoyed listening to rakugo they were already familiar with performed in a foreign language.[214]

From that point on, his management team seized the golden opportunity and organized various "Rakugo in English" performances in Tokyo, Kyoto, Nagoya, and Yokohama. In June 1987, he embarked on his first overseas tour of Honolulu, Los Angeles, and Vancouver (all cities with a sizeable Japanese population) under the sponsorship of the East-West Culture Center at the University of Hawaii.[215]

Back in Japan, on February 25, 1988, Shijaku was elected the vice president of the Kamigata Rakugo Association. But declined the position, stating that it was not suitable for him. He continued to

---

[213] Braun, John. "Rakugo and HOE International." English rakugo, July 10, 2013. https://englishrakugo.wordpress.com/rakugo-and-hoe-international/.
[214] Morioka and Miyoko. *Rakugo*.
[215] Morioka and Miyoko. *Rakugo*.

perform energetically thereafter and enjoyed success as a rakugo storyteller. But his depression reared its head once again.

In 1997, when he was appearing in front of a small audience on *Shijaku Banashi no Kai*, his debilitating anxiety made it difficult for him to perform. Shijaku gave what was to be his last rakugo performance on January 14, 1998, in Takamatsu City, Kagawa Prefecture.

Shijaku was about to turn 60, and during summer that year, he showed his friend, Toda Manabu, his plan to give 60 performances in 20 days (three shows per day) to help commemorate his birthday. Two publications, the *Complete Works of Shijaku's Rakugo* and a *Photobook of Shijaku Katsura* were also planned for that year.[216]

Sadly, those plans were never realized, and a brilliant career came to a tragic end on April 19, 1999, when Shijaku died of heart failure. He had been in a coma for a month following a failed suicide attempt at his home in Suita, Osaka. It was a paradoxical end for a man who spent his lifetime making others laugh.[217]

---

[216] "桂枝雀（2代目）(Katsura Shijaku II)."
[217] "Shijaku Katsura II." Wikipedia. Wikimedia Foundation, December 26, 2019. https://en.wikipedia.org/wiki/Shijaku_Katsura_II.

Shijaku's master, Katsura Beicho, was deeply distressed by the death of his disciple. He said he had always wanted to see how Shijaku's performance would have evolved as he grew older.[218]

Today, there are a number of amateur and professional Japanese rakugoka who perform in English; however, Shijaku was the first to perform in English and take his show overseas, making an otherwise inaccessible Japanese art form available to non-Japanese-speaking audiences.

---

[218] "桂米朝、海原小浜の上方笑芸繁盛記 2" ("Katsurabeichō, Unabarakohama No Kamigata Shōgei Hanjō-Ki 2'). YouTube, 2016. https://www.youtube.com/watch?app=desktop&v=Ss5V6HLtH3w.

17. Katsura Kaishi

> "I want people to know that rakugo isn't something difficult to understand. Everybody can see it and enjoy it."
> —Katsura Kaishi, January 24, 2012

A disciple of Katsura Bunshi V, Katsura Kaishi, is a contemporary Kamigata storyteller who is known for performing rakugo in English. He was a student at the Takasaki City University of Economics when he saw Bunshi's performance and fell in love with the art of rakugo. After graduating from the university in 1994, he officially began his apprenticeship with Bunshi.

Kaishi was born in Amagasaki City, Hyogo Prefecture on May 7, 1969. Unlike most other young apprentices who pursue careers as professional rakugo performers after graduating from college, he did not belong to an ochiken as a university student. He attributed this lack of experience to not being given a stage name until his first public performance in March 1995. Just two hours before his performance was scheduled to begin, his master said to him, "Now you can begin," and gave him the stage name Katsura Kaishi. Kaishi means beginning in Japanese.

When Kaishi began performing rakugo, he performed only in Japanese; however, one day in 1997, he came across a foreigner at a bar who asked him to perform rakugo. Although Kaishi had started learning English as a junior high school student, he did not know how to convey rakugo stories in any language other than Japanese. He was uncertain as to whether Japanese humor could actually make foreigners laugh. The experience at the bar motivated him, and he began testing different rakugo stories in English.

Among the stories Kaishi tested were the classical stories "Chiritotechin" ("Rotten Tofu") and "Dobutsuen" ("The Zoo"). The first story is about a man who wants to teach a lesson to one of his friends who has a know-it-all attitude, and offers him rotten tofu as chiritotechin, a rare Chinese delicacy that does not actually exist. As expected, the friend says that he knows it and eats it in agony as he keeps saying, "This is delicious!"[219] The second story is the same story Katsura Shijaku performed in English, which he called "The White Lion."

After devoting one year to writing stories and performing them for foreigners in Japan, Kaishi made his first overseas appearance in Colorado in 1998. The performance was a success, and he was very

---

[219] "桂かい枝 (Katsura Kaishi)." Wikipedia. Wikimedia Foundation, February 14, 2021. https://ja.wikipedia.org/wiki/%E6%A1%82%E3%81%8B%E3%81%84%E6%9E%9D.

surprised that he had managed to make people outside of Japan laugh.

Ten years later, he was appointed as the Japan Cultural Envoy for the Agency for Cultural Affairs and embarked on a six-month tour of the United States. Traveling in a camper and accompanied by his wife and two daughters, he visited 30 cities, including New York, Los Angeles, and Chicago. Kaishi performed in clubs, bars, schools, and even a fire department. He was willing to perform at any place where people gathered in his effort to spread rakugo outside Japan. During a show in New York, he adopted an unconventional approach to performing rakugo by projecting photographs onto a screen behind him. In doing so, he violated rakugo's sacred tradition of only using a hand towel and a fan as props.

In addition to his success overseas, Kaishi received numerous awards in Japan including the 2003 Agency for Cultural Affairs Art Festival Award and the 2004 NHK Newcomer Performing Arts Award (Rakugo Category).

To date, he has traveled to 93 cities in 15 countries, performing rakugo in English. In an interview given to *The Japan Times* in 2012, he said, "I'm hoping that rakugo, as one kind of Japanese humor, will be accepted by more people around the world as a form of entertainment rather than just as part of traditional Japanese culture."[220]

---

[220] Mimizuka, Kayo. "Storyteller Broadens Appeal of 'Rakugo'." The Japan Times, January 24, 2012. https://www.japantimes.co.jp/news/2012/01/24/national/storyteller-broadens-appeal-of-rakugo/

18. Rakugo with Subtitles

> "The audience at each of my performances laughed a lot and listened with uninterrupted concentration, rapt attention, and sparking eyes [to] my clumsy rakugo stories (in Japanese with subtitles, and in English). In fact, I think that their reaction exceeded the response I normally receive in Japan, probably because they were interested in the culture of traditional performance arts, while Japanese tend to take it for granted."
> —Katsura Utazo
> The Japan Foundation Wochi Kochi Magazine, 2015

Most Japanese rakugo performers do not perform in English simply because they do not speak the language. However, a growing number of storytellers who cannot speak English but are interested in communicating rakugo to a foreign audience are attempting to perform rakugo with English subtitles. Yanagiya Kyotaro, Yanagiya Sankyo, Yanagiya Kyonosuke, Shunputei Ichinosuke, Katsura Koharudanji III, and Katsura Bunshi VI are among the rakugoka who have performed rakugo with subtitles.

Osaka-born Koharudanji entered the world of rakugo after dropping out of Ritsumeikan University in August 1977 and apprenticed under Katsura Harudanji. He was promoted to shinuchi in April 1999 and subsequently adopted the name Koharudanji III (the second generation Koharudanji was Tsuyu no Gorobei II).

After his promotion to shinuchi, Koharudanji became interested in helping to expand rakugo outside Japan. He first began performing for non-Japanese audiences in Japan, and in August 2000, he embarked on a tour of France, Germany, Bulgaria, and the United Kingdom.

He also became the first Japanese rakugo performer to participate in the Edinburgh Fringe Festival. During the festival, Koharudanji performed "Otama-ushi" ("Otama the Cow"), a story about a young man who tries to sneak into the room of a woman named Otama at night, unaware that her father had replaced her with a cow as he knew about the pending arrival of the unwelcome visitor. Koharudanji performed the story in Japanese; a native English speaker had translated the script and transcribed the subtitles, that were projected onto a screen behind Koharudanji during the show. He presented the story speaking at a much slower pace than usual to give the audience enough time to read the subtitles. Although he had initially thought the language barrier would be a hurdle for a non-Japanese audience trying to fully appreciate the value of rakugo, his experiences have taught him otherwise. He now believes that his audiences enjoy his subtitled rakugo in a similar way to how people enjoy subtitled foreign movies.

After being appointed as the Japan Cultural Envoy on June 20, 2006, Koharudanji established the International Rakugo Promotion Association, the first rakugo non-profit organization for rakugo artists. The following year, he traveled to New York, where he attempted rakugo with English subtitles at the Florence Gould Hall. He returned to New York in 2010 to perform in front of over 200 United Nations officials and staff, utilizing subtitles projected on a screen behind him in Chinese, English, French, and Spanish, Koharudanji plans to continue to use subtitles because he feels uncomfortable performing rakugo in English.[221]

Rakugo celebrity Katsura Bunshi VI has also dabbled in presenting rakugo with subtitles. In 2016, he gave multiple performances that relied on English and Japanese subtitles. The first show, called "Katsura Bunshi (subtitled) Rakugo," took place at the Jinbocho Kagetsu theater in Tokyo. The performance was intended for audience members with challenges such as hearing impairments

---

[221] Murakami, Asako. "'Rakugo' Artist Takes Sit-down Shtick to Edinburgh Festival, with Subtitles." The Japan Times, August 6, 2000. https://www.japantimes.co.jp/culture/2000/08/06/stage/rakugo-artist-takes-sit-down-shtick-to-edinburgh-festival-with-subtitles/

and for foreign tourists who otherwise might not be able to enjoy rakugo due to not understanding Japanese well.[222]

And there are rakugoka who are able to perform in English, but they sometimes use subtitles in other languages when they tour abroad. One such storyteller is Katsura Utazo, the disciple of rakugo master Katsura Utamaru.

Utazo began his apprenticeship with Utamaru in December 1991, at the age of 27. Before entering the rakugo world, he traveled to England to join the karate dojo run by Jean-Jacques Burnell, a member of the British punk rock band, The Stranglers. The rakugo storyteller, who was promoted to shinuchi in 2005, also holds a professional boxing Class C license, which he earned in 1994.

Following his promotion to shinuchi, Utazo has performed rakugo in English in 16 countries. But when he traveled to Vietnam in 2012, he performed rakugo in Japanese using Vietnamese subtitles.

In an interview he gave to the *Daily Bruin* in 2012, Utazo, who performs rakugo in both Japanese and English said, "I enjoyed English rakugo overseas much more than Japanese rakugo. English

---

[222] 株式会社 MANTAN. "桂文枝：リアルタイム多言語字幕付きで落語を披露 (Katsura Bunshi: Rakugo with Real-Time Multilingual Subtitles)." MANTANWEB（まんたんウェブ. MANTANWEB, June 5, 2016. https://mantan-web.jp/article/ 20160605dog00m 200030000c.html.

is the universal language, so all the reactions from the audiences varies (based) on the country."[223]

Rakugo without borders is a noble concept, and I am highly in favor of introducing the art form to non-Japanese audiences. However, I believe that subtitles are not well-suited for rakugo. My reason is that a rakugo storyteller masterfully conveys a myriad of non-verbal subtleties during the storytelling process by developing characters, engaging the audience, and encouraging them to use their imaginations. Forcing the audience to read subtitles from a screen prevents them from picking up on these subtleties and it also takes away from enjoying rakugo as it is meant to be enjoyed. This author believes that live rakugo is meant to be watched and listened to, not read.

---

[223] Allred, Laurie. "Rakugo Master Utazo Katsura to Share Traditional Japanese Storytelling in English." Daily Bruin, February 24, 2012.
https://dailybruin.com/2012/02/24/rakugo_master_utazo_katsura_to_share_traditional_japanese_storytelling_in_english.

In the Words of the Rakugoka

19. Katsura Sunshine

"I want to travel all over the world and do English rakugo, and make rakugo part of the Western vocabulary"
—*Katsura Sunshine*

Born Gregory Robic on April 6, 1970, Katsura Sunshine is a professional Kamigata rakugo storyteller who hails from Canada. After having worked as a playwright and composer for musical theater in Toronto, he traveled to Japan in 1999 to study kabuki and learn about Japanese culture. He originally intended to stay in Japan for only six months. But he ended up falling in love with the country and its culture, and decided to make Japan his second home.

Sunshine had been living in Yokohama for almost five years when he encountered rakugo for the first time. That encounter, in a small tatami-floored theater above a *yakitori* (grilled skewered chicken) shop, galvanized him to become a rakugo performer. He left Yokohama and traveled to Osaka, where he enrolled in the graduate program at the Osaka University of Arts. He studied under Aiba Akio, a leading researcher and authority on Japanese traditional comedy and the author of several books on the subject.

In 2008, acting on a friend's suggestion, Sunshine approached rakugo master Katsura Bunshi VI and asked to become his apprentice. Sunshine made his professional debut as a rakugoka in Singapore on April 26, 2009, and completed his three-year rakugo apprenticeship in November 2011.

He brought his acclaimed rakugo show to New York on September 19, 2019. After a six-month run, he was nominated for the "Best Unique Theatrical Experience" in the 2020 Off-Broadway Alliance Awards. (The performances at the famous New World Stages, like all New York City venues, were suspended due to the COVID-19 pandemic.)

Sunshine is currently experimenting with musical rakugo and even has his own line of denim kimonos.

KO: I have read that you experienced rakugo for the first time in 2004. As a playwright and composer, what appealed to you most about this traditional style of Japanese storytelling?

KS: *Although I had acquired some Japanese language skills, I only understood about one tenth of the actual rakugo story at the time. Unlike kabuki, where you really do not have to know the language to appreciate the art form, rakugo requires fluency in the language to be understood and appreciated. Plus, I was watching Edo rakugo where they sometimes use an antiquated manner of speaking with a lot of different words that I was not familiar with. The makura was much easier to understand.*

The makura was similar to stand-up comedy; the storyteller was just telling jokes, basically. When the story began, and he started acting out all of the parts, I thought it was great! I watched two storytellers perform two stories each and recognized the pattern. There was a little bit of comedy, a little bit of drama, and it all ended with a punchline. I fell in love with rakugo simply by watching the audience and how they reacted to it.

I thought to myself, "This is incredible. I was born to do this. I have to do this!"

KO: How did you manage to learn Japanese? Were you taking Japanese classes?

KS: *No, actually I went to the yakitori shop every single day and mingled with the locals who did not speak English. That was the best way to immerse myself in the language.*

KO: You decided to pursue rakugo. What happened next?

KS: *The yakitori shop owner tried to dissuade me. He said there were no foreigners in rakugo and that I would have to apprentice myself for three to four years. Apprenticeship would involve cleaning my master's house and serving him every single day. He advised me to come up with a routine where I can tell some comic stories while playing the accordion. He offered to include me in the local shows he was producing. He mentioned that I could get to know the local rakugoka this way. He further added that he did not believe there was a rakugo master anywhere who would take me on as an apprentice.*

So, I came up with an act and he put me in a show. I went into the gakuya (backstage area) and witnessed the interactions and camaraderie. I saw how everyone cooperated to ensure that the audience enjoyed the entire show. There was a balance, unlike stand-up comedy where each individual comedian strives to kill the audience with laughter.

This further galvanized me to become a rakugoka. I fell in love with the world of rakugo.

KO: How did you come to select Katsura Bunshi as your shisho?

KS: *A friend of mine, who is actually my senpai (senior) suggested that I approach him. She was an apprentice to one of Bunshi's disciples.*

At the time, Bunshi was known as Sanshi and he was the president of the Kamigata Rakugo Association. She told me to go talk to Sanshi Kaicho (president of a society). She said that "He is incredible; he does new stories and he is always searching for new and different things. He may be open to taking you on as an apprentice."

I went to see him perform and heard his original rakugo. It was incredible. I loved it and wanted to translate it. I didn't watch TV at the time and was unaware that he was such a huge television personality. I liked him, purely based on his rakugo. Plus, I saw how he devoted his time to his fans. I watched him interacting with his fans and taking photos with them after the performance on a freezing cold November night. It was love at first site, basically.

KO: Life as a rakugo apprentice is very challenging, even for those born and raised in Japan who are familiar with the hierarchy—vertical relationships which exist in Japanese society. As a foreigner, it must have been particularly challenging. How would you describe those years?

KS: *It was very strict. It is a different world entirely, not at all like normal Japanese society. But my seniors were very supportive. They said things like, "We were worse than you are, so don't worry about it. If you get criticized, it is because your master cares about you and wants you to do your best."*

At the same time, there was a laid-back atmosphere; I wasn't rushed to learn stories. Instead, I was asked to focus on my master and make him as comfortable as possible, carry his bags, fold his kimonos, work on the lighting and sound during the shows, etc. After all of that was finished, I had an opportunity to concentrate on my rakugo a little bit. It was difficult to understand back then, but I understand now. I think knowing what I know now, I would be a much better apprentice.

KO: After receiving your stage name, Sunshine, your master ordered you to bleach your hair. Please tell me a little about that.

KS: *During your apprenticeship, you are not supposed to stand out. But my master has the mind of a producer in addition to being a genius storyteller and TV star. That's why I am now on Broadway! I thank the stars that I became my master's apprentice because he always emphasized that in addition to learning the stories, we had to always focus on what we could do differently; how to attract people, how to attract the media. He said to always keep those things in mind, otherwise you are just parroting stories.*

My master embarks on an all-Japan tour every year and he takes his apprentices with him. One year, he decided that we were going to perform an ogiri, similar to Shoten. There were four or five apprentices on stage and he was playing the part of the host. The ogiri begins in the second half of the show, and as the curtain slowly rises the apprentices rise up from a bowing position. In a large theater of 500 to 1,000 people, it is hard to distinguish a foreigner with brown hair from the rest of the apprentices on stage. So, he told me that I did not look foreign enough. He told me to dye my hair blonde.

Of course, during the ogiri he pointed me out to the audience and said things like, "He sticks out a bit too much for my taste; he is a little too old to be an apprentice, but he promised to translate my stories and perform them abroad," etc. He got big laughs from the audience, particularly in reference to my name. All in all, he literally changed my life by naming me Sunshine. I have been dying my hair ever since.

KO: I have read that there was a time when you were called "Canadatei robu reta (love letter)." Can you tell me a little about performing under the name Canadatei? Was that a name you came up with or did it originate with someone else?

KS: *There is an old Japanese song called "Canada Kara no Tegami" (Love Letters from Canada), which became a huge hit. When I walked into the yakitori shop in Yokohama and mentioned that I was from Canada, the proprietor began to sing the song. Eventually, I began to get this reaction everywhere I went. It was really funny.*

When I started to perform as an amateur, a friend suggested that I adopt a version of this song title as my stage name. So, I became Canadatei robu reta.

KO: Kairakutei Black (Henry Black) was the first foreign-born rakugoka in Japan during the Meiji era. When you entered the world of rakugo, you became the second. How do you feel about this?

KS: *When I went on tour in Australia, I was asked if my role as a rakugo performer was to pick up the baton for Black.*

I don't think so, because I believe what I am doing is the complete opposite of what he was doing. He entered the rakugo world when the art form was on the decline. Sanyutei Encho was trying to revitalize rakugo by adapting stories from China and Europe. He took Black under his wing and explained to him that they needed to reinvigorate rakugo and make it interesting once again. They were focused on Japan and bringing stories from the outside. I am the complete opposite of that. I am learning traditional rakugo and bringing it to Broadway, Netflix, and Spotify.

I performed "Tameshi Zake" based on Kairakutei Black's original story, "Biiru no Kakenomi" (The Beer Drinking Bet) on Broadway and people loved it.

KO: You brought rakugo to New York and enjoyed a successful six-month run, and would have had a full twelve-month run had it not been for the pandemic. With your previous experience as a playwright, have you ever considered turning traditional rakugo stories into stage plays or musicals?

KS: *I can't wait to do that. I have been planning that for a long time, but there is so much to do right now. It took five years to bring rakugo to Broadway. I not only co-produced the show, but I raised the money to put the show on. I met with investors; I flew back to Japan twice a month to meet with them. I had to turn down performances because I was uncertain about where I would be at any given time.*

But now that Broadway is on hold due to the pandemic, I can focus on a few other things until the performances resume. I am actually composing rakugo rap these days and I would like to do a rakugo opera someday.

xxiv. Katsura Sunshine (Russ Rowland)

20. Sanyutei Koseinen

> "I want to make people laugh in Japanese."
> —Sanyutei Koseinen

Sanyutei Koseinen, whose real name is Johan Nilsson Björk, was born in Uppsala, Sweden in 1985. While growing up, he enjoyed performing in front of people and making them laugh. He wanted to pursue a career in acting but thought it was a good idea to have something to fall back on. He decided to major in Japanese at Stockholm University. As a high school student, he had taken a rudimentary Japanese class and he had a fondness for Japanese culture, particularly Japanese anime.

During his second year at Stockholm University, Koseinen applied to Nanzan University in Nagoya as an exchange student. The exchange program ended after four months, but Koseinen wanted to further pursue his Japanese studies. He returned to Japan as an exchange student during his senior year and enrolled at Chuo University in Tokyo.[224] At Chuo University he discovered rakugo

---

[224] Tokuhashi, Isao. "If I Made an Unfunny Joke, I Could Say, 'I Guess It's 'Cause I'm from Sweden.' Do You Know Why?" My Eyes Tokyo, April 23, 2017. https://www.myeyestokyo.com/johan-nilsson-bjork/.

for the first time and decided to become a professional rakugo performer.

On July 15, 2016, Koseinen became the tenth disciple of rakugo master Sanyutei Koraku, a long-standing member of *Shoten*. In August 2020, he was promoted to the second level of futatsume and given the name Koseinen.

KO: First of all, congratulations on your recent promotion to futatsume. Are you getting used to your new stage name, Koseinen?

SK: *I'm not used to my new stage name yet, and I sometimes have to correct myself when I speak on the phone and introduce myself.*

KO: Previously, your kozamei was Jubei, but prior to that you were known as *Borubo-tei Ikeya* (a combination of the names of two well-known Swedish companies, Volvo and Ikea.) How did that come about?

SK: *Borbotei Ikeya was a name that a Japanese friend came up with. "You're Swedish so, what's Swedish... IKEA! And Volvo! ... IKEA Volvo!"*

I thought it was a bit embarrassing, but the Japanese liked it. Many assumed I would get a similarly quirky name as a pro, but my master chose to go in a different direction in naming me.

KO: You once aspired to become an actor and now you are a professional rakugoka. How did you make the transition?

SK: *To me, rakugo is still basically acting, although it differs from film or stage acting in some regards. So, it felt natural to me.*

KO: Japan's traditional apprenticeship system—we don't have anything like it in the West. Did you find the zenza life challenging?

SK: *Yes, the zenza life was very hard; it felt very strenuous and draining. I had to constantly be aware of the seniors around me, and take care of them.*

There were many rules of conduct that are typical to Japanese society. I really felt like I had to become Japanese for this.

And then there are very specific details pertaining to how to serve the tea, how to fold the masters' kimonos neatly and quickly, and how to play the taiko drums. The Japanese concepts of "reading the air" (reading between the lines), and not being able to decline invitations to go drinking, etc., made it very hard. As a non-Japanese I tried my best to show that I could play along, but it was very tiring.

KO: You stated that you learned your first rakugo story after just one month as a deshi. What was that story? How many stories do you currently have in your repertoire?

SK: *My master initially taught me a few short stories, then I learned the story "Kohome"("Complimenting A Child"). My master's style of teaching involves quickly bringing his disciples up to the level where they can start performing in front of an audience.*

I currently know roughly 45 stories.

KO: You know Kairakutei Black, the first foreign-born rakugoka who performed in Japanese. He was admired for not only learning Japanese, but also for being able to make a Japanese audience laugh in a language that was not his own. How does that relate to your own experiences as a performer?

SK: *Of course, I know about Kairakutei Black. He was a pioneer in rakugo during the Meiji era. He was a resident of Japan from an early age, so he more than likely spoke like a native speaker. He also did not go through the strict training other*

> *apprentices had to go through, although I think he experienced other hardships.*
>
> *The Japanese audience's reaction to a foreign performer probably has not changed much through the years. "A foreigner who can speak Japanese! How quaint!" is still the vibe I get, even today.*
>
> *I've read a good deal about Black, and his story was fairly tragic.*

KO: You primarily perform in Japanese, but you have also performed in English and Swedish. Is this something you would like to do more of in the future?

SK: *I hope to perform regularly in all three languages in the future. I think I can attract a decent audience if I perform in English in Japan; not as much if I perform in Swedish.*

> *I will probably perform online as well, though rakugo is really meant to be performed in front of a live audience.*

KO: You translated classical rakugo stories into English and Swedish, and you have also written your own original stories. What topics do you favor? What topics do you stay away from?

SK: *When writing stories in Japanese, I tend to focus on the differences between the Japanese and Western cultures. It is easy to do, and audiences are interested and sometimes shocked by those stories.*

Stories about politics and religion do not work well in Japan. Although I think I am shielded by the fact that I am a foreigner, and audiences tend to think that I do not know better, I still have to tread lightly. Especially when it comes to the Japanese emperor. One cannot joke about him. It is very different in Sweden; people are free to take potshots at the Swedish king.

KO: Rakugoka like Tatekawa Danshi acted in films and TV shows, and he also did voice acting. Shunputei Shota is another rakugoka who engages in acting. Would you like to pursue acting sometime in your career?

SK: *I would love to do some acting as well. We will see what opportunities arise in the future.*

KO: You related what it was like to be a zenza earlier. You have recently been promoted to futatsume. While the experiences of being a zenza are still fresh in your mind, what has changed? Do you now face a new set of challenges?

SK: *After being promoted to futatsume, most of my previous responsibilities as a zenza were eliminated.*

I no longer have to clean and run the yose, and I am allowed to perform my own style of rakugo. As a zenza, I was only allowed to perform exactly as I was taught. I no longer have to call my master every day, although I sometimes accompany him as I did before. I only have to help my master with his kimono, serve him tea, etc.; I do not have to look after the other masters.

I do, however, need to find opportunities to perform on my own. As a zenza, I was provided with a sustainable income, and [my] living expenses were covered, but now I only have myself to depend on as a performer. This has become a bit more complicated by the ongoing pandemic, of course.

KO: We were discussing Kairakutei Black earlier, and you mentioned that a Japanese audience's reaction to a foreign performer has not changed very much. I would like to ask you if you noticed that perhaps you were being treated differently by your peers as well because you are a foreigner? Did your ani-deshi treat you differently?

SK: *In general, I was not treated differently. My master apparently instructed the others to treat me like any other zenza. I performed all of the tasks required of a zenza and apprentice, and my ani-deshi were very strict. Although on occasion some offered more of an explanation with regard to doing things the Japanese way, overall, I was treated the same as anyone else in my position.*

KO: I know it is still too early to touch on this subject, but every rakugoka eventually develops his own style of performing. Each is known for something in particular. Do you have a vision as a performer? Is there something specific you would like to achieve in your career as a performer?

SK: *Hmm... It's still too early to tell, but I first want to master classical rakugo, as best as I can. Later, I would like to take the good elements of Japanese comedy and acting and combine them with the humor and performance styles of the West to create something truly unique. In this way, I believe my art will evolve into something new eventually.*

xxv. Sanyutei Koseinen (Shimamura Ryota)

21. Tatekawa Shinoharu

> "Some of the classical stories are more than 300 years old. They are still very much alive, which teaches us that humans haven't changed that much. The idea that humans make the same mistakes, no matter when or where they are from, is part of rakugo's charm. You can jump right in and enjoy it."
> —Tatekawa Shinoharu

Tatekawa Shinoharu was born in Toyonaka City, Osaka Prefecture on August 14, 1976. A graduate of Yale University, he worked for the prestigious trading company *Mitsui Bussan* (Mitsui & Co., Ltd.) before pursuing a career in rakugo.

Unlike many of his peers in the rakugo world, Shinoharu did not appreciate the art form until his mid-twenties and only after he stumbled upon Tatekawa Shinosuke's live performance. He approached Shinosuke and asked him to take him on as an apprentice. However, the master rakugo performer turned him down and advised him to continue working for Mitsui & Co. Six months later, the determined Shinoharu quit his job and asked Shinosuke to take him on as an apprentice once again. This time, Shinosuke agreed.

Shinoharu was promoted to futatsume in January 2011. He attained the level of shinuchi in April 2020.

KO: I understand that you initially thought rakugo was intended for "old people," and didn't appreciate it until you stumbled upon Shinosuke shisho's live performance. What was it about that performance that made you change your mind?

TS: *It was simply hilarious. I had never laughed so much in my life. A few seconds into the show, that image of rakugo as an "old people's hobby" disappeared. I was also astonished by Shinosuke's power to create a lively image in the audience's mind. It felt as though the story was not being told, but it was unfolding right in front of my eyes.*

KO: You worked for one of the largest trading companies in Japan at the time. How difficult was it for you to leave a prestigious position and enter the world of rakugo? Did you find the zenza life challenging?

TS: *It wasn't difficult at all, actually. I was somehow convinced that rakugo was the thing for me. Zenza life was challenging because I had no money and no time, but more so because for the first time in my life, I had to live my life according to someone else's values and rules.*

KO: I read that Shinosuke shisho initially refused to accept you as a disciple. He advised you to remain at Mitsui & Co. and pursue rakugo as an amateur performer. What drove you to become a professional rakugoka?

TS: *I knew I had to pursue a career as a professional. I also knew that advising me to remain at Mitsui was not my master's true intension.*

KO: You obviously began your rakugo apprenticeship by learning Japanese rakugo and delivered your first English rakugo performance at the Singapore International Storytelling Festival in 2012. What made you want to transition to English rakugo?

TS: *I actually gave an English rakugo performance earlier than that, when I was still a zenza. It was during the Ginza Rakugo Matsuri event, where Shinosuke hosted an English rakugo show. I performed "Tenshiki," and it was quite a success. I had never received so much laughter from the audience before, and I thought to myself, "This is not right. If I get addicted to this, it'll ruin my Japanese rakugo," and did not perform in English until being invited to Singapore. I simply accepted the offer because I wanted to go to Singapore.*

KO: You lived in the United States for seven years and you graduated from Yale University. Did those experiences impact your rakugo in anyway?

TS: *Definitely. First, the idea that you have to follow a certain career path when you go to a certain school was never deeply engrained in me, which made my decision-making rather easy.*

Second, the experience of choosing to go to a university in the U.S. amidst all the objections, prepared me for a similar situation when I decided to enter the rakugo world.

Third, when it came to composing original rakugo stories, the debating habit in American classes helped a lot.

Finally, being aware that different taboos exist across different cultures helps when translating stories into English. I believe those earlier experiences have had a far-reaching impact in my life.

KO: You wrote an original rakugo story about the infamous geisha/murderer Abe Sada. It is a very unique choice! What made you choose her as the subject for your story?

You mentioned earlier, "Being aware that different taboos exist across different cultures helps when translating stories into English." Do you adhere to the same principles when creating your own original stories?

TS: *Why I chose Abe Sada as the topic for my new story is a combination of several reasons.*

I decided five years ago to begin a tsuyabanashi or simply a shimoneta [vulgar material] show to perform erotic stories that I could not perform elsewhere. I've done that once a year, for five years now.

There were several reasons for that. One, I found that there are many classical rakugo stories which deal with sexual matters, and they are actually very funny. I thought it was a pity that these stories were not being performed any longer.

Second, I wanted to change my image. You may know, Japanese people are quite obsessed with gakureki, or educational background. So, no matter how many original stories I created in Japanese, or how many shows I performed, I could not get away from being referred to as "the Yale-mitui bussan guy" (the Yale-Mitsui Co. guy), or "the guy who performs in English."

Every interview I received since becoming a futatsume was about my career choice before becoming a rakugoka. I initially thought that those labels were "catchy," but they were also limiting how I was being perceived. So, in order to change that I decided not to tear apart those labels, but to put on as many new labels as possible; and shimoneta was one of them.

Further, I didn't want the show to be male-oriented, like most shimoneta in Japan tend to be, so I made it a point to do something that female audiences can enjoy as well. In the process, I started creating original stories. It's interesting that for the past five years, the male-female ratio at these shows has always been around 3:7. There is a much higher percentage of female audience members in attendance.

I think it was just by chance that I chose Abe Sada as a topic in my fourth year. Originally, it was because of the theme I selected for that year. First year's theme was shimoneta in general. Second year, I selected the love doll as a topic. Third year, the theme was condoms. Fourth year, it was S&M. I had also written an original story based on a real person, Sakata Sankichi, a legendary shogi master, before that, and wanted to write another story about a real person.

> *As I read many books about Abe Sada, my image of the incident itself changed. I began to want to shed a new light on the incident, and that is why I started working on the subject. I thought it was the perfect subject for rakugo.*
>
> *"Rakugo wa ningen no goh no koutei" is a famous phrase by Tatekawa Danshi, which states that rakugo is an affirmation of human faults and weaknesses. I wanted to do that. Since it is rakugo, I think the story is more comical than what you would expect of an Abe Sada story.*

KO: How many original stories do you currently have in your repertoire?

TS: *I have written about 30 original stories so far.*

KO: You share some commonalities with your shisho: you graduated from Yale, he graduated from Meiji; you worked for Mitsui, he worked for an advertising agency. Do you find that these shared experiences helped you with regard to your master/disciple relationship?

TS: *I think it made it quite rough, actually. Because I shared some commonalities with him, and because he thought that it could work in a negative way in rakugo disciple training, he tried to break me and erase my pride and self-*

consciousness. Compared to my fellow disciples, the number of times that I was told to quit, or go away, was tenfold.

KO: You mentioned that you met with a lot of objections when you decided to go into rakugo. Did those people who objected most to your career choice change their minds after witnessing your success in the field?

TS: *I guess most people changed their attitudes for the better. But I still get comments like "mottainai" (what a waste), which is one feeling I have never had. Not doing something you instinctively know you want to devote your life to, is mottainai for me.*

KO: What was the first rakugo story you performed in front of a live audience? Can you describe what that experience was like?

TS: *The first story was "Tsuru." It was in Yokohama Nigiwaiza. It was sudden. I was told to go up on stage five minutes before the show started, I did not even have the time to get nervous.*

I got up, told the audience that it was my first koza [a term used among rakugoka to indicate taking the stage], got a big applause, and then, just silence. No laughter. I remember being relieved that I made it till the end.

My two ani-deshi [older brother apprentices] told me it went well, which I found out later was a common phrase to say to first-timers.

KO: In the 1950s and 60s, television and radio brought rakugo to people who did not have access to it earlier. With the advent of the Internet, YouTube, and technologies such as Zoom, what do you project for the future of rakugo? Do you think more rakugoka will utilize these tools to spread rakugo?

Also, rakugoka gauge their performances by observing their audience. The audience's reaction is very important to the storyteller. With performances going online these days, how does that impact you as a performer? Obviously, you cannot tell if people are laughing and reacting to your story.

TS: *My initial attitude toward performing online was negative. As you said, I always thought rakugo was a cooperative entertainment between the performer and the audience. We're the projector, and each audience member's mind is the screen. The images on each screen may be slightly different, but they move simultaneously. With people, including the performer, sharing similar images at the same time and same place, rakugo becomes very powerful. That would not be possible during an online performance, I thought.*

I was forced to go online, though. With all shinuchi promotion events canceled, and no real, physical shows in sight for an extended period, I had to create opportunities for exposure by myself. Online was the only choice for me.

I started uploading my past performances on YouTube in May, and did my first live streaming show in mid-June. It was a bit late, because until late May, I still hung on to the belief that my first show as a shinuchi must be in person. But at that point, I thought to myself that if I hung on to that belief any longer, I'd be completely forgotten.

What I found out after my first live streaming show in June was that it was mentally quite tough. Without the usual laughter and reaction, I couldn't be certain if I was able to deliver the story to the audience. Even when I received no reaction during a real show, I still knew for sure that I failed. In the case of an online show, I did not know if I succeeded or failed, and that uncertainty was intolerable. That uncertainty lasted until I started receiving positive comments on SNS and email.

But along the way, I found some new things. I found out that I must be more careful with my movements on an online show, because I would be captured up close by the camera. That is something that I did not care so much about in a real show (though I probably should have). I also found out that to deliver a story successfully in an online show, you have to focus more on portraying the characters more precisely and vividly, and capturing the core of the story, since you cannot rely on the atmosphere.

During a live show I was focused more on telling a story in an energetic way, to create an overall atmosphere where the audience can fully enjoy the story. I had to build my performances in a way so that it stands by itself without the exciting atmosphere of the venue. I think those new findings made me a better rakugoka technically, and they will help a lot when I start performing live again.

So now, I'm starting to enjoy online shows much more than I used to. I also started doing a talk session after my shows using the online chat functionality, to make it a two-way communication. That helped in reducing the uncertainty because I get feedback right after the show.

I think 80 percent of the rakugoka still think about online shows as I did before. Quite negative, something to avoid as much as possible. The biggest reason is, they have not tried it yet. And the reason they have not tried it, is I think, out of fear.

The biggest fear is, when you screw up, it will be spread out to the entire world. But from my experience, I have found that to be false. Be it YouTube, or live streaming shows, it is extremely difficult to have people who do not know you to come see you. So people who come to see me online are mostly people who have seen me live already. The entire world is very far. My new challenge now is to reach the entire world.

xxvi. Tatekawa Shinoharu (Shimomura Shinobu)

22. Yanagiya Tozaburo

> "Kabuki, sumo, and sushi are all commonplace in America now. Rakugo is still unknown, and I want to change that."
> —*Yanagiya Tozaburo*

Born on September 28, 1976, Tokyo native Yanagiya Tozaburo dropped out of college, with only one year remaining until graduation, to pursue rakugo. He officially became the disciple of rakugo master Yanagiya Gontaro III in April 1999. He was promoted to futatsume three years later, and he attained the rank of shinuchi in 2014.

Tozaburo has since given performances at countless yose and other theaters all over Japan, the United States, and Canada. He even made an appearance on the popular Japanese television program *Shoten*.

KO: You were studying creative writing at Nichigei (Nihon University College of Art) when you decided to leave and become the disciple of Gontaro shisho. What influenced you to leave school and study rakugo? When did you first become interested in rakugo?

YT: *I was a fan of rakugo since the age of 16, and I wanted to become a rakugoka from the time I was a high school student. But as time went by, I became less sure of pursuing the path of becoming a rakugoka. I enrolled at Nichigei with the intention of becoming a novelist or a copywriter. I later learned that my college had a rakugo club (ochiken), so I signed up to learn rakugo.*

On December 29, 1998, I went to see Gontaro's performance at the yose. As a fan, I frequently attended his rakugo performances. On that particular day, I instinctively knew that I would be studying rakugo with Gontaro.

KO: When you decided to become a disciple of Gontaro shisho in 1998, how did you approach him? Was it in person or did you write a letter?

YT: *I obtained Gontaro's address from Takarai Kinsei, a Kondanshi [kodan storyteller] acquaintance. Afterwards, I went to Gontaro's home without an appointment. I felt certain that it would not be possible to ask to become a rakugo master's disciple by simply writing a letter, so I* went directly to his house to beg him to allow me to become his disciple.

KO: How long did it take for Gontaro shisho to accept you as a disciple?

YT: *Our first meeting took place on April 29, 1998. We met a second time on May 3, when my parents accompanied me to the meeting. Overall, it took five days to be officially accepted as a disciple.*

KO: Did you find the zenza life difficult?

YT: *The life of a zenza differs depending on who the master is, and what his plan and strategy happen to be. My master Gontaro is very strict, so my life as a zenza was very hard. I also worked at the yose and at other rakugo events (rakugokai).*

KO: You performed rakugo in Japanese at the yose and other theaters all over Japan. What made you want to perform rakugo in English?

YT: *In 2016, I received the Agency for Cultural Affairs (ACA) National Arts Festival Award for "Outstanding Performance for the Kanto Area." Offers for me to perform rakugo increased as a result.*

Then, my father passed away on January 11, 2017. Since most of the rakugo stories I performed on stage were based on a father and son relationship, I became confused and I did not want to perform rakugo any longer. I left Tokyo and settled in Kyoto.

While in Kyoto, I began writing a novel about my father and rakugo. I also did some commercial work where I portrayed a rakugo performer. These things made me miss rakugo and I wanted to perform again.

I have since devoted my life to spreading rakugo all over the world. To do so, I decided to perform rakugo in English.

KO: How did you decide to compete/participate in this festival?

YT: *In 2014, I was searching for opportunities to perform as a newly promoted shinuchi and the Agency for Cultural Affairs Arts Festival came to mind. This is a very big festival and I saw it as a good opportunity to showcase my performance.*

KO: I read that you studied English in the Philippines. Can you tell me a little about that?

YT: *Cebu Languages English School in the Philippines sponsored me to learn English at their school. That is how I came to study in the Philippines.*

KO: You arrived in New York in October 2018. What made you decide to come to New York? Did you consider other cities?

YT: *First, I went to Toronto, Canada and later traveled to New York City (from February to April). After I returned to Japan, I really thought about moving to New York and performing rakugo there.*

I felt that the Japanese rakugo community was already too saturated and I wanted to find new opportunities to perform rakugo. I have toured many places in the United States, and I love America; but I feel that New York is a special place for a comedian and a theatrical actor.

I also love standup comedy and Jazz. These things have influenced and motivated me creatively. I have since established myself in New York; I founded a theatrical group and I have disciples here.

I don't consider myself to be the typical rakugo performer; I really feel in my element in New York.

KO: You said that the Japanese rakugo community is too saturated. Do you feel that rakugo will continue to be popular in Japan in the next ten years? Twenty years?

YT: *I think that rakugo has become more popular now because of the Internet and social media. Its popularity is no longer tied only to television. Since rakugo is based on invariable human emotions, I think it will continue to appeal to audiences.*

KO: You mentioned that you are not the "typical" rakugoka – can you describe how you are different?

YT: *Many rakugoka only focus on rakugo, but I focus on theatrical dramas and films as well. I have founded a theatrical company in the U.S. and established connections with a variety of different performers and artists. These associations have inspired and influenced me as a performer.*

KO: You like standup comedy and jazz. Do you have any favorite performers in comedy and/or music?

YT: *I have been following the Hong Kong-American actor and stand-up comedian Jimmy O. Yang. I also like comedy films, like those directed by Woody Allen. As far as music is concerned, I love Miles Davis and Roy Hargrove. My favorite instrument is the trumpet.*

KO: You are writing novels also. Did you finish your novel about your father and rakugo? If so, what is the name of the novel, and how can readers find it?

YT: *Yes, I am still working on that novel. I am not sure when it will be finished.*

KO: In 2010, you created and performed a version of Anton Chekhov's The Darling, commemorating the 150th birth anniversary of the author. How did you pick this story for a rakugo story?

YT: *I wanted to adapt a Russian novel into a Japanese rakugo story. I am very familiar with Anton Chekhov's novels and I felt that The Darling was well-suited for this purpose. Other rakugo performers choose theatrical scripts to serve as the basis for their rakugo stories, but I wanted to do something that was unique.*

xxvii. Yanagiya Tozaburo (Izima Kaoru)

23. Kanariya Eiraku

> "Rakugo embodies every underlying character trait: happiness, sadness, anger, sorrow, jealousy, and most importantly, humor."
> —Kanariya Eiraku

Kanariya Eiraku is a Tokyo-based English rakugo storyteller who has been studying and performing rakugo for over thirty years. After earning his bachelor's degree in English at Sophia University, he joined the Tatekawa-ryu group, where he studied rakugo for several years.

In 1990, while watching an English rakugo performance by Katsura Shijaku II, Eiraku came to the realization that rakugo can be conveyed and appreciated in any language. He established his Japanese rakugo classes in 1991 and founded the Canary English Rakugo Company in 2007.

With over 50 members, the Canary English Rakugo Company holds regular recitals all over Tokyo. The group began touring overseas in 2015 and gave performances in the United States, the United Kingdom, Georgia, Kazakhstan, Denmark, Laos, New Zealand, and Australia.

In October 2020, Eiraku established the English Rakugo Association in Japan. The association's primary goal is to use English rakugo to introduce Japanese culture to foreign audiences both in Japan and overseas.

KO: Several rakugo performers have studied acting at one time or another, and you are no exception. Was it your ambition to pursue a career as an actor originally? What inspired you to become a rakugo performer?

KE: *I studied acting in Los Angeles in 1984, but it was not with the intention of becoming an actor. I was more interested in directing and I thought learning how to act would help me become a better director. Eventually, I gave up both acting and directing, and leaned toward rakugo.*

I was greatly influenced by Tatekawa Danshi in Tokyo and Katsura Shijaku in Osaka. They both inspired me to delve into rakugo not only through their performances, but also by how they each interpreted rakugo as an art form.

Danshi once said, "Rakugo is the acceptance of human nature." Shijaku added, "A laugh is drawn by the release of tension." ²²⁵ *I thought these statements were very profound and they touched me deeply.*

In 1990, I saw Shijaku perform rakugo in English at Yurakucho Mullion Hall in Tokyo. I was impressed by his performance and decided to try it myself someday.

KO: Your rakugo family name is *Kanariya*. How did you establish that name? Does it have a special meaning?

KE: *Kanariya means "deer cry." I managed a language and music school during the 1990s. The school's name was Canary. I searched for the Chinese characters (kanji) that would represent the name Canary. I came up with various combinations of characters and I thought* 鹿*(deer) and* 鳴 *(cry) looked best visually.*

*These characters can also be pronounced Roku-mei, which reminds some Japanese people of the two-story building in Tokyo called Rokumei-kan (*鹿鳴館*). The building became a symbol of Westernization during the Meiji period. During its heyday, it hosted countless parties and balls, and served to introduce Western customs and manners to high-ranking Japanese. It is still a fixture in the cultural memory of Japan.*

---

²²⁵ Yu, A. C. Ochi (the punch line of a joke) - Japanese Wiki Corpus. Accessed March 10, 2021. https://www.japanese-wiki-corpus.org/culture/Ochi%20(the%20punch%20line%20of%20a%20joke).html.

So, our group name represents learning or trying something new. Ya (家), which commonly represents "house," means "group" in this instance.

KO: You mentioned that you were most influenced by Tatekawa Danshi and Katsura Shijaku. Were there others who influenced and shaped your own performance style?

KE: *Yes, Kokontei Shincho. He was a fervent rival of Danshi, but I liked both of their styles. Shincho's performance was traditional and elegant. Danshi's performance was innovative and philosophical. Shincho tried to adhere to the traditional way of conveying rakugo stories while Danshi sometimes changed the concept of the story and tried to talk about life through rakugo.*

When I translated "Shibahama" ("Shiba Beach") into English, I referred to Danshi's script. When I performed "Bunshichi-mottoi" ("Bunshichi's Hairband Shop"), I modeled it after Shincho's performance.

KO: You have translated a significant number of rakugo stories into English. Aside from the inability to translate certain things due to obvious cultural differences, what influences you when it comes to choosing which stories to translate and which ones to leave alone?

KE: *Basically, I translate my favorite stories and the stories that Danshi loved.*

KO: Your rakugo students essentially come from all walks of life and represent various age groups. How do you choose who you will accept as a student?

KE: *I accept anyone who demonstrates a certain level of English comprehension. My students range in age from 10 to the mid-80s. Most of them are office workers, businessmen, tour guides, teachers, housewives, and retired salaried workers. It is interesting how their whole life seems to be reflected in their performances in one way or another.*

KO: English rakugo is not structured and regulated like Japanese professional rakugo is. How do you determine when a student has developed enough to move on to a level equivalent to that of a master storyteller? Do you currently have students who wish to have their own students some day?

KE: *Yes, I have a few students who aspire to be professionals. At the amateur level, they can begin teaching rakugo if they have mastered 50 stories.*

KO: There is a growing number of professional Japanese rakugo performers who are branching out to perform rakugo in English these days. How do you feel about that?

KE: *It is a positive phenomenon. When it comes to English rakugo, there is no clear distinction between amateurs and professionals, so I would like to collaborate with some of them.*

In 2020, I began collaborating with Sanyutei Koseinen, a Swedish rakugoka, who is a disciple of Sanyutei Koraku, one of the members of Shoten.

Since we have different backgrounds and different affiliations, I believe we will be able to create something new and unique.

KO: What is your ultimate goal as a rakugo performer? What would you consider to be the pinnacle of your career?

KE: *I would like to perform English rakugo in various countries to help people outside of Japan gain a better understanding of Japan and Japanese culture. Unlike kabuki, Noh, or kyogen, rakugo is intended for the common people. For example, there are rakugo stories based on less sophisticated topics such as flatulence, urinating, and yawning. Most stories are rather unpretentious.*

I would also like to perform foreign stories in the rakugo style such as the works of William Shakespeare. So far, I have adapted King Lear and Hamlet into rakugo. Every country has their own unique collection of wonderful and interesting stories. If I can convey those stories in the rakugo style, they might be enjoyed and appreciated even further. So, what I am aiming for is not only introducing Japanese stories, but also introducing the Japanese style of storytelling.

To date, I have performed over 60 stories. Within the next ten years, I would like to reach the goal of performing 100 stories.

With the establishment of the English Rakugo Association (ERA), I hope we can pave the way for a new era of rakugo.

xxviii. Kanariya Eiraku

24. Kanariya Eishi

> "The world of rakugo is full of imperfections. Something is almost always wrong with those lovable characters."
> —Kanariya Eishi, April 9, 2019

Kanariya Eishi is a Japanese rakugo storyteller who resides in Auckland, New Zealand, and presently is the only rakugo performer in the entire country.

Born in Yokohama and raised in Oiso in Kanagawa Prefecture, Eishi has been involved in theater for over twenty years. He has worked as an actor, stand-up comedian, and even a theater clown, having trained under Rone & Gigi, the celebrated clown duo. He has been a student of Kanariya Eiraku since 2016 and aspires to spread rakugo all over New Zealand.

KO: Judging from the past, it seems that you have performing in your blood. What made you gravitate toward rakugo?

KE: *Rakugo was and always has been my first love. When I was 9 or 10, I stumbled upon a cassette tape recording of Koganemochi by Kokontei Shinsho V, in which a man steals* money from the stomach of a dead monk. I was horrified and captivated at the same time by this story. I have been a huge rakugo fan since.

My stage career actually started in a school choir. It was a very well-known choir, and we won multiple national championships. As a choir boy, I even had an opportunity to perform at Nippon Budokan and NHK Hall.

I entered the rakugo club at Meiji Gakuin University when I was 18 with the intention of becoming a professional rakugo performer after graduation. I was already planning to perform rakugo in English someday, so I majored in English Literature. This was a major mistake. The curriculum was unbelievably boring.

To kill the boredom, I decided to take a year off to study Theatre Arts in America, hoping that it would contribute to my rakugo career later. What I hadn't expected was that America in the mid-90's really suited my personality. I fell in love with America. I soon quit Meiji Gakuin and transferred to a college in California.

At this stage, I was still intending to become a rakugo performer after graduation. But in my final year at the university, I met a woman from New Zealand when I was visiting Japan for the summer holiday. We got married, and

I moved to New Zealand permanently. She was the only reason why I did not go through a traditional apprenticeship.

As I thought pursuing a rakugo career was no longer realistic, I chose the closest thing that was available—stand-up comedy. Thanks to my rakugo background, my comedy career took off quickly, and I won the national championship in Raw Comedy Quest at the New Zealand International Comedy Festival 2005.

In 2009, a theatre producer approached me, saying, "You said your stand-up is heavily influenced by rakugo; show it to me." I translated a story called "Mount Head" ("Atamayama") in about half an hour and performed it for him, some actors, and several playwrights. They loved it. My rakugo became a part of a month-long season of Asian Tales: Native Alienz at Herald Theatre, and I later performed at another theatre festival as well.

I could have continued creating rakugo, but I wanted more authenticity. I did not want to keep performing rakugo my way; I had too much respect for the rakugo tradition.

I contacted some masters in Japan who I thought might teach me rakugo remotely, but all except one said no.

> *Actually, none of those naysayers took me seriously; they simply ignored my emails.*
>
> *The only person who said yes was my beloved master Kanariya Eiraku. To summarize, rakugo has always been my love and passion, and through the theatre producer and Eiraku shisho, I was only brought back to where I had started as if it had been the most natural thing for me to do. It was like Paulo Coelho's The Alchemist.*

KO: You are obviously training in English rakugo. Would you ever consider performing rakugo in Japanese if the occasion called for it?

KE: *No, I made a vow never to perform rakugo in Japanese even though I am still able to. This is out of respect for the rakugo performers who went through the traditional apprenticeship. I have no right to represent Japanese rakugo, and I only inherit and represent English rakugo through Eiraku shisho. I am very old-fashioned and almost stubborn in some ways.*

KO: You said you wanted to spread rakugo all over New Zealand. Would you like to tour other countries performing rakugo?

KE: *Yes, I definitely would! My peculiar accent, the strangest concoction of Japanese, Kiwi, and American, would surely confuse the audience, which would probably add to their comedic experience!*

KO: You accept acting jobs on occasion. How would you feel if you were ever offered a role as a rakugo performer?

KE: *I am very fortunate that I have been performing rakugo full-time, mainly thanks to performances and workshops at educational institutions, but rakugo is still nowhere near the mainstream in New Zealand. I have been feeling the need to take more acting jobs for the sake of promoting rakugo; the more visible I become as a performer, the more widely recognized rakugo will be. I do not like the limelight, but gaining a little more fame might be a necessary evil for the sake of rakugo. So yes, I would love a role as a rakugo performer! I'd especially love to be in a Sci-Fi rakugo movie with some love story elements in it!*

KO: Your master is based in Japan and you are in New Zealand. What is it like being instructed in rakugo long-distance? Would you recommend it to others outside of Japan who would like to enter the world of rakugo?

KE: *First of all, I am eternally thankful to Eiraku shisho for opening up the door for me. As I can only see him directly when I visit Japan or when we meet elsewhere, self-discipline is the hardest aspect of learning rakugo this way. I think this long-distance relationship was only possible because I had already learned the basics of rakugo before departing Japan. I also remained a rakugo nerd while I was pursuing other comedy careers.*

Having said that, Eiraku shisho has started opening up to long-distance students from overseas. This is a great opportunity for them to learn the art as a hobby, but if they are serious about it, they will probably need to at least spend a few years in Japan and breathe the culture to really understand the world of rakugo.

KO: You recently had an opportunity to perform with your shisho in New Zealand. What was that experience like? Did you walk away with any lessons learned?

KE: *It was a great privilege for me to monopolize him during his stay in New Zealand. He generously imparted his knowledge and philosophy to me, but what I really learned was how to be as a performer – through his presence. He is completely himself wherever he is, and he mingles right*

> *along in a second as if he was in Kitasenju. His principles in rakugo serve as my anchor so that I wouldn't get swept away by my peculiar sense of humor. Most importantly, I was inspired to become a better storyteller, not just a better comedian.*

KO: Every rakugoka strives to find themselves as a performer. What makes you unique among other rakugoka, or simply among rakugoka who perform in English?

KE: *I think my attempt to create New Zealand rakugo would make me really different from others. I incorporate the Māori language and culture into my rakugo stories, too. Also, my background as a professional stand-up comedian who is trained in Western acting, theater clowning, and comedy improv give me really quirky edges as a rakugo performer.*

KO: You are the father of two wonderful boys. How would you feel if one or both came up to you and told you that they wanted to be a rakugo performer? Would you encourage them?

KE: *If they want, why not? At this stage, they don't seem very inspired, though—maybe I am not good enough! But I would love to see the second generation of New Zealand-based performers someday. My dream is to see them grow New Zealand rakugo like Brazilian jiu-jitsu.*

xxix. Kanariya Eishi

25. Kanariya Ichirin

> "In the past, the audience was mainly men, but nowadays, rakugo is entertainment for everyone."
> —Kanariya Ichirin

Kanariya Ichirin is a female English rakugo performer and a member of the Canary English Rakugo Company. She has been studying the art of rakugo for the past eight years, and she has toured with the group giving performances in the United States, the United Kingdom, and Georgia. When she is not involved in rakugo, Ichirin lectures at Kanda University of International Studies in Chiba City, Japan.

She earned her Bachelor's degree in American Studies from the University of Connecticut and her Master of Arts degree in English Language Teaching and Applied Linguistics from King's College London. She has been teaching English for over 35 years.

KO: You indicated that you are a college lecturer. What inspired you to become a rakugo performer?

KI: *I teach the English language at a university. I had been thinking that rakugo can be an excellent tool to nurture students' speaking skills.*

Eiraku was and still is my colleague, so I thought of doing it myself since he started offering English rakugo classes. I joined his class eight years ago, and ever since I've performed at various places, and it has become part of my life now.

As for using English rakugo as a means to teach English, I haven't done much, but I'd love to do that from this point on.

KO: Do you perform in both English and Japanese?

KI: *Yes, I do. I started performing English rakugo at first, but it didn't take long until I realized that without a solid understanding of Japanese rakugo, English rakugo never sounds like rakugo.*

KO: Rakugo is an art form that has traditionally been dominated by men. Did you find that it was difficult to enter the world of rakugo as a woman?

KI: *More than 500 stories written during the Edo, Meiji, and Taisho eras (before World War II) are still performed in modern Japan, and many of these stories were written from the men's perspective. Some of the themes are unacceptable from the women's point of view (i.e. a father sells his own daughter to pay off his debts), and female performers do not usually perform these stories. The stories woman can perform are limited in this sense, but many other stories deal with universal themes, so female performers should not have a problem.*

In the past, the audience was mainly men, but nowadays, rakugo is entertainment for everyone.

The apprentice system still exists, but apprentices are not required to live in their masters' household as was a norm in the old days, so women should not be at a disadvantage regarding this, either.

Economically, it takes a long time for most of the performers to become financially independent, so it's a challenging profession for both men and women, I think.

KO: I understand that you have toured in the United States, the United Kingdom, and Georgia. What is your perception of audiences overseas as compared to Japanese audiences?

KI: *The reactions are very different. Audiences overseas generally laugh aloud and react emotionally. Japanese audiences show their emotions in moderation. I think this is partly because some audiences in Japan do not understand English well, but others are a bit reserved.*

Rakugo is an interactive thing. When the audience directly reacts to what we perform, our performance gets better. So we really enjoy performing overseas. By performing overseas, we notice what is universal and what is unique to the Japanese.

For example, tanuki, a kind of animal, appears in many Japanese folk tales and children's stories as an adorable character. But when it comes to taking the stories overseas, we notice the creature is unique to East Asia and we Japanese have a special attachment to it.

KO: It is evident that story selection is somewhat limited for female storytellers. Have you ever considered writing your own original rakugo stories to perform on stage?

KI: *Someday, I'd like to try. But rakugo stories are well planned and devised in calculated manners so it is not easy to create a story. Unlike improvised stories, well-written stories can last 300 years.*

KO: Of the existing classical/contemporary rakugo stories, do you have ones you favor or enjoy performing?

KI: *My favorite is "Tenshiki."* (*)

                (*) The story "Tenshiki" involves a Buddhist priest who goes to a doctor with complaints of stomach pain. During the examination, the doctor uses the word "tenshiki" and the priest pretends to understand its meaning even though he doesn't.

                Afterwards, the priest sends a novice to search for the meaning of tenshiki. The townspeople also pretend they know the meaning of word, creating a situation ripe for farce.

xxx. *Kanariya Ichirin*

xxxi. Jugemu (The story of the boy with the very long name) by Kei Ohsuga

English Rakugo Scripts

> "Rakugo must find its authentic form in the space between the unreal and the real. If you are good, the tension between the two will not be obvious in your story."
> —Yanagiya Kosan IV (1888-1947)

The beauty of rakugo is that it was created for the average person; therefore, the stories are based on fundamental human characteristics such as instincts, habits, and emotions. This is a feature that has helped rakugo survive for over 400 years. What audiences laugh at today are essentially the same things people laughed at 400 years ago!

Since laughter is universal, what people in Japan find funny can also elicit the same reaction from audiences overseas. Humor has the ability to transcend cultural dissimilarities. Although there may be elements of a story which may get lost in translation, rakugoka who translate and perform in English make every effort to convey these stories in such a manner that they can be fully understood and enjoyed by audiences regardless of their cultural or social background.

The classical rakugo scripts featured here were translated and performed by Kanariya Eiraku to English-speaking audiences both in Japan and overseas. Several of his original scripts appear under the "Adaptations" category. These scripts will provide you with the background knowledge of specific rakugo stories and enable you to anticipate and appreciate them when they are performed live.

The greatest appeal of rakugo is that a story can be enjoyed no matter how many times it is repeated, for each performer (and sometimes even the same performer) will incorporate certain variations into the storytelling process which will make every retelling unique.

Common Characters in Rakugo Stories

In rakugo, certain stock characters will appear in multiple stories. This is because these particular characters represent a common personality type that is relatable or easy to understand from the audience's perspective. These characters are similar in both Edo rakugo and Kamigata rakugo, but they bear different names depending on the style of rakugo being performed. Upon hearing a particular name, the audience will instantly associate an age, occupation, sex, social status, and certain habits with that character.

It is important to stress that the characters are similar, but not the same. For instance, Edokko are considered quick-tempered compared to the people living in the Kansai region, who are generally viewed as friendly, outgoing, and humorous.

Let's meet some of these stock characters.

Characters Common to Edo rakugo:

Gonsuke	Is a manservant from the countryside. He is responsible for doing housework and serving his master.
Hachigoro **Kumagoro**	These characters are very similar. They are both craftsmen and simpletons. They live in a nagaya, are quick-tempered, thoughtless, and sometimes create a big scene.
Kinbo	Is a typical male child in Edo.
Kisegawa	Is a high-class courtesan who works in the Yoshiwara pleasure district.
Kotaro	Is an irresponsible young master who is always playing around. He can be found frequenting the pleasure quarters.

Yotaro	Is a complete but likeable fool.

Characters Common to Kamigata rakugo:

Omatsu	Is a housewife or housekeeper who lives in a nagaya. She is domineering and outspoken.
Sakujiro	Is similar to Kotaro in Edo. He is a young master who does not take matters very seriously and can frequently be found playing around.
Seihachi **Kiroku**	They are similar to Hachigoro and Kumagoro in Edo and also live in a nagaya.
	They are not merchants, but they are often given similar qualities. Kiroku is about thirty years old and Seihachi is slightly older. Kiroku usually calls on Seihachi when he cannot figure something out. Seihachi helps Kiroku,

but not without teasing him first. Kiroku is the more unreliable of the two.

Characters Common to Edo and Kamigata rakugo:

Ippachi Is a taikomochi or male geisha.

Jinbei In Edo rakugo, he is a good-natured man.

In Kamigata rakugo, he is similar to Inkyo (characterized below). He lives on one of Osaka's backstreets. He is good-natured, and knowledgeable, and answers any and all questions brought to him.

Okiyo Is a housekeeper.

Osaki Is a wife.

Sadakichi Is an adolescent apprentice.

Tora	Is a male child.

Characters Who Represent a Profession or a Position in Society:

Banto	Is a head clerk. He is often ordered to keep an eye on the merchant's young son. Banto is the name of his position, not his actual name.
Bugyo	Is a judge.
Inkyo	Is a retired old man who lives on one of Edo's side streets. He is the source of wisdom for the community, but his vanity will not allow him to accept his lack of knowledge. He is sometimes known to disperse misleading information to cover up his ignorance.
Ohya (*Edo*)	Is a landlord.
Ienushi (*Kamigata*)	Is a landlord.
Osho	Is a priest.
Tanako	Is a tenant.

xxxii. Another Bottle of Sake by Kei Ohsuga

Another Bottle of Sake (*Kawarime*)

Characters:

R: Rickshaw Puller
M: Man
W: Man's Wife

☙

M: *(Staggering)* One little, two little, three little bottles...

Four little, five little, six little bottles...

Seven little, eight little, nine little bottles...

Ten little, 11 little, 12 little bottles...

13 little, 14 little, 15 little bottles...

16 little, 17 little, 18 little bottles...

19 little...

Oh, gosh, this song doesn't end.

Someone, please stop me!

R: Hey! Mister—you are hopelessly drunk.

Would you like a ride?

M: Where are you taking me?

R: I'll take you wherever you like.

M: Wherever I like?

That's interesting.

Then take me to Kamchatka!

R: Are you kidding?

	How can I take you to such a distant place up north?
M:	But you just said you would take me wherever I wanted to go.
	How about Sakhalin?
R:	Sakhalin is still too far.
M:	Then take me to Hokkaido.
R:	Don't make a fool out of me.
	Now, get on!
M:	I see.
	If you insist then, I cannot refuse.
R:	Mister, are you seated now?
	Then we will get started.
	Where would you like to go?
M:	You cannot go backward.
	So why don't you go forward?
R:	Mister, I cannot just go forward.
	Tell me where you want to go.
M:	Rickshaw puller, can you let me off?
R:	Oh, you just got on.
	What now?
M:	Can you knock on the door of this house?
R:	Knock on this door?
	At this time of night?
	Is he your acquaintance?

M: Yes, kind of.

R: *(Knock, knock)* Hello!

(Knock, knock) Excuse me!

W: Yes, I'm coming.

Don't knock on the door so hard!

It's already late at night.

I'll open the door now.

Oh, are you a rickshaw puller?

R: Yes, this guy asked me to…

Hey, you, don't go inside.

Hey, you, stop!

W: It's all right.

He is my husband.

R: He is?

W: I'm sorry.

When he is drunk, he always makes a fool out of a rickshaw puller.

Where did you pick him up?

R: Well, I picked him up right here.

In front of the entrance to your house.

W: Oh, my.

Right in front our house?

I'm sorry.

This is only a small amount of money, but please take it.

R: No, I can't.

	I didn't take him anywhere.
	I just knocked on the door.
W:	You deserve it.
	You took care of a drunken man.
R:	Really?
	Then I'll take it.
	Thank you. Good night!
W:	*(Softly)* Take care.
	Good night!
W:	*(Loudly)* What in blazes are you doing, you fool!
M:	Hey, don't scare me.
	You were so kind to that rickshaw puller, and now you are barking at me like a dog.
	Can't you talk to me like you talked to him?
	You even gave him some money.
	It's no wonder we are so poor.
	Now I understand.
	You give all the money I earn to that rickshaw puller!
W:	What are you talking about?
	Who did you drink with tonight?
M:	With Tome. I haven't seen him for a long time.
	We ate and drank and talked on and on.
	We couldn't stop.
	I have a good idea.

	Shall we go someplace to have a few drinks?
W:	Stop joking.
	Why do I have to drink with you at this time of night?
	It's almost midnight. You already drank enough.
	So, go to sleep.
M:	What?
W:	I said you already drank enough. So, go to sleep!
M:	No! I'm at home now.
	Drinking outside is one thing. Drinking at home is another.
	I can't go to sleep without having some sake at home.
W:	But I already turned off the stove.
	So, go to sleep.
M:	No! I don't want to.
W:	Then, what do you want?
M:	You don't have to warm up the sake. Cold sake is all right with me.
	So why don't you say, "I know you already had a lot of sake. But drinking outside is different from drinking at home. I know you would like to be accompanied by a young girl, but tonight let me give you another bottle of sake."
	Then I will say, "I understand. It's already late at night. So, I'll go to sleep."
	You understand what I mean?

W: I see. If I say so, you'll go to sleep?

All right. I know you already had a lot of sake. But drinking outside is different from drinking at home. I know you would like to be accompanied by a young girl, but tonight let me give you another bottle of sake.

M: Is that right? Then I cannot refuse.

Give me another bottle of sake!

W: Come on! You tricked me.

M: Give me sake.

And you have some food, right?

W: No, I have no food at home today.

M: I remember we had some pickles.

W: I ate them all.

M: You did?

I remember we had some cucumber and eggplant.

W: They are not pickled yet.

It takes time to pickle them.

M: I see. How about soy beans?

I remember there were 35 soy beans left from last night.

W: I ate them all.

M: You did?

I remember we had some dried fish.

W: I ate it.

M: You did?

	I remember we had some boiled shellfish.
W:	I ate it.
M:	What? You ate everything!
	You are always eating or sleeping.
	That's not good for your health.
	I want some food while drinking.
W:	Then should I go out and buy some oden?
M:	Oden! Yes, that's a good idea.
	I like boiled food. Hey, wait!
	Ask me what kind of ingredients I would like.
W:	All right. What kind of ingredients would you like?
M:	I want "saw."
W:	What do you mean by saw?
	Are you going to cut wood or something?
M:	No, I mean sausage.
W:	I see. What else?
M:	I want "cab."
W:	What do you mean by cab?
	Are you going somewhere now?
M:	I mean cabbage.
W:	I see. Anything else?
M:	Hmmm. I want "pot."
W:	What do you mean by pot?
	Are you going to cook something for yourself?
M:	Don't you understand? It's potato.

	We the men in Edo are short-tempered, so we always make long words short.
W:	They are not long at all. Sausage, cabbage, and potato. They all have only a few syllables.
	You are just lazy.
M:	Shut up!
	I also want "rad."
W:	You mean radish?
M:	Bingo! Now you are getting what I'm trying to say.
	What are you doing, Osaki?
	You don't have to put on makeup now.
	You are just going out to buy oden.
	Don't forget to bring a bowl.
	Now go out and get them!
M:	She's gone. What a good wife she is!
	Going out to buy oden late at night.
	Nobody will do such a thing except my wife.
	All of my friends say, "Kuma, you have a good wife. She is too good for you."
	I think so, too. She lives with such a selfish man like me. I cannot thank her enough. But I can never say that to her.
	I always have to be harsh toward her.
	"Do this and do that, you idiot!"

I know she is not an idiot. It is me who is an idiot.

When she is not at home, I always put my hands together and thank her or apologize to her.

"You are my God. I cannot live without you."

(He looks at the door) Oh, you are still here!

The Summer Burglar (*Natsu Doro*)

Characters:

        B: Burglar
        C: Carpenter

ଓଞ୦

B: Oh! The door is unlocked.

Is there anyone home?

It stinks of mosquito repellent.

What a dirty house!

But folks living in houses like this usually save up a ton of cash.

Oh, there's someone sleeping in the corner.

Hey, wake up!

C: What?

B: I said, wake up!

Give me all your money.

C: What?

Give you my money?

Who are you?

B: Who am I?

C: Yeah, who are you?

What are you doing here?

B: You know what I'm doing.

C: You know what you're doing, but how should I know what you're doing?

B: I'm a burglar.

C: Oh, a burglar.

Then, I have nothing to worry about.

B: What?

I'm a burglar!

C: Don't shout.

You must be a novice.

A burglar shouldn't raise his voice.

The neighbors might hear you.

B: Shut up!

Give me all your money.

Or else you're a dead man.

C: I have no money.

B: Don't lie to me.

C: I mean it.

B: I don't believe you.

If you don't give me your money, I'll kill you.

Do you see this knife?

C: I see.

Kill me, then.

B: What?

When I say I'll kill you, I really mean it.

I'm not kidding.

C: I was thinking about ending my life.

So you've come at a good time.

Go on. Kill me!

B: Hey, don't shout!

The neighbors might hear you.

You are still young.

Why do you want to die?

C: Because I have nothing to eat.

B: Nothing to eat?

Why don't you go to work?

C: I'm a carpenter, but I don't have carpentry tools.

B: What happened to your tools?

C: They are in the pawnshop.

B: In the pawnshop?

How much do you need to buy them back?

C: Three yen.

B: Three yen?

That's not a lot of money.

You can get it somewhere.

C: No, I can't.

That's why I'm thinking about dying.

Come on, kill me!

B: Don't shout.

The neighbors might come.

With three yen, you can buy your tools back, right?

C: Right.

B: All right, I'll give you three yen.

C: Wait, you are giving me three yen?

That's funny.

B: What's so funny?

C: You are a burglar.

B: Yes, I am.

C: Then you have to take my money, not the other way around.

B: Yeah, but I can't just watch you die of starvation.

Here's three yen.

Go back to work.

C: Thank you.

You should quit being a burglar.

You're such a nice guy.

B: Am I?

C: Yes. I have a lot of friends, but none of them ever came here and gave me money.

For a complete stranger like you to help me out, well, I just don't know how to thank you!

(Pause) But I really should return this money.

B: Why? You just took it.

C: Three yen is just the principal.

	I need to pay off the interest, too.
B:	Interest?
	Do I have to pay off your interest, too?
	Oh, I had a bad dream yesterday.
	Fish were flying, birds were swimming, and all the human beings became robots.
	What a strange dream!
	Somehow, I knew something terrible was going to happen to me.
	All right, I guess I'll help you pay the interest too.
C:	Thank you.
	(A short pause) But still, I should return everything to you.
B:	Why, don't be so modest.
C:	I'm not being modest.
	You see, I have nothing to wear.
	I can't go to the pawnshop only with this loincloth on.
	It's better if you just kill me.
B:	There you go again.
	I'll give you three more yen for clothes.
	That's good enough, right?
C:	Thank you, but…
B:	But what?
C:	I need some food, too.
	I haven't eaten for ten days.

B: All right. Here's one more yen for your food.

Get something to eat with this.

C: Thank you very much, but…

B: You want more?

Your "but" is really starting to scare me.

You have what you need for tools, clothing, food…

C: I have to pay my rent.

I haven't paid it for five months.

B: You can pay your rent after you earn some cash.

C: My landlord is very kind.

He always waits for my rent payments.

But he wants me to pay as soon as I start working.

I have to pass in front of his house whenever I go to work.

I can't take that!

So go on, kill me!

B: There you go again.

Keep your voice down.

How much is the rent?

C: Five yen.

B: All right. Here's 10 yen.

C: That's for two months.

B: That should be good enough for now.

C: Yes, thank you.

B: You took all the money I had.

But today I feel like I did something really good.

Work hard from now on.

Goodbye!

C: Hey! Mr. Burglar.

B: Don't shout!

And don't call me a burglar.

I did all that I could do for you.

C: Sorry, but I don't know your name.

B: What more do you want?

C: Could you please come again next month?

Browsing in the Pleasure Quarter (*Nikai Zomeki*)

Characters:

- Y: Young Master
- M: Master
- B: Banto (Head Clerk)
- S: Sadakichi

೧೪೮೦

During the seventeenth century, the Tokugawa Shogunate officially established several pleasure districts in major cities throughout Japan. The one in Edo was known as Yoshiwara. It was originally based in Nihonbashi, but was relocated to Asakusa after a devastating fire. Yoshiwara was in operation until 1958 when a law was passed prohibiting such places.

A lot of men visited Yoshiwara to have a good time with the women who worked there, but some men were satisfied with just browsing the district. The following story is about a young master who loves to browse in Yoshiwara.

B: Young master.

Y: Yes.

B: Your father is furious.
 Do you know why?

It is because you go to Yoshiwara every day, come home late at night, and knock on the door.
He said he can't stand it any longer.
He said he has no other choice but to disown you.
Young master, please listen to me.
You don't have to go to Yoshiwara every night.
Why not go once a week or once every two weeks?

Y: You know, Banto, when the night comes, I can't help visiting Yoshiwara. It's my nature, I can't resist.

B: Is that so?
I can't blame the master for getting angry with you.
If you go to Yoshiwara every day to see a girl, why don't you let her stay at your house instead?
It's much more economical and convenient.

Y: I don't care about girls.

B: What do you mean?
If you are not seeing a particular girl, why do you go to Yoshiwara every night?

Y: I like its atmosphere.

B: You mean, you are just browsing?

Y: Yes.
So, you see, there is no point in letting a girl stay at my house.
If you can bring Yoshiwara home, I won't go out.

B: How can I bring Yoshiwara to your house?

Well, let's see.

How about this?

The second floor of the store is huge, and it is not being used right now.

So why not build a Yoshiwara on the second floor?

Then you can browse the second floor instead.

Y: Is that possible?

B: I know a very skillful carpenter, so I think it's possible.

Y: Well, if it works…

B: Good!

I'll ask him if he can do it. I'll keep it a secret from your father.

B: Masagoro-san, you know our young master goes to Yoshiwara every day and his father is furious about it. The young master said that if you can build a Yoshiwara on the second floor of the store, he won't go to Yoshiwara any longer.

Can you do it?

C: Well, building Yoshiwara is not an easy job, but if it prevents the young master from getting disciplined, I will try.

B: Thank you.

You will have to go to Yoshiwara and get its map.

C: No need.

I know everything there is to know about Yoshiwara. When I was a young man, I spent more time in Yoshiwara than I did at home.

The carpenter and his colleagues finished building Yoshiwara on the second floor of the store.

B: Young master, it's finished.
Y: What's finished, Banto?
B: You forgot?
I'm talking about the second floor.
The second floor has just been renovated.
So why don't you go upstairs and browse through it?
Y: All right.
Thank you.
If it serves me well, I won't have to go all the way to Yoshiwara from now on.
B: Take your time, young master.
You can enjoy it until late at night.
Y: Yes. But if I don't feel comfortable, I'll come down right away.
What matters is its atmosphere.
See you soon.
B: Yes, see you later.

Y: Oh, wait.

Banto, can you get me a kimono from the closet?

B: But you are wearing a kimono now.

Y: This one doesn't work.

I should wear a kimono suited for browsing.

B: But you are just going upstairs.

Y: No, Banto, you don't understand.

I want to feel like I am really browsing in Yoshiwara.

B: Hmm. Is that so?

Which kimono do you want?

Y: The one with wide sleeves.

B: Why do you need a kimono like that?

Y: Oh, you don't know what goes on in Yoshiwara.

The place is always crowded.

So, you sometimes bump into somebody.

Then, you start fighting.

Do you know what's important when you fight?

You have to make the first move.

You hit him before he hits you.

If you wear a kimono with narrow sleeves, it takes a little longer to hit him.

That's why.

B: So you go to Yoshiwara to fight.

Y: Why not?

I also need a hand towel.

B: What are you going to do with a hand towel?

Y: I will wear it around my head.

B: Why?

Y: Because it's winter now.

 I may get wet from the night dew.

B: But you are just going upstairs.

 There is no night dew on the second floor.

Y: Banto, you don't understand at all.

 I want to feel like I am really browsing in Yoshiwara.

 I want to enjoy its atmosphere.

B: All right.

 Suit yourself.

Y: Yes. I'm off.

 If someone comes, don't let him go upstairs. OK?

B: I understand.

 If you stay there until late, you can sleep overnight.

 See you.

Y: All right.

 Humph, Banto is always complaining about me, but he is also concerned about me.

 I don't want to go all the way to Yoshiwara actually.

 If I can browse on the second floor, that's good enough.

 (Goes upstairs and starts looking around) Wow! It really looks like Yoshiwara.

That carpenter and his colleagues are very skillful!

This is amazing.

The willow tree right here.

Every guy looks back at the pleasure quarter from here after they had a good time.

They don't want to go home.

And here is the Big Gate.

It's so exciting to pass through this gate.

You enter a totally different world.

All the tea houses are just the same as those in Yoshiwara.

Miura-ya, Tama-ya, Izumi-ya, Kado-ebi.

It's great browsing here.

On the left is Fushimi-cho Street, and there is Edo-cho Street over there.

This area is called Waiting Space because they sometimes wait for important guests here.

I want to be such an important person someday.

There's nobody around here today.

Usually there are lots of guys in Yoshiwara, but when there are events in other towns, Yoshiwara is deserted like this.

It's all right with me.

It's easier to walk around.

♪ *Chitonchintotechinton-Horete kayoeba senrimo ichiri...*
If you are in love, thousands of kilometers feel like only a few kilometers. ♪

G: Hi, how are you doing, young master?
Why not come into our store?

Y: No. I'm sorry.
I'm just browsing.
I'll come again.

♪ *Nagai tambo mo hitomatagi...It is nothing to walk across a large paddy field.* ♪

G: Come in, young man!

Y: No, I'm sorry I can't.
I have a lot of things to do tonight.
I'm busy.

G: Come on.
Don't talk such nonsense.
Busy people cannot come here at this time of day.
What time do you think it is now?

Y: Yes, she is right.
If you are busy, you don't have time to browse here.

♪ *Chitonchintotechinton-Tsukini muragumo hananiwa arashi...Clouds to the moon, and storm and rain to the flowers.* ♪

G: Young master, we have a new face today.

	She is a good girl. Why not come in and have a good time with her?
Y:	Sorry, I'm just looking around.
	I like the atmosphere of this district.
	♪ *Tokaku ukiyoha mamanaranu…It's hard to live in this world.* ♪
G:	Oh, young master, why not come in and smoke a pipe?
	Here you go.
	Is it good?
	Oh, are you going?
	You just smoked a pipe and now you are leaving?
	Are you broke?
	You have no money?
	Are you penniless?
Y:	Shut up!
	Don't call me broke and penniless.
	If I like you, I'll come in and spend a lot of money on you.
	Don't make a fool out of me!
Man:	Hey, stop it!
	Don't fight with a girl.
	I'll fight for her if you want.
Y:	Who are you?
	Where did you come from?
	All right.

	If you say so, let's fight.
	Oh, you hit me first, bastard!
	Take this!
Man:	Ouch!
	Do you see this knife?
	I'll kill you!
Y:	Oh, you took out a knife.
	OK, then, kill me.
	Hey, kill me, kill meeee!
M:	(*Looking upstairs*) What's all the fuss upstairs?
	What is he shouting about?
	It appears that there are several people up there.
	Sada, Sadakichi!
S:	Yes, master, what can I do for you?
M:	Why don't you go upstairs and tell them to be quiet.
S:	I understand. The young master is always like this.
	(*Goes upstairs*) Wow, these houses are gorgeous!
	I see. So, this is what they call Yoshiwara.
	There is a guy over there covering his head with a hand towel.
	Is he a burglar?
	But burglars usually don't shout like him.
	Ah, I see.
	He is the young master.

He is fighting.

But he is fighting alone.

He is grabbing his own kimono and shouting at himself.

Has he gone crazy?

Young master, young master!

Y: You, bastard!

Don't hit me.

Take this. Take this!

S: Excuse me, young master. Excuse me!

Y: I don't know who you are, but don't stop our fight.

Take this!

I will never forgive you.

S: Young master!

Y: Don't tap my shoulder. Don't stop our fight.

I'm not asking for arbitration.

I can never forgive him.

What! Sadakichi?

Oh, my goodness. Why are you here?

This is no place for a boy like you.

Sadakichi, when you go home, don't tell my dad that you met me here.

Faceless Ghost (*Nopperabo*)

Characters:

K:	Kichibei
L:	The Lord
Y:	Young Girl
S:	Soba Noodle Salesman
W:	Kichibei's Wife

☙❧

Once there was a street peddler named Kichibei who lived in Yotsuya, Tokyo.

Kichibei made and sold combs, hairpins, cosmetics, and accessories for swords. One of his customers was a lord in Akasaka. The two loved playing the game Go, and they were very competitive.

One evening, Kichibei went to the lord's mansion to deliver his orders and they started to play Go. They played several rounds until late at night. Usually, each would win a few games and lose a few games, but tonight was a strange night for Kichibei. He lost every single game.

L: What happened today, Kichibei?

You are no match for me.

Would you like to play one more game?

K: No more tonight.

I'm out of luck today, and it's too late.

I should go home.

L: Don't say such a thing.

Let's play one more game.

K: Sorry, my wife is waiting for me.

I must be going.

L: Is that so?

(To Oku) Hey, Oku, what time is it now? What, that late?

(To Kichibei) Sorry to have kept you for such a long time, Kichibei.

K: I'll come again. Goodbye, Lord.

(To Oku) Okusama, I'll bring your orders next week. Goodbye.

Kichibei left the mansion. As he was getting ready to cross the Benkei Bridge over the moat in Akasaka as usual, he saw a young girl crouching under a willow tree near the bridge. She was 16 or 17. She appeared to be graceful and wore a beautiful kimono with gorgeous sleeves. Her hair was arranged like that of a young girl from a good family. She was facing the moat and praying with her hands placed together. Thinking that she

> *might jump into the moat and drown herself, he rushed to her and caught her by her sleeve.*

K: Wait! Don't do that!
   Don't jump into the moat!

Y: *(Weeping)*

K: Don't cry like that.
   This is no place for a young lady to be late at night.

Y: *(Weeping)*

K: Please, please listen to me.
   Do not cry.
   Tell me what is troubling you.
   If there is any way to help you, I'll be glad to.
   (Slowly she rises up, and stops crying)

Y: *(Hiding her face with her sleeve)*
   Do you really want to know why I want to die?

K: Yes, tell me all your troubles, and you'll feel much better.

Y: Would you really listen to a girl with a face like this?
   (Stroking her face)

K: Gyaaaa!
   (He runs away)

K: Where am I?
   Yotsuya-mitsuke?
   What is that?
   It looks like the gleam of a firefly.

(He continues to run)

It's a lantern of a soba stand.

(Flinging himself down at the feet of the soba seller)

Soba-man!

S: Hey, what's the matter?

You bumped into my stand.

K: *(Gasping)* Hah, hah, hah.

S: What happened?

Did somebody hurt you?

K: No, nobody hurt me.

S: Robbers?

K: Not robbers. Not robbers.

I saw a young girl under a willow tree at the Benkei Bridge.

I thought she was going to drown herself and I went to help her.

When she turned to me, I found she had no eyes, no nose, or mouth.

S: So you saw a Nopperabo.

K: Do you know her?

S: Yes, she lives in that moat and appears on a warm night like this.

You were lucky.

If you had stayed there for a little longer, you would have been drawn into the moat and drowned.

By the way, that young girl you saw by the bridge—did she look like this?

K: Gyaaaa!

(He runs away)

K: Where am I?

Oh, it's my house!

K: *(Knocking on the door)* Open the door, open the door!

W: *(Unlocking the door)* I'm coming, I'm coming.

Don't shout.

It's already late at night.

Our neighbors are sleeping.

K: *(Enters the house. Gasping)* Hah, hah, hah…

W: What's the matter with you?

K: Listen. I went to the lord's mansion in Akasaka today, on business.

I played Go with the lord until late at night.

When I was going to cross the Benkei Bridge, I saw a young girl trying to kill herself.

I asked her what the trouble was, and she turned around and looked at me.

She was a Nopperabo.

She had no eyes, no nose, or mouth.

I was scared and ran away.

Then I saw the lantern of a soba salesman.

I flung myself down at his feet and told him the whole story.

Then he said, "Did she look like this?"

He was also a Nopperabo!

I saw two Nopperabos in one night.

I was scared and ran away.

I don't remember where I ran, but somehow, I was in front of my house.

W: No kidding?

Such things can't exist in this world.

What? It's a true story? How horrifying!

Those stories make me feel sick.

You had such an experience because you played around until late at night.

By the way, did they look like this?

K: Gyaaaa! (*He faints*)

W: Darling, wake up. Wake up.

K: Where am I?

Where's the Nopperabo?

W: Nopperabo?

What are you talking about?

Did you have a bad dream?

K: A dream?

Oh, thank god.

It was just a dream.

          I went to the lord's mansion and played Go until late at night.

          On the way home, I saw a young girl trying to drown herself.

          I tried to help her, but I found that she was a Nopperabo.

          I was scared and ran away.

          Then I found a soba salesman and told him the whole story.

          He was a Nopperabo too.

          I was terrified and rushed home and told you the whole story.

          Then, don't be surprised.

          You were a Nopperabo, also.

W: *(Laughing)* Ha, ha, ha. What a dream!

          You didn't go to the lord's mansion today.

          You had no orders from them, so you started to drink here in the evening and fell asleep.

          You had such a dream because you drank too much.

          By the way did they all look like this?

K: Gyaaa!

The Father and Son Who Love Drinking (*Oyako Zake*)

Characters:

    F: Father
    S: His Son
    W: Wife

ଔଷଓ

F: You are still very young.
Sake could ruin your health.
You should stop drinking.
I will stop drinking too.

S: I see.
(A few weeks later)

F: I'm a little tired today.
Is there anything I can refresh myself with?

W: How about drinking Pokari Sweat?

F: It's a sports drink.
I mean, something more stimulating.

W: How about Kakkonto?

F: That's Chinese medicine.
I'm not sick!
I want some…sake…

W: No!

It's you who said you would stop drinking and told Kotaro not to drink.

When he comes back, what will you say?

F: One bottle before he comes back, and I'll go upstairs and go to sleep.

Only one bottle.

W: No!

F: Don't be so mean.

We've been married for a long time, so why can't you be more lenient toward me?

W: Well, OK, if you insist.

It'll really be only one bottle.

F: Yes, one bottle. That's fine.

(But of course, that is not the way sake works.)

F: One more bottle!

W: This should be the last.

F: One more, please.

W: You should stop now.

F: I should stop now?

Who do you think I am?

Who brings home the bread and butter?

Get me one more bottle!

No more sake?

Did I have enough already?

What are you talking about?

Am I drunk?

(He attempts to put tobacco leaves into a pipe and tries to light it, but it doesn't work too well)

No kidding.

I'm sober.

You think I'm drunk because you were watching me drink.

I'm all right. What?

If you want to say something, do not mumble away to yourself.

You should get it straight. What!?

Our son came back?

Why did he come back so early?

Honey, put away all the bottles and plates.

Tell him that I have some work to do, so have him wait at the threshold for a while.

(He continues to smoke. He tries to look sober)

F: Who's that? Kotaro? Come in.

S: Hi, Dad. I'm home.

(Son collapses on the floor with a crash)

S: Well, I went to Mr. Yamato's house in Kojimachi as you instructed me.

He was enjoying some sake and asked me to join him.

(He hiccups) I told him I had promised my father not to drink, but he just got angry.

He said I could never visit his house again if I didn't drink with him.

(He hiccups again) I told him I didn't care, and I wouldn't drink.

Then he said, "That's the spirit.

You have great courage.

Such a courageous person should drink a cup of sake."

So I said, "Thank you very much."

We drank five liters between us.

You know dad, you can't give up what you like.

F: You idiot! You're really hopeless.

I tried so hard to get you to stop drinking.

Just look at me. I can't even stand the sight of sake.

The reason why I am strict with you is…

(He yawns) I worry about your health.

(He stares at his son and blinks his eyes) What's that?

(Calling his wife) Honey, come here, he's got seven, no, eight faces now.

He is a monster.

Hey, I can't leave my estate to a monster like you.

S: Ha ha ha ha ha. Who are you kidding?

I don't want to inherit a house that spins round and round like this.

xxxiii. Foxes in Oji by Kei Ohsuga

Foxes in Oji (*Oji no Kitsune*)

Characters:

M:	Man
F:	Fox
SF:	Small Fox
S:	Store Clerk
O:	Otake
MA:	Master

෬෨

There are times when animals appear in rakugo stories. The most common animals to appear in these stories are foxes and raccoon dogs. These creatures characteristically play tricks on human beings.

Raccoon dogs have the ability to shapeshift into dice, money, or carp in an effort to try and cheat humans; however, they are usually unsuccessful. Raccoon dogs are not very intelligent; they are known more for being attractive and charming.

Foxes, on the other hand, are smarter and more cunning than raccoon dogs. They can take on human form and play clever tricks on people. They trick us by serving us noodles, which in reality are earthworms; sake, which is actually horse's urine; and rice cakes, which are in fact horse manure.

They are mischievous animals. But they have been worshipped by people through the ages, as they are believed to be messengers from God. Statues of foxes can be found at the gates of specific types of shrines known as an Inari shrines.

This story is about a man who decided to visit the Oji Shrine. It was the day after a festival, so there weren't many people around. As he was walking around in the back of the shrine, he encountered a fox that was placing grass on its head. Curious, the man watched to see what would happen. Then, right before his eyes, the fox changed into a beautiful woman.

M: Oh my! This is the first time I've ever seen a fox change into a human being.
She must be planning to trick someone.
But, who? There's no one around here.
That means…she must be planning to trick me.
Oh, that's interesting.
I'd like to play along.

In the old days, Japanese people wiped their eyebrows with saliva to ward off evil spirits. This practice is similar to saying "knock on wood" in Western culture.

M: *(Wiping his eyebrows with saliva, he approaches her)*
Tama-chan. Aren't you Tama-chan?

F: Oh, hello, young man!
It's been a long time.

M: *(Talking to himself)* She answered me.
She said it's been a long time.
She is pretending that she knows me!

F: What are you mumbling about?

M: Oh, never mind.
I was just talking to myself.
I didn't expect to find you here.
What are you doing here?

F: I prayed at the shrine.
The weather is fine today, so I've been walking around, feeling refreshed.

M: I've been to the shrine, too.
Tama-chan, you have grown into such a beautiful woman. How old are you now?
Twenty-two?
Then it's about time you got married.

	Your parents must be expecting you to tie the knot soon.

Your parents must be expecting you to tie the knot soon.

Do you have a boyfriend? No?

Then, I will introduce you to one of my friends.

Let's go to a restaurant together and chat for a while.

F: Is that all right with you?

M: Sure! There's a restaurant named Ojiya down this street.

Let's talk over lunch.

F: Sounds nice.

M: Hello.

S: Hello. Are you here to have lunch?

This floor is full, so would you mind going upstairs?

There are still some rooms available upstairs.

M: Thank you. This is a great room.

It commands a wonderful view.

(To the waitress) Could you take our order?

Bring us some sake first.

Yes, one small bottle and two cups.

Tama-chan, what kind of food would you like?

Do you have any likes and dislikes? No?

(To the waitress) Could we have some sushi and tempura?

Tama-chan, it's been quite a while since I saw you last.

I never expected to see you and have lunch with you.

How lucky I am!

I'd like to see your parents one of these days.

Yes, the sake has arrived. Good!

Please put it here.

Now, let's have some sake first.

F: I don't drink.

M: Don't worry.

This cup is very small.

If you get drunk, I'll take care of you.

Let me have some, too.

(Wiping his eyebrows with saliva)

Hmm, it tastes very good.

This sake is the real thing, it's not horse's urine.

F: I beg your pardon?

M: Oh, never mind.

I just said this sake is really tasty.

Tama-chan, have some sushi and tempura, too.

They ate and drank a lot. Soon she got drunk and fell asleep. While she was sleeping, he went downstairs.

S: Oh, are you leaving?

M: Yes. My girlfriend is sleeping upstairs now.

Don't worry, she just had a little too much sake.

She'll be fine soon.

I have an uncle who lives nearby.

I'd like to visit him and bring him a souvenir.

What would you recommend? Rolled omelette?

That's fine. Then, please wrap three pieces of rolled omelette.

My girlfriend will pay for everything, so give her the bill when she wakes up.

When you wake her up, don't do it in a loud voice.

If you surprise her, she might jump up.

S: Jump up? Why?

M: Oh, never mind.

I just want you to be careful.

Is the rolled omelette ready?

Thank you. Goodbye.

S: Otake, would you wake the guest upstairs?

It's getting late.

O: I see.

(She goes upstairs) Well, excuse me.

Oh, she is sleeping so well.

Excuse me, please wake up.

It's getting late.

Wake up, please.

F: Oh, sorry. I'm so drunk.

Where is that young man?

O: He said he was going to visit his uncle nearby.

He bought some rolled omelette and left.

F: My goodness!
 He left without even saying goodbye to me.
 What about the check?
O: He said you will pay for everything.
F: What?

She was so surprised that she lost her magical powers and turned back into a fox. Looking at her long ears, her big mouth and tail, Otake was shocked and she fell down the stairs.

O: Help me!
S: What's the matter?
 Otake!
O: The guest upstairs…
S: Yes, what happened to her? What?
 When you asked her to pay the bill, she became a fox?
 Is that so? I thought something was wrong with her from the beginning.
 When I saw her walking up the stairs, I saw something in between her legs.
 Now I understand. That was her tail.
 Hmm, what should I do?
 Otake, gather together some strong guys.
 We'll go upstairs and catch the fox.

They went upstairs and fought the fox. The fox was beaten badly and injured. When they were just about to catch the fox, it expelled the smelliest gas imaginable and jumped out of the window. Just then, the master of the restaurant came back.

MA: I'm back.
S: Welcome back, master.
MA: What's all the fuss upstairs?
S: We had a fight with a fox.
It came to our restaurant disguised as a woman.
She drank a lot and fell asleep.
When Otake asked her to pay the bill, she was surprised, lost her magical powers and changed back into a fox.
We beat and injured her, but she expelled the smelliest gas imaginable, jumped out of the window, and ran away.
MA: What an awful thing you did!
S: Awful thing?
MA: Yes, where are we? We are in Oji.
This area is under the protection of the Inari Shrine.
Don't you know that a fox is a messenger of the shrine?
In other words, it is a messenger of God.
When you see a fox, you have to be hospitable.
How can you beat her, you fool!

         She may curse you later.

         Let's call it a day today.

         Take a cold bath and purify yourselves.

         And burn some sacred wood and ask for her forgiveness.

S: I see.

M: Hey, uncle. How are you?

U: Good. What's new?

M: I visited the Oji Shrine today, so I decided to drop by.

         I missed the festival yesterday.

         I brought a souvenir for you.

         Rolled omelette from Ojiya.

U: Thank you. I like their rolled omelette.

         It must be very expensive.

M: No. I didn't pay for it.

U: You didn't pay for it?

         Then who paid for it?

M: A fox.

         When I was at the Oji Shrine today, I encountered a fox.

         It changed into a beautiful woman.

         I took her to Ojiya where we ate and drank a lot.

         She got drunk and fell asleep.

         I left the restaurant with this souvenir when she was sleeping.

U: You mean you tricked her?

M: Yes, I did.

U:	Are you out of your mind?
	Don't you know that a fox is a messenger of the shrine?
	In other words, she is a messenger of God.
	You missed the important festival at the shrine yesterday, so she felt sorry for you and appeared.
	She will curse you.
	See, your mouth is getting bigger, your ears are getting longer, and a tail is growing out of your butt.
M:	Stop it! Don't scare me.
U:	I mean it. Go home now and you will discover that your wife has turned into a fox.
	She will bite your throat.
M:	My goodness. What should I do?
U:	You have to visit Oji again tomorrow and apologize to her.
	(The next morning)
M:	*(Carrying a souvenir)* Man is the lord of all creation.
	I never thought I would apologize to a fox.
	I should have paid the bill yesterday.
	She must be around here. Hmm?
	I hear somebody groaning back there.
	Oh, there's a small fox.
	Excuse me, do you know who is groaning back there?
SF:	She is my mom.

	She was tricked and beaten by human beings yesterday.
M:	I'm sorry. It's me who tricked her.
	I came here to apologize to her.
	I have a little souvenir for her here.
	It is just a token of my regret.
	So would you give it to her?
	I'm leaving now, so please give her my best regards.
SF:	I see.
	(He rushes home) Mom, I'm back.
F:	Be quiet! You know I'm not well.
	If you go out, you may be bullied by human beings like I was.
	Why don't you stay here?
SF:	I just saw the man who tricked you yesterday.
F:	You did?
	How could he find this place?
	Is he still there?
SF:	No, he's gone.
F:	What did he say?
SF:	He said he came here to apologize to you.
	He brought a souvenir for you.
	He said it is a token of his regret.
	He also told me to give you his best regards.
	Mom, here's his souvenir. Can I have it?

F: *(Wiping saliva on her eyebrows)* You have to be careful.
Human beings today are so cunning.
Why not unwrap it in front of me?
If it looks safe, you can have it.

SF: *(He unwraps it)* Mom, it's rice cakes.
They look so delicious!

F: Rice cakes?
(Wiping saliva on her eyebrows)
No, no, don't eat them.
They must be horse manure!

Gonbei and the Racoon Dog (*Gonbei Danuki*)

Characters:

    G: Gonbei
    D: His Daughter
  YM: Young Man
    R: Raccoon Dog

ෲ

There once was an old man named Gonbei who lived on the mountain. He was barber by trade. His wife had died seven years ago, and his only daughter got married and moved away.

Gonbei is a grandfather now, but he still lives alone.

D: Dad, why won't you move away from the mountain?
       I know life on the mountain is good, but life in town is also good.
       Why don't you come live with us?
G: Thank you for your suggestion.
       But I like life on the mountain.
       You know, the wind blows differently each season on the mountain.
       The sounds of the rivers and the shapes of the clouds also tell me how the season changes.

The birds wake me up every morning and cheer me up.
I like living with nature.
It teaches me everything I need to know in life.
I was born on the mountain and will die on the mountain, just like the plants and animals here.
Besides, I am the only barber on the mountain.
Everybody comes to me when they want their hair cut.
I will be happy if you come to see me with your children once in a while.

At night he drinks alone and remembers his wife. One night, as he was getting ready to go to bed, someone knocked on the door and called his name.

R: *(Knock, knock)* Gonbei!
   (Knock, knock) Gonbei!
G: Who is it? I'm not asleep yet.
   Come in! Is it you Sagoju, or Risuke?
R: *(Knock, knock)* Gonbei!
   (Knock, knock) Gonbei!
G: Come in! The door is not locked, I said.
R: *(Knock, knock)* Gonbei!
   (Knock, knock) Gonbei!
G: OK, OK. I'm coming.

You don't have to keep repeating my name.

(He opens the door) What? There's no one here.

Is someone playing a trick on me?

All right. I'm going to go to bed.

(He closes the door)

R: *(Knock, knock)* Gonbei!

(Knock, knock) Gonbei!

G: Hey, who are you? Don't make me angry.

Come in! I said, come in!

Oh, I see. It must be a raccoon dog.

They often try to make fools out of human beings.

OK, I'll catch him.

The raccoon dog stood with his back against the door and knocked on the door with the back of his head. Gonbei crept to the door quietly and slowly opened the door. It caught the raccoon dog by surprise; he lost his balance and rolled into the house.

G: You rascal!

R: Gonbei!

G: So, you're still calling my name.

Gonbei fought with the raccoon dog. It was a tough fight, but he managed to catch the animal. He tied all four of his legs together and hung him from the ceiling. The next day, a young man from the village came to visit him.

YM: Good morning, Gonbei-san.

G: Good morning.

YM: You got up so early.

G: When you get old, you wake up early.

That's how it is.

Are you going to the field?

YM: Yes. My dad tells me to go to the farm early in the morning.

He always says, the early bird catches the worm.

But there are too many worms in the field now.

My work is just to kill them.

G: I see. Working in the field is always tough.

Why not come in and have some tea?

YM: Thank you. By the way, you have a lot of injuries. What happened?

G: Look above your head.

YM: How can I look above my head?

G: I mean, look at the ceiling.

YM: Ceiling? What's that?

G: It's a raccoon dog.

YM: Where did he come from?

G: I don't know.

Last night when I was going to bed, he called my name many times.

Gonbei, Gonbei.

When I opened the door, there was no one there.

He played a trick on me.

Finally, I found him.

I had a fight with him and managed to catch him.

YM: I see. He came to my house at midnight, too.

He knocked on the door and said in a loud voice, Jinjiro, Jinjiro!

It lasted all through the night.

I could not sleep even for a moment.

I tried to catch him, but I couldn't.

What will you do with him?

G: Do you have any ideas?

YM: Let's eat him.

I would like to have some soup made with his meat.

I like raccoon dog soup.

It's delicious, nutritious, and makes you warm.

It's my dad's favorite too.

So, give me some of his meat.

G: Well, that's a good idea, but actually today is the anniversary of my wife's death.

You know, she died seven years ago.

	I don't want to kill anything on such an important day.
YM:	Never mind that.
	He bothered us, so he deserves it.
	Let's kill him and eat him.
G:	I know how you feel.
	But let's not eat him today.
	Look, he looks scared!
	He knows what we are talking about.
	(To the raccoon dog)
	OK, I will bring you down now.
	Sit down here.
R:	Thank you, Gonbei.
G:	You still call me Gonbei.
	You should thank my wife.
	If today was not the anniversary of her death, you would have been turned into soup.
	Jinjiro, bring me the razor blade.
	I'll shave the hair on his head.
	Then he will be ashamed of his appearance and he will stop tricking us.
YM:	And what are you going to do with him afterwards?
G:	I'll just let him go.
YM:	Let him go?
	Why not tear off his skin?

And then you can let him go.

G: I'm serious!

OK, raccoon dog, listen.

I'm going to shave your head, so don't move.

It takes just a second.

Don't worry. I'm a professional barber.

Gonbei shaves the racoon dog's head.

Now, look at the mirror and see how terrible you look.

You should feel ashamed, and stop playing tricks on human beings.

All right? Now, I'll let you go.

The racoon dog looked at Gonbei for a while, bowed to him dozens of times, turned his back and ran away. The next day when Gonbei woke up...

R: *(Knock, knock)* Mr. Gonbei!

(Knock, knock) Mr. Gonbei!

G: There he is again. That stupid raccoon dog!

This time he called me Mr. Gonbei.

Why did he suddenly become so polite?

R: *(Knock, knock)* My dear Gon! My dear Gon!

G: My dear Gon!

This time he became so friendly.

What must he be thinking?

Gonbei became angry, walked to the door and opened it. Instead of just one racoon dog, there were many raccoon dogs standing in line in front of his house.

G: What's this?

R: Well, when I came back, they saw my shaved head. They thought it looked cool, and now they want their head shaved like mine.

G: What? Didn't they think you looked horrible?
Who are they?

R: They are my parents, grandparents, my brothers and sisters, my uncles and aunts, and my cousins.

G: So, all of your relatives are here?

R: Yes. This is the first time for them to get their hair done, so they are very excited.

G: I can't believe it. But why are you here?
Do you still want something?

R: Yes, this time, I want you to shave my beard.

Gonsuke's Lantern (*Gonsuke Jochin*)

Characters:

> H: Husband
> W: Wife
> M: Mistress
> G: Gonsuke

ଔଊ

> *In the old days, it was common for a wealthy man to maintain a mistress with his wife's knowledge. Oftentimes, the mistress lived in an elegant house surrounded by a black fence with a pine tree planted near the fence. Passersby admired the esthetic beauty and charm of the mistress' house.*
>
> *The relationship between the wife and the mistress was unique, as you will see in the following story.*

H: The wind is getting stronger.
W: Yes, I'm afraid there might be a fire somewhere tonight.
H: Indeed.
W: Did you close the books?
H: Yes, I'm almost done.
   It's already late. Let me go to sleep.
   It's really getting windy.

W: Darling, I'm worried about your mistress in Shinmichi.

H: Why?

W: She lives alone, doesn't she?

She always expresses her gratitude for you.

If a fire broke out, she would be in a big trouble.

She must be afraid of a fire breaking out.

I know you are tired, but why don't you go and stay with her tonight.

It's not very far from here.

H: You are too kind.

She always expresses her gratitude for you.

If she knew how considerate you are, she would be even happier.

OK, if you say so, I'm willing to stay with her tonight.

Is anyone in the household still awake?

Did they all go to sleep?

Oh, yes, Gonsuke is still around.

I'll have him accompany me tonight.

Gonsuke, Gonsuke!

G: Yeeeees.

H: Your answer is too long.

Make it shorter.

I'm going to Shinmichi now.

So light a lantern.

G: Oh, you want me to burn it down?

It's too wasteful.

H: What are you talking about?

When I tell you to light a lantern, I mean light the candle inside the lantern.

G: I see. Which lantern?

H: What do you mean, "Which lantern?"

G: Decorative or non-decorative?

H: Why do you ask such a question?

A decorative lantern is for a long-distance trip.

I'm just going to the next town.

A plain lantern is good enough.

G: You are going to see your mistress, right?

Is it a secret visit or an open visit?

H: It is an open visit.

Everybody knows about her.

She is indeed good natured, so I'm taking care of her.

G: Then, why don't you use a decorative one?

H: That's none of your business, Gonsuke.

Light a lantern. Now!

G: Yeeees.

H: Your answer is too long.

H: Here we are. Please wake her up.

G: It's late at night. I don't think she will wake up.

H: Don't say anything before you try.

G: If you say so.

	(Knocking on the door) Hey, wake up!
	The man who gives you an allowance every month is here to see you.
H:	Gonsuke, don't talk like that!
M:	Yes, who is it?
H:	It's me.
M:	Oh, master. You came very late at night.
	I'll open the door now.
	Are you on your way home?
G:	No, I was working until midnight, and I was going to sleep when the wind grew strong.
	My wife said if a fire broke out, you would be in big trouble.
	So she asked me to stay with you tonight.
M:	Oh, how kind she is!
	Wives are usually jealous of their husband's mistresses, but she is so different from other wives.
	I appreciate her kindness, but I cannot let you stay here tonight.
	I feel guilty about it.
	So please go back home tonight.
H:	I see. Gonsuke, Gonsuke!
G:	Yeeees.
H:	I told you that your answer is too long.

	She told me to go home.
G:	Ha, ha, ha, ha.
H:	What's so funny?
G:	I know you are a great master, but you were driven away by your wife earlier and now your mistress.
	I feel sorry for you.
	You are homeless.
	I'm better off than you are.
	At least, I have a place to sleep.
H:	Keep your mouth shut, Gonsuke!
	Let's go home.
	(Arriving at his house)
	I'm home.
W:	Oh, why did you come back?
	Why didn't you stay with her?
H:	She was very glad to see me.
	She appreciates your thoughtfulness, but she feels guilty about letting me stay.
	She asked me to go home, so I've come back.
W:	Oh, what a great girl!
	But I would like her to understand how I feel about her.
	If something happens tonight, I can't take any responsibility for it.
	So, stay with her tonight.
H:	I see. Gonsuke, Gonsuke!

G: Yeeeees.

H: Make your answer shorter.

I told you many times.

Light a lantern.

G: Ha, ha, ha.

I was waiting without putting it out.

H: Why do you do such a stupid thing?

G: Did I do something wrong?

H: Yes, you wasted the candle.

Don't keep the lantern lit in the house.

Even if it's only 15 or 20 minutes, it is wasteful.

Merchants should always try not to be wasteful.

You have to keep that in mind.

G: May I ask you a question?

H: Yes, what is it?

G: You said merchants should always try not to be wasteful.

H: Yes.

G: Does it only apply to the lantern, or can it be applied to anything else?

H: It applies to everything.

I'm not only talking about a lantern.

G: Then, you should also keep that in mind.

H: What do you mean?

G: Your mistress is a waste.

You give a lot of money to her every month.

Think how many candles you can buy with that money.

H: That's none of your business.

G: I don't think so. You are selfish.

H: Shut up. Bring the shoes.

G: I'm wearing them.

H: I'm not talking about *your* shoes.

Bring me *my* shoes.

G: Why don't you go out barefoot?

It will cool you down.

H: I know what I am doing.

Come with me to Shinmichi.

G: OK. OK, I can't fight the master anyway.

H: *(Arriving at the mistress's house)*

Here we are. Wake her up.

M: Yes, who is it?

H: It's me.

M: You are here again?

It was very cold, wasn't it?

Did you forget something?

H: No. When I went home and talked with my wife about you, she praised you a lot.

But she said if something happened, she wouldn't be able to take responsibility for it.

So she wants me to stay with you tonight.

M: Oh, did she say so?

H: Yes.

M: When she is so considerate to me, I should also be considerate to her.

I cannot let you stay here tonight.

So please go home.

H: I see. I will. Gonsuke, Gonsuke!

G: Yes.

H: I'll go home.

Light a lantern.

G: I don't have to.

H: Why not?

G: It's already morning.

xxxiv. Okiku's Dishes by Kei Ohsuga

Okiku's Dishes (*Okiku no Sara*)

Characters:

    H: Hachi
    I: Inkyo
    O: Okiku
    F: Hachi's Friend

H: Hello Inkyo, I brought my friends.

I: Oh Hachi! Come in, come in everyone.

H: Inkyo, we have a question, so we came to ask you.
Do you know anything about a ghost in these parts?

I: Ghost? Are you talking about the haunted mansion in Bancho?

H: What is that?

I: There was once a mansion in Bancho.
It was owned by Lord Aoyama Tessan.
Tessan was a very arrogant and mean man.
Since it was a big mansion, there were many maids working there.
One of the maids, Okiku, was very beautiful.
Tessan fell in love with her.
He said to Okiku, "Hee Hee Hee…Be my wife? I love you, Okiku. Hee Hee Hee…"

She turned down his proposals because she had a fiancé. But Tessan kept saying, "Be my wife." And she kept saying, "No, I can't."

"Be my wife."

"No, I can't."

"Be my wife."

"No, I can't."

H: Ah, I see. So she refused him.

I: Yes. Tessan got mad at Okiku.

He decided to do something horrible to her.

The greatest hate springs from the greatest love.

Tessan had a priceless family treasure; a set of ten beautiful dishes.

He asked Okiku to take care of them.

One day, he deliberately hid one of the dishes.

He called Okiku and said, "I want to see that beautiful set of dishes."

Okiku brought them to him and started counting.

"One dish, two dishes, three dishes, four dishes, five dishes, six dishes, seven dishes, eight dishes, nine dishes… oh my, one of them is missing!!"

"Hey, Okiku! Where is it?"

"I don't know, sir."

"How dare you, Okiku! Did you steal one of them?"

"No! I didn't."

"I'm sure you did."

"No! I didn't."

H: I see. So, she never admitted it.

I: No. Tessan said, "You are still lying to me!"

Tessan hung Okiku upside down in the well, and said, "Be honest. Tell me the truth! But if you become my wife, I'll forgive you."

But Okiku said, "No, I have a fiancé. His name is Sanpei. He is a rakugo performer. I enjoy being with him, so, I can't marry you. I didn't steal your dish."

"All right, all right, you will regret this. Stay still and close your eyes. You will feel no pain!"

Tessan took his sword out and slashed Okiku.

Then he cut the rope above her.

Okiku fell and sank deep into the well.

She died.

H: What an awful story!

I: But the story is not finished yet.

After the incident, Okiku's ghost appeared every night from the well and counted the dishes at his bedside.

"One dish, two dishes, three dishes..."

Tessan was terrified. He went mad and finally died.

H: Wow, so she punished him!

I: Yes. But the story is not finished yet.

H: Not yet?

I: The ghost still appears every night.

H: What? Okiku's ghost still appears, even now?

Okiku was very beautiful.

She must be beautiful as a ghost, too.

Hey guys, why don't we go to see Okiku?

I: Stop it!

They say whoever listens to Okiku count to nine will go mad and die.

Even if you hear her count to seven or eight, you will be in big trouble.

H: Hmmm, OK. I have an idea.

If we leave just as she counts to six, we should be OK. Right?

I: Maybe so.

H: OK, let's go.

I: Hey fellas, be careful.

Make sure you leave when she counts to six.

H: *(Walking)* Well, I've never seen a real ghost.

Isn't this exciting?

F: Hachi, I'm scared.

H: Hey! Don't be such a chicken!

F: I'm not a chicken!

What will happen if Okiku is mean, and she starts counting slowly, one, two, three, four, five, then suddenly, she starts to count fast, six, seven, eight, nine?

We will have no time to run away!

We will be dead.

H: Take it easy.

It is not going to be like that.

I don't think she is that type of a ghost.

Here we are.

Oh, this is really an old mansion!

This must be the well Inkyo told us about.

It was after midnight and the temple bell rang. Goooon! Then, a small fireball appeared. A cool wind blew. Okiku loomed out from the well.

O: I hate you, my lord, Tessan.

I curse you.

One dish, two dishes, three dishes...

H: She is counting the dishes!

Did anyone see her? No?

Then, let me take a look.

Wow! She is beautiful.

Hey, guys! Look at her.

F: Yes, you are right.

She is beautiful!

O: Four dishes, five dishes, six dishes…

H: She's reached six!

Let's get out of here!

(Pause) That was close.

It was so scary.

But let's come back tomorrow night.

The story about Okiku spread and more and more people gathered to see her. They even formed an Okiku fan club.

One day, when Hachi and his friends went to see Okiku, there was already a huge crowd of people gathered. There was even a group of foreigners among the crowd.

Soon the temple bell rang. A small fireball appeared. Okiku's ghost floated up from the well.

O: Hi everyone!

Thank you for coming every night.

I'm very happy to see you.

Oh, are you from China? *Ni Hao!*

You are from Korea? *Ahn nyong ha se yo!*

And you? From Thailand. *Sawadee kha!*

Namaste, Aloha, Bonjour, Hola, Shalom!

Thank you for traveling so far to see me.

	Then, let me start.
	One dish, two dishes, three dishes…
M:	Hey Okiku, may I take a photo with you?
O:	Sure. Go ahead.
M:	Thank you. Wait a second.
	Let me use my selfie stick. (*Click*)

As she became more popular, she appeared every day, seven days a week, rain or shine. The crowds grew so big that ticket booths were set up. People had to book their reservations months in advance. One promoter built a stadium for the Okiku show. Many stalls appeared outside the stadium. They sold beer, popcorn, and hot dogs. They also sold Okiku cards, Okiku folders, Okiku tablets, Okiku smartphones, Okiku video games, and many other souvenirs with Okiku's name.

H:	It's a big show, like the ones in Las Vegas.
	There are many food stands and souvenir shops!
F:	Hachi. I found something interesting — Okiku cookies!
H:	Cookies are not interesting.
F:	Yes they are. Look!
	It says ten cookies outside, but there are only nine cookies inside!
MC:	Ladies and gentlemen, welcome to Okiku's show! Before we start, please listen to a song by the Okiku Sisters!

♪One little, two little, three little dishes, four little, five little, six little dishes, seven little, eight little, nine little dishes, one little dish is missing. ♪

Then, all the lights were turned off. The temple bells started ringing. Spotlights were cast on the well. Big fireworks were shot off in the air. A drumroll began; dondon dondon dondon.

Finally, Okiku rose up out of the well.

O: *(In the kabuki style)* I hate you, my lord Tessan.
I curse you.
H: Gosh, her performance is becoming more like kabuki, isn't it?
F: Yes, she is overacting now.
Besides, she gained a lot of weight recently.
She doesn't look like a ghost anymore.
She used to be thin and I felt sorry for her.
But now she looks like a Sumo wrestler.
H: You are right.
I hear she is eating a lot sushi and tempura these days.
O: *(Cheerfully)* Ladies and gentlemen, thank you for coming to my show.
Nice to see you once again. Please enjoy.
Here we go!

O: One dish, two dishes, three dishes, four dishes, five dishes…

H: Get ready, everyone!

O: Six dishes….

H: OK! Let's get out of here! Move! Move! Hurry up!

F: No, we can't.

H: What's happening?

F: We are stuck!

There are too many people.

It is impossible to move forward.

H: What? Hey, what should we do?

We are going to die!

O: Seven dishes, eight dishes…

H: She counted to eight!

Move, move forward!

O: Nine dishes.

H: Wow!! We'll all be dead!

O: Ten dishes, eleven dishes…

H: Wait! What's happening?

She is counting over nine and we are all still alive.

O: Twelve dishes, thirteen dishes, fourteen dishes…

H: She still keeps counting.

O: Fifteen dishes, sixteen dishes, seventeen dishes, eighteen dishes. And it finishes!

H: Oh, god. Okiku, is this a cheap joke?

You are not supposed to count over nine. What's going on?

O: Shut up! It is not your business.

I counted up to eighteen because I will take a day off tomorrow.

Peach Boy (*Momotaro*)

Characters:

    F: Father
    S: Son

ೞ

In rakugo, there are several stories based on traditional folk tales. These stories include: Jugemu, Matsuyama Mirror (Matsuyama Kagami), Head Mountain (Atama Yama), and Peach Boy (Momotaro).

This is the story of Peach Boy.

F: Kinbo, it's time to go to bed now.
If you stay up late, a ghost will appear from the closet and eat you.

S: Ghosts? Oh, I'm afraid of ghosts.
I'll go to bed right now!

F: OK, then, I'll tell you an old story. So listen, and then go to sleep.

A long, long time ago, in a certain place, there lived an old man and an old woman. The old man went to the mountains to gather firewood, while his wife went to the river to wash clothes.

One day, while the old woman was down at the river washing clothes, a big peach came floating down the river. She took it home and cut it open. Then, a boy came out of the peach. The old couple decided to call him Momotaro, which means Peach Boy. He grew up to be very strong.

This was the time when demons from Demon Island were attacking the villagers and causing them harm. Peach Boy decided to go to Demon Island to defeat the demons.

The old woman made him dumplings, known as kibi-dango, for his long journey. On the way, a dog, a monkey, and a pheasant joined him. Together, they fought against the demons and defeated them. The demons apologized and gave all of their treasure to Peach Boy. He took the treasure to the old couple and they lived happily ever after.

How's that, Kinbo? Kinbo.
Oh, he went to sleep.
How innocent kids are these days!

This is what happed before the war. Kids are different now.

F: Ken, Ken.

S: What? What?

I'm busy playing a video game right now.

You bought me a PlayStation 5 for my birthday last week.

F: I did, but I told you not to play for more than an hour a day. It's already late at night.

Go to bed!

S: I'm not sleepy.

F: If you stay up late, a ghost will appear from the closet and eat you.

S: A ghost? Are you trying to scare me?

Do you really believe in ghosts?

Don't talk nonsense, buddy.

F: Don't call me buddy.

I'm not your friend.

I'm your father.

Do you know what filial piety means?

You have to respect your parents.

You cannot buy your parents.

S: I can't sell them, either.

F: What? Are you going to sell us?

They say that by the time you think of doing something for your parents, they are already gone.

S: Well, I don't want to do anything for my parents, and they're still alive.

F: Stop it! Hold your tongue.
I'll tell you an interesting story.
So listen, and go to sleep.

S: That's impossible.

F: Why?

S: If I listen to your story, I cannot go to sleep.
If I try to go to sleep, I cannot listen to your story.
How can I solve this contradiction?

F: Contradiction! Where did you pick up such a big word?
Anyway, just listen to my story and go to sleep.
(Getting him ready for bed)
I'll tell you an old story.

S: Dad, can you tell old stories?
You cannot even tell modern stories.

F: Shut up. Don't make a fool out of me.
A long, long time ago...

S: How long ago?

F: A long time ago is a long time ago.

S: In what era?
We have the name of an era based on the reign of the emperor.

So there is Meiji, Taisho, Showa, Heisei—now we are living in a new age called Reiwa.

In the Edo period, there was Genroku, Bunka, Bunsei, Tempo….

F: Hey, Osaki, do you know when Peach Boy was written? No?

(To his son) Don't bother with such details.

A long time ago, in a certain place…

S: Where? What's the name of the province?

What's the zip code?

F: Don't bother with such things.

S: I can't. It is not realistic.

There were names for places in the old days, too.

F: I don't know.

There lived an old man and an old woman.

S: What are their names?

F: Be quiet. Don't interrupt me.

They didn't have names.

S: They didn't have names? Why not?

F: Because they were so poor, they sold their names.

S: How did they sell their names?

Then why do you have your name?

If poor people have to sell their names, you had to sell your name a long time ago.

F: Shut up, Ken. Let me continue with the story.

The old man went to the mountains to gather firewood.

S: What's the name of the mountains?

How high above the sea level?

F: I don't know. That's not important.

And his wife went to the river to wash clothes.

Don't ask me the name of the river. OK?

One day, while the old woman was down at the river washing clothes, a big peach came along.

S: I see.

F: *She took it home and cut it open.*

Then, a boy came out of the peach.

S: What? If such a thing were to happen, there would be so many babies at grocery stores.

How would they manage with all those babies?

F: I don't know. That was a special peach.

You just listen, OK?

They decided to call him Momotaro, which means Peach Boy.

He grew up to be very strong.

This was the time when demons from Demon Island were attacking the villagers and causing them harm. Peach Boy decided to go to Demon Island to defeat the demons.

The old woman made him dumplings, known as kibi-dango, for his long journey. On the way, a dog, a monkey, and a pheasant joined him. Together they fought against the demons and defeated them. The demons apologized and gave all of their treasure to Peach Boy. He took the treasure to the old couple and they lived happily ever after.

So, you have to make us happy in the future, too.

Why aren't you asleep?

S: How can I go to sleep?

You are such a bad storyteller.

Can't you tell this story as if you were talking about love?

F: What are you talking about? This is not a love story!

S: This is the story called Momotaro, right?

F: Oh, you know about it.

S: This is one of the best-known stories, and it can be compared to the tales written by the Grimm Brothers of Germany or by Hans Christian Andersen of Denmark.

(Getting up)

You don't seem to know the essence of this story.

It begins with "*A long time ago, in a certain place.*" The time and place are not determined. They are not determined deliberately, because if the story was based in Tokyo, children in other provinces may not be so interested.

By not mentioning the names of a particular place and time, any child in any age will be interested.

An old man and an old woman appear in the story.

They are actually a young couple.

But in the old days, the grandparents were very close to the children, so it was changed to the old couple.

The old man went to the mountains to gather firewood, while his wife went to the river to wash clothes.

Actually, his wife went to the sea.

Since you can't wash clothes in the sea, it was changed to the river.

This part means a father's love is higher than the mountains and a mother's love is deeper than the sea.

In other words, the story tries to explain how important parents are to the children.

F: Is that right? I didn't know that.

Hey, Osaki, come here and listen to what Ken has to say. And?

S: *While the old woman was down at the river washing clothes, a big peach came along. She took it home and cut it open. Then, a boy came out of the peach.*

Here, the peach is a metaphor for life. Otherwise, there would be too many babies at grocery stores.

He grew up very strong. So he decided to go and defeat the demons living on Demon Island. There is no such place as Demon Island. It is a metaphor for the real world. Our world is not Disneyland.

There are many bad people like demons in our society and we have to punish them. That's why Peach Boy went to fight the demons.

The old woman made him dumplings, known as kibi-dango, for his long journey.

Kibi or millet is a lower quality grain than rice. This means you must live a modest life. Luxury is the enemy.

F: Osaki, come here and listen.

Ken could be the governor of Tokyo someday. And?

S: *On the way, a dog, a monkey, and a pheasant joined him.*

Do you know why those three animals appear in the story? A dog is faithful, a monkey is wise, and a pheasant is courageous.

They represent three important virtues all human beings should possess: faith, wisdom, and courage.

F: I see. Osaki, what are you doing?

Ken could be Prime Minister someday. And?

S: Peach Boy and the others went to Demon Island. They won the fight and got all the treasure from the demons. Peach Boy took the treasure to the old couple. This treasure is a metaphor for trust. You need to be trusted when you build friendship and when you do business. So, in a nutshell, this story teaches us how we should live in society.

You need to be a good storyteller to convey the essence of this story.

If you want to tell this story outside, you should attend a rakugo class and learn how to tell a good tale.

(Looking at his father) Dad, daddy... Oh, he went to sleep. How innocent parents are these days!

Test Sake (*Tameshi Zake*)

Characters:

    M: Master
    O: Omiya
    K: Kyuzo

ଓଃଡ

M: Omiya-san, why don't you stay for a while and have some sake?

I've been looking forward to seeing you.

O: I would like to, but I have to visit several more clients.

Besides, there's a man waiting for me outside.

M: Oh, is there someone accompanying you?

Then call him in, he can join us.

O: No, I can't introduce him to you.

He is from the countryside, so he has no manners. Besides, he drinks too much.

M: Oh, how much does he drink?

O: I think he can drink five sho.

M: Five sho?

You mean 10 liters or 20 pints at one time?

No way!

If it is one or two sho, I can believe it, but five sho?

No, nobody can drink that much.

Not even a sumo wrestler.

O: I think he can.

M: Really?

If it's true, I would like to see him drink that much.

There's a man waiting outside.

Please bring him in.

(Pause) Oh, someone's coming in. Is he your man?

O: Yes. Come over here.

K: What's the matter?

O: Why not say hello to the master of this house?

K: Hello, master.

M: Hello.

Glad to meet you.

May I have your name?

Kyuzo-san?

I see.

We've been talking about you.

Is it true that you can drink five sho at one time?

K: What's five sho?

M: Oh, you don't know what a sho is?

K: No, I don't.

I drink a lot of sake, but I never thought about how many sho I drink.

M: Why don't you try?

If you can drink five sho, I will give you some money.

K: What?

You'll treat me to sake and give me money?

I feel sorry for you.

(To his boss) Boss, what should I do?

O: Why not try?

Be his guest.

K: I see.

Then I'll be his guest.

Master let me try.

M: Great. But, Kyuzo-san, what would you do if you can't?

K: Then, should I give you some money?

M: I don't intend to get any money from you.

Why don't you sing a song or dance?

K: Ha, ha, ha, I can't do that.

But if I lose, I can have a sumo bout with you.

O: Hey, Kyuzo, what are you talking about?

Master, see, he's such a stupid guy.

How about this idea?

If he can't, I will take you to a hot spring in Hakone for a couple of days and treat you to a gorgeous dinner.

M: I see.

That's great.

Thank you.

K: Wait.

If I fail, are you going to take him to a hot spring and treat him to a dinner?

How much does that cost?

O: You don't have to worry about it.

K: No. Please tell me how much it costs.

O: I told you.

That's not something you need to worry about.

K: Mmm. Master, could you give me some time to go outside and think about it?

M: All right.

(Kyuzo leaves the house) Ha, ha, ha, Omiya-san, I'm sure he won't come back.

It's impossible to drink five sho.

O: Well, I don't know.

K: Sorry to have kept you waiting.

O: Oh, Kyuzo. I was worried about you.

The master thought you'd give up and leave.

K: Why would I do that?

Master, I'm ready for those drinks now.

M: Wow, I didn't think you would come back.

Look at this cup.

It's about two liters, or four pints.

In order to win the bet, you have to finish five cups.

K: This is huge!

I've never seen such a large cup.

M:	Can you pour him the first drink?
K:	Thank you.
M:	Now, you start, Kyuzo-san.
K:	Yes.
	(He finishes the cup instantly) I'm done!
M:	Amazing. You downed it in no time!
K:	Whoa... I drank too fast.
	I don't remember how it tasted.
	I'll take my next drink slowly and savor the taste.
M:	The next round!
K:	Thank you.
	(He drinks) This sake tastes really good.
	Do you drink this sake every day?
	Boss, the sake we drank last time was terrible.
	Let's drink this sake from now on.
M:	Kyuzo-san, I have a question.
	What do you like best in this world? Sake?
K:	What do I like best? I like money.
M:	Oh, money.
	Are you going to work hard and buy some land in your hometown?
K:	Why would I do that?
	I would like to drink sake.
M:	That means you like sake best.

K: Oh, yes. You are probably right.

There are a lot of heavy drinkers in my hometown.

M: Is that so?

Where are you from?

K: I'm from the west, a place called Tamba.

There is a mountain where a man called "the God of Sake" lives.

Once he starts drinking, he doesn't stop.

He is my relative.

M: You are kidding me.

K: Ha, ha, ha, I'm sorry.

There can't be a man like that.

(He finishes the second cup)

M: You can still drink that fast?

I can't believe you.

Next round!

K: Thank you.

(He drinks) You said you want me to sing songs if I lose our bet?

Actually, I can sing songs. I learned some songs in Tokyo.

♪ *Shiba de umarete Kanda de sodachi imaja Hikeshi no ano Matoimochi* ♪

M: Sounds great.

Do you know what it means?

K: Yes. I was born in Shiba and brought up in Kanda, now I'm a fighter holding that banner.

In the Edo period, firefighting was the most popular job among boys.

Every boy wanted to be a firefighter.

And the chief firefighter was holding a banner.

How about this one?

Can you guess who I am singing about?

♪Born in Austria, working in America, he became the California state governor and Terminator. ♪

M: Yeah. I think I know this guy.

He must be Arnold Schwarzenegger.

K: Bingo! Then how about this one?

♪Born in Mongolia, working in Japan, now he is a Yokozuna and a businessman. ♪

M: I know this guy, too.

He must be Asashoryu.

K: Yes, you're right.

He was a selfish guy, so people hated him.

But I liked him.

(*He finishes the third cup*) I'm done.

How many cups have I finished?

M: Three.

K: How many more cups do I have to drink?

M: Two more.

Hmmmm, Omiya-san, maybe you're right about him being a heavy-weight, but I'm not giving up yet.

He won't be able to handle the last two.

Pour him his fourth round.

K: Thanks! I love this sake.

M: Look! Look at how he drinks, Omiya-san.

One, two, three, one, two, three.

He seems to be singing a song.

It looks like the sake wants him even more than he wants the sake.

The sake and Kyuzo-san seem to be one.

There goes the fourth cup.

Hmmm, I might lose this bet, but I can't give up yet.

The last one must be impossible.

That's the way it is.

Bring him the final drink.

K: Is this the last one?

(He starts drinking and stops) Oh, my stomach is getting full.

(Pats his belly) Can you hear all the sake sloshing around in my stomach?

Let me take a rest for a while.

M: Sure.

(To Omiya) Ohmiya-san, did you hear that?

He can't take much more of this.

K: (He starts drinking again. He tries to jump up and down)

M: Kyozo-san, what are you doing?

K: I'm trying to make some space in my stomach.

The sake is going down.

Now, I've got space here.

M: Is that right? I can't believe it.

K: (He keeps drinking and finally finishes the last cup) I'm done!

M: Incredible! You did it, Kyuzo-san!

Here's the money I promised to give you.

Now, I would like to ask you just one thing.

K: How many more cups should I drink?

M: No, no, that's not what I mean.

You went out before you decided to accept this bet.

Did you take some stomach medicine or chant a prayer

or something so that you wouldn't get drunk?

If there is a trick to it, then let me hear your secret.

K: Nah, master, nothing like that!

I really didn't know if I could drink five sho of sake. So I

went to a liquor shop nearby and drank five sho as a test.

xxxv. Toki Soba (Time Noodles) by Kei Ohsuga

Time Noodles (*Toki Soba*)

Characters:

N1:	Noodle Salesman #1
N2:	Noodle Salesman #2
C:	Customer
M:	Man

☙❧

In Japan, there are many noodle stands where people can enjoy soba and udon noodles. You can find one at almost every train station.

In the past, people ate soba noodles at portable stands throughout town. The noodle salesmen carried their stands on their shoulders and searched for an appropriate spot to set up shop. Once they found a spot, they placed the stand down on the side of the street and commenced doing business.

If you go to the Fukagawa Edo Museum in Kiyozumi-shirakawa, you can see replicas of these portable stands and gain an insight into the food culture during the Edo period.

You may or may not know this, but in Japan it is customary to slurp your noodles. It may be considered rude in other cultures, but in Japan slurping while eating noodles is natural.

Therefore, please do not be offended by the sounds I make when I eat the noodles.

N1: *(Holding a portable stand on his shoulders)* Soba noodles! Would you like soba noodles?

C: Oh, that's a soba stand.
   Hello, it's cold today, isn't it?

N1: Yes, it's very cold today.

C: What kind of noodles do you have?

N1: I have seaweed noodles and fish cake noodles.

C: Then I would like a bowl of fish cake noodles.

N1: Sure. Thank you.

C: By the way, how's business these days?

N1: Not so good.

C: That's good.

N1: Why good?

C: Bad is a good sign.
   There are ups and downs in business.
   Bad times are followed by good times.

N1: I hope you are right.

C: By the way, what's that sign?
   There is a mark and an arrow which hits the center of the mark.

N1: That's my shop's name, "On the Mark."

C: On the Mark!

That's a good name.

I'm going gambling later.

N1: Are you?

I wish you luck.

Here you are, sir.

C: Thank you.

That's very quick.

I was born and raised in Edo, so I'm short-tempered.

I get irritated when things are slow.

Oh, you use new chopsticks.

At other stands, chopsticks are sometimes old and wet.

Your bowl is clean, and the edges are not chipped.

If you use a good bowl, the noodles inside also look good.

Oh, it smells good.

I can tell whether it is good or bad by its smell.

(Sipping the soup) The soup is perfect.

It's rich in flavor.

You made the broth using lots of bonito [skipjack tuna] flakes.

At other stands, the soup is sometimes too salty or too sweet.

This soup is just right.

> *(Eating the noodles)* These noodles are thin, firm and tasty. At other stands, the noodles are sometimes thick and soft.
>
> It's not good.
>
> And this fish cake is big.
>
> Can you make a profit from this? That's great.
>
> At other stands, the fish cake is sometimes so small and thin that it's hard to find.
>
> *(Finishing the noodles and the soup)* I'd like to have one more, but I'm already full.
>
> I'll come again.
>
> Well, how much is it?

N1: Sixteen mon, please.

C: I have only small change today.

Can you hold out your hands?

N1: Yes.

C: Here you go.

One, two, three, four, five, six, seven, eight, what time is it?

N1: Nine.

C: Ten, eleven, twelve, thirteen, fourteen, fifteen, sixteen. Goodbye!

> *Another man was observing all of this from the corner and thinking about what had just happened.*

M: What a strange man!

He only said nice things about everything.

The chopsticks are new.

The bowl is clean, and the edges are not chipped.

The noodles are thin, firm, and taste good.

The soup tastes perfect and the fishcake is big.

With so many compliments, I thought he was going to ask for a discount or run away without paying money.

But he paid. And he paid using small change.

When he was counting the money, he got as far as eight and asked for the time. Why?

One, two, three, four, five, six, seven, eight, what time is it, nine, ten, eleven...hmmm??

(Counting on his fingers) One, two, three, four, five, six, seven, eight, what time is it, nine, ten... when you count to ten, this little finger should be up, not the ring finger. Ah, I see!

He cheated the noodle salesman out of one mon.

What a smart trick!

That salesman will never notice this trick.

(Looking at his wallet) I don't have enough coins today, so I'll try exactly the same thing tomorrow!

Next day, he collected enough coins and found a different soba noodle stand

M: Hello, it's cold today, isn't it?
N2: No, it isn't so cold today.
Yesterday was very cold.
M: Oh, yes. What kind of noodles do you have?
N2: We have seaweed noodles and fish cake noodles.
M: Then I would like a bowl of fish cake noodles.
N2: Sure. Thank you.
M: By the way, how's business these days?
N2: Very good.
M: Very good?
N2: Yes, they say the economy is slow these days, but my shop is making good profits.
M: Good profits?
That's too bad.
N2: Why bad?
M: Good is a bad sign.
There are ups and downs in business.
Good times are followed by bad times.
Oh, what am I saying?
N2: I don't know, but maybe you are right.
M: By the way, what's that sign?

There is a mark and an arrow which hits outside the mark.

N2: That's my shop's name, "Off the Mark."

M: Off the Mark?

That's a bad name.

I was going to go gambling later, but I should not go today.

It doesn't work like yesterday.

Is my order ready yet?

N2: Sorry, it takes time to boil water.

M: Are you still boiling water?

All right, all right.

I was born and raised in Edo but I'm rather long-tempered.

Take your time.

N2: Sorry to have kept you waiting, sir. Here it is.

M: Thank you.

Oh, you use old chopsticks and they are wet.

And there is a slice of onion on the tip.

That's OK. I'll wipe it with my kimono.

(*He wipes the chopsticks with his kimono*) What's important is not the chopsticks but the bowl.

The bowl is…so dirty and there are lots of chips on the edge.

I have to be careful not to injure my mouth.

That's all right. I'm not going to eat the bowl.

What's important is the soup and noodles.

Oh, it smells good.

I can tell whether it is good or bad by its smell.

(He sips the soup but soon he spits it out) God, it's too salty.

Put some water in it.

It's OK. What's important is not the soup but the noodles.

(Eating the noodles) Oh, my goodness, these noodles are so thick and soft and sticky.

(Searching for the fish cake) Where is the fish cake?

Are you sure you put it in?

Ah, yes, it's stuck to the bowl.

It's so thin that I thought it was part of the design of the bowl.

How did you cut it?

With an ordinary kitchen knife?

How skillful you are!

I thought you used a carpenter's plane.

I can see your face right through this.

(Eating the fish cake) Oh, this fishcake is not real.

It tastes like rubber.

Oh, this is enough. Sorry, I can't finish this.

(Returning the bowl to the salesman) Well, how much is it?

N2: Sixteen mon, please.

M: Oh, this part is the same as yesterday.

Sorry, but today, I have only small change.

Can you hold out your hands?

N2: Yes.

M: Are you ready to get paid?

Ha, ha, ha, the poor salesman.

N2: What's so funny?

M: Oh, nothing.

I was just talking to myself.

Here you go.

One, two, three, four, five, six, seven, eight, what time is it now?

N2: Four.

M: Four!!

(Disappointed)..... five, six, seven, eight.

—*Adaptations*—

King Lear *(Lear Oh)*

Characters:

L:	King Lear, King of Britain
G:	Goneril, the king's eldest daughter
R:	Regan, the king's second daughter
C:	Cordelia, the king's youngest daughter
K:	Kent, King Lear's servant

ଔଓ

William Shakespeare was born in 1564 and he died in 1616. In Japan, this time period corresponds to the late Muromachi period through the early Edo period. When you think about that time period, what Japanese historical figures come to mind?

Tokugawa Ieyasu, Japan's first shogun and the man who is associated with the start of the Edo period, was born in 1542 and he died in 1616, the same year during which Shakespeare passed away. So, please remember that Shakespeare and Tokugawa Ieyasu died in the same year, but Tokugawa lived 22 years longer than Shakespeare.

Shakespeare wrote forty plays in his lifetime, twelve of which are considered tragedies. Among them are Hamlet, King Lear, Macbeth, and Othello.

The story of King Lear, which you are about to hear, is somewhat similar to the story of Katabo, in which an old man tries to bequeath his property to his three sons and in doing so tests their love for him.

L:	Kent, as you know, I'm getting old. And I have to think about who will inherit this kingdom.
	I have three daughters, Goneril, Regan, and Cordelia.
	Who do you think is best suited to succeed the throne after I die?
K:	Oh, lord, it's very difficult to say who will be the best successor.
	Why don't you ask them a question?
L:	What kind of question?
K:	Ask them how much they love you.
L:	That's a good idea.
	Would you please call them?
Daughters:	Yes, father, did you summon us?

L: Yes, my lovely daughters. As you know, I'm getting old. And I have to think about who will inherit this kingdom.
I have divided the kingdom into three estates.
I will give these estates to whichever daughter loves me most.
So, tell me how much you love me and what you want after I die.
Goneril, you are the eldest daughter.
You tell me first.

G: Father, I love you more than words can say.
I love you more than I love myself.
Since I am the eldest daughter, I think I have the right to inherit the largest estate.
I'm sure my husband, the Duke of Albany, and I will be able to successfully reign over the largest estate together.

L: I see.
Goneril, look at this map.
I will give you the largest estate, the area between this line and this line.
There are dense forests, fertile plains, rivers with lots of fish, and spacious meadows.

	This will belong to you, your husband the Duke of Albany, and to the children that will be born to you.
	And now, Regan, tell how much you love me.
R:	Father, I love you as much as my sister does.
	Please think of me as you think of my sister.
	My sister has already said all I wish to say. However, I'd like to add one more thing.
	My happiness consists only of loving and respecting you.
	I'm sure my husband, the Duke of Cornwall, and I will be able to successfully reign over the second largest estate.
L:	I see.
	I'll give the second largest estate to you, your husband the Duke of Cornwall, and your future children.
	The land is rich and beautiful.
	And now Cordelia, tell me how much you love me. I may give you the remaining one third of my kingdom, which is the smallest but the richest among all the estates.
C:	Father, I have nothing to say.
L:	Nothing?
C:	No, nothing, father.

L: Nothing comes out of nothing.
C: Unfortunately, I cannot say in words what I have in my heart.
       I love you as is my duty to love you--not more, not less.
L: What's the matter with you, Cordelia?
       Be careful how you speak, or you will regret it.
C: You have brought me up with love.
       So, in return, I will love you as it is my duty as a child.
       I will obey you.
       I will love you.
       I will respect you.
       But, if I should marry, I would have to give at least half of my love to my husband.
       I don't know why my sisters got married if they love only you.
L: Do you really mean what you say?
C: Yes, father.
L: You are young, so you are lacking in tenderness.
C: I am young, but I speak the truth.
L: OK, then.
       Let your truth be your dowry.

By the light of the sun, and by the darkness of the night, I swear that I no longer consider you as my child!

K: Oh, my lord!

L: Be quiet, Kent.

Do not come between me and my anger.

I hoped she would be kind to me, but she has treated me like this.

She is no longer my child!

Let Cordelia marry her own pride.

Goneril, Regan, I give you the remaining one-third of my kingdom.

Divide it between yourselves.

I give you all the powers and all the honor that I have.

And as proof of my words, I give you these crowns.

Goneril, Regan, let me stay with you, alternating between your estates monthly.

Goneril, I will stay at your estate next month.

Regan, I'll visit you the month after next.

Kent, it's already late at night.

I'd like to go to sleep.

Good night.

G: Father, you are always causing so much trouble.

If you stay here, we will have no more peace in this palace.

You are scolding everybody for the most trifling reasons and your attendants are all so rough. That's why I reduced the number of your attendants from 100 to 50.

L: Oh Goneril, how dare you talk to me like that!

My attendants are all fine men.

I am ashamed that I gave you the power to treat me like this.

But, if you say so, I won't stay here any longer.

I'll go to Regan's palace and I will stay with her from now on.

Goodbye, Goneril.

I'll never see you again.

L: Regan, how are you?

R: Oh, father, what's the matter?

You are supposed to come here next month.

Come in.

L: Thank you.

Regan, your sister is a wicked woman, a cruel woman who has made me suffer great pain.

R: You mustn't talk that way, father.

I don't think you understand my sister.

You are old.

And you decided to give everything to me and my sister.

So, please return to the Goneril's palace, and ask her to forgive you.

L: What! Ask her to forgive me?

Do you want me to kneel before her and say, "I am a useless old man, so give me clothes to wear, food to eat, and a bed to sleep in?

Is that what you want me to do?

R: Father, stop talking like that. And go back to Goneril.

L: Never! She reduced the number of my attendants to half.

And she also spoke to me most harshly.

R: Father, you mustn't talk like that.

Go back to Goneril, and stay until the end of this month.

Right now, I am not ready to receive you.

And next month, reduce the number of your attendants to half and you may come and live with me.

L: What! You want me to reduce my attendants, too? I see. Now I understand you never loved me.

You and your sister have made this old man so miserable.

I won't come to your palace, and I will never see you again.

(Pause) How terrible they are, and how miserable I am!

I'd like to go to Cordelia, but I didn't give her anything.

Not a single penny.

Why did I treat her like that?

How foolish I was!

(Pause) Oh, where am I?

I'm in the wasteland.

It's a dark and stormy night with lightning and thunder.

Blow, wind, blow!

Rain, flood the earth!

(He falls down)

K: My lord! Wake up!

Wake up, my lord!

L: Oh, Kent, where're my two terrible daughters?

K: My lord, did you have a bad dream?

L: A dream? Oh, thank God, it was a dream.

Kent, Goneril and Regan betrayed me.

First, I went to the Goneril's palace, but she didn't like what I was doing, and she dismissed many of my attendants.

After that I went to the Reagan's palace, but she told me to go back to Goneril, and she said she would dismiss my attendants, too.

They didn't love me at all.

I have mistreated Cordelia.

I can't believe it was only a dream.

Everything seemed so real. Kent, I think I'd better overturn my decisions.

I will give all the estates and powers to Cordelia, and her future husband.

How about that?

K: Lord, I believe it is the best decision.

I'm sure she is the kindest daughter among them.

A few days later, Goneril and Regan rush in.

G: Father, I heard you gave all the estates to Cordelia.

It's not what you said you would do.

You said you would give me the largest estate and the second largest to Regan.

R: Father, my sister is right.

You also said you would give us the remaining one third.
But you gave all the estates and all the powers to Cordelia.
Why, father?
Why didn't you tell us the truth?

L: You want to know why I didn't tell you the truth?

G: Yes, I'd like to know why you didn't tell us the truth.

L: Because I am not King Lear. I am King Liar.

The Replacement of Enma (*Enma no Irekawari*)

Characters:

    E: Enma, the King of the Afterworld
    K: Kikunosho, a rakugo performer
    R: Red Demon
    B: Blue Demon

ೞ೦

There once was a very popular rakugo performer named Kikunosho. He was just 50 years old when he became sick and passed away. Therefore, he was widely known not only in this world, but also in the Afterworld.

It is said that after we die, we are taken to the Afterworld. Enma, the King of the Afterworld, and his two demons, the Red Demon and the Blue Demon, greet the recently deceased at the entrance to the Afterworld.

Enma poses questions to the recently deceased, and based on their answers, he decides whether their soul is sent to Heaven or condemned to Hell.

E: Are you Kikunosho?
           Come over here.

You earned a lot of money by talking, gesturing, and cheating people.

You are going to Hell!

K: Ye…yes, sir.

E: Come closer, Kikunosho.

As a matter of fact, I have never seen nor heard real rakugo before.

I would like you to perform here in front of me.

If you do it well and make me laugh, you can go to Heaven.

K: Yes, sir!

E: Hurry up.

K: Certainly.

But I can't perform down here on the ground like this.

I would like to perform on a koza, an elevated stage.

E: I see. What can I do?

K: Let me perform where you are sitting.

E: I see. Then you can come up here.

K: And one more thing.

I can't perform wearing such a thin white kimono like this.

E: I see. Then what can I do for you?

K: I would like to wear a gorgeous kimono like the one you are wearing.

E: I see. Then you can use mine.

After exchanging their kimonos, Kikunosho climbed up to the koza and Enma came down to the ground level.

E: Your kimono is really thin.

          I'm so cold.

          Can you start now?

K: Yes. *(He bows to Enma)*

༻✦༺

This is a story about a man who is always suspicious of his wife. He rented a condominium near his office, so that he can come home during his lunch break to check up on her.

༻✦༺

(H: Husband; W: Wife; E: Enma)

H: I'm home.

W: Oh, it's you.

          What's going on?

H: It's lunchtime now.

          I was worried about you.

          I was wondering if you were flirting with another guy.

W: Don't be silly.

          After you left home, I cleaned the house, I did the washing, and now I am going to have lunch.

          I have no time to be with another guy.

H: Is that so?

Someone may be hiding in this apartment, though.

After saying so, the husband started searching in the closet and looking in the drawers, but there was no one inside. He went outside onto the balcony and looked down. There, he saw a man pulling up the zipper of his trousers. He thought the man must be the one who was with his wife. The thought drove him crazy. He picked up the refrigerator in the kitchen and threw it down off of the balcony. The refrigerator landed on the man and killed him instantly.

Later, he learned that the man was simply a passerby. He felt so guilty that he jumped from the building and died.

At the gate of that world, the two men met Enma, the king. By the way, 'that world' is called 'this world' and this world is called 'that world' in that world.

E: Next! Come in. Sit down.

How did you arrive in this world?

M1: I am really an unlucky man.

In that world, I was a door-to-door salesman.

One day, while I was out working, I had to pee. But I couldn't find a public bathroom.

I didn't know what to do, but I found a condo nearby.

I talked to the janitor of the building, and he let me use the bathroom.

After finishing my business, I thanked him and left the building, pulling up my zipper.

Then, all of a sudden, a fridge came down from the sky and killed me.

E: You were smashed by a refrigerator? What bad luck!

OK, you can go to Heaven and rest peacefully.

M1: Thank you.

E: Next! Come in and sit down.

How did you get here?

M2: I am a very sinful man.

I thought my wife was cheating on me.

I threw a refrigerator at a man who had nothing to do with my wife, and killed him.

Then I killed myself out of guilt.

E: Oh, so you are the man who killed him.

What a sinful guy!

You have to go to Hell.

(Pause) Oh, there is another guy waiting.

Come over here. How did you get here?

M3: I really don't know.

I died while hiding inside a refrigerator.

K: *(He bows to Enma)*

Well, how did you like it?

E: Ha ha ha ha ha.

That's so funny.

You told a story about Enma to the real Enma.

How smart you are.

Yes, you must have been the best rakugo performer ever.

Let me hear some more.

As Enma relaxed, Kikunosho dashed down to him, drew his sword and said…

K: Red Demon and Blue Demon come here!

This is the man who earned a lot of money by talking, gesturing, and cheating people.

Take him to Hell.

The Demons rushed to Emma and pinned him to the ground.

E: What are you doing?

I'm the true Enma.

I am your lord!

R: Don't make a fuss.

Stay still!

E: What are you doing?

I'm the real Enma!

It's me.

Did you forget my voice?

I'm the king.

B: You are a great actor.

You speak in the same voice as our lord.

The Demons threw Enma into a huge, burning pot in Hell.

E: Ohhhhhh.......

This is how Kikunosho replaced Enma. From that day forward, all rakugo performers go to Heaven.

Scary Hamburgers (*Hanbaga Kowai*)

Characters:

J:	John	B:	Ben
H:	Henry	C:	Carlos
L:	Long	E:	Elvis
A:	Abe	D:	Dick

൘൛

J: Is everyone here?

A: Yes, eh, except one person.

J: Who's not here?

B: Long.

J: What happened to him?

    It'd be more fun with Long here.

    Oh, well, let's begin the party.

L: *(Panting)* Sorry, I'm late.

J: What's the matter with you, Long?

    You look pale.

    Have you been chased?

L: No, I saw a snake.

    I'm afraid of the snakes.

    I'm afraid of eels, earthworms, or anything that is long.

H: Really? But your name is Long.

L: Yes, so my name scares me.

H: Oh, that's too bad.

You'd better change your name.

Well, they say even a hero has one or two weak points.

Is there anything you are afraid of, Abe?

A: I'm afraid of frogs.

J: Why?

A: Because they open their mouths wide.

I'm afraid they will swallow me up.

J: I see.

How about you, Ben?

B: Spiders.

I don't like anything that produces thread.

Even a sewing machine scares me.

J: Really?

I'm sorry about that.

And you, Carlos?

C: Centipedes.

They have so many legs.

When I think about how many shoes they need, it scares me.

J: Are you worried about their shoes?

What a strange guy!

How about you, Dick?

D: Ants, because they march in line.

When they meet each other, they whisper something.

	I'm afraid they are speaking ill of me.
J:	You shouldn't be worried about that.
	Next, Elvis?
E:	Horses, because they kick you.
	Ever since I got married, I have been kicked by my wife.
	Now I have a strong fear of horses.
J:	You are not afraid of horses.
	You're afraid of your wife.
	How about you, Henry?
H:	*(Shrugging.)*
J:	Why are you shrugging?
H:	*(Shrugging)* Nothing.
J:	Aren't you afraid of anything?
	It's all right.
	You don't have to put on airs like that.
	We're having fun, so why not join us?
H:	Why do we have to talk about the things that scare us?
	We are men!
J:	Are you really not afraid of anything?
	How about snakes?
H:	I eat them.
J:	You eat them?
H:	Yes, I eat them more often than I eat eels.
	When I have a fever, I coil one around my head.

J: How about frogs?

H: They are my favorite.

           I like horses too.

           I like to eat their meat raw.

           It gives me a lot of energy.

           And ants. I like them, too.

           I eat them with rice.

           I also like spiders.

           I put their threads in natto, fermented soybeans, when the beans are not sticky enough.

J: Amazing. You can eat anything.

           But there must be a thing or two that scares you.

H: Don't keep asking.

           I'm actually trying to forget it.

           I don't want to confess my secret to all of you.

J: Tell us! Come on!

           I'm not asking you to tell us a state secret.

           It's only a game.

           It's nothing to be embarrassed about.

H: If I tell you, you will laugh at me.

J: No, I won't laugh, I assure you.

           Don't be bashful.

           What are you afraid of?

H: You promise not to laugh?

           I'm… afraid of…no, you will laugh.

J: No, I won't. I promise.
H: I… I'm… afraid of… ham…ham…
J: Hamsters?
H: No, not hamsters… ham…burgers.
J: I beg your pardon?
H: Hamburgers.
J: Hamburgers.
What kind of animals are they?
H: I mean, hamburgers you can buy at McDonalds, Burger King, Wendy's, Jack In The Box, and Sonic.
J: What? You're afraid of those hamburgers?
Ha ha ha …
H: Don't laugh.
J: I'm sorry.
I couldn't help it.
I won't laugh any more.
I like hamburgers.
Especially Jack In The Box burgers.
Actually, my favorite is the spicy chicken sandwich at Jack In The Box.
H: Don't talk about it.
I'm afraid of the spicy chicken sandwiches the most.
J: You are afraid of a spicy chicken sandwich?
You are a chicken.

H: Oh, that's a bad joke.

Please don't make fun of me.

J: I'm sorry.

I like a double cheeseburger, too.

H: A double cheeseburger…that's twice as scary.

I'm afraid of cheese, too.

J: When I'm really hungry I even try a triple burger.

H: Triple… no, never talk about a triple burger.

It's three times as scary!

J: Last month, I went to Sasebo in Nagasaki, and tried Sasebo burgers.

They are the best hamburgers in the world!

H: Sasebo? Don't talk about that city.

I went there on a business trip last week.

When I saw all those Sasebo burger shops lining the street, I fainted.

J: Is that a fact?

H: Yes. I'm very ashamed of myself.

Oh no, I'm getting dizzy — probably because I remember Sasebo.

Let me rest for a while.

J: All right, then.

Go lie down in the next room.

Did you hear that, everyone?

Henry is quite a coward.

	I have a good idea.

Let's buy dozens of hamburgers and place them at the head of his bed.

We can get him for his usual arrogance.

L: That's a good idea.

Let's scare him with hamburgers.

J: Then go and get some right away.

L: We are back.

J: Oh, you bought a lot of hamburgers.

Please put them here.

A hamburger, a bacon cheeseburger, a triple cheeseburger, and a spicy chicken sandwich; I'm sure this will scare him the most.

A Whopper, a Big Mac, a Quarter Pounder, a Western Bacon Cheeseburger, and a Super Star® with Cheese.

What's this?

A ramen burger?

I've never seen this before.

Oh, this is a Sasebo burger.

Where did you get it?

In Yoyogi? Great!

This is a great collection.

Long, put them on a tray and leave them next to his bed.

L: All right, John. *Putting them next to Henry's bed.)*

J: Now let's wake him up.

L: Henry, how do you feel?

H: I had a terrible dream.

I was surrounded by hamburgers.

L: Did you hear that?

He was surrounded by hamburgers in his dream.

He doesn't know his dream is about to come true.

H: Oh, my god!

Where did all these hamburgers come from?

Oh, are you trying to kill me?

Good heavens! Help!

J: He is screaming.

This serves him right.

H: I'm scared!

(Holding the spicy chicken sandwich and eating it)

I like this spicy chicken sandwich.

Chicken is my favorite.

This is a Big Mac.

The double patties of 100% beef are perfectly complimented by the famous secret sauce.

I'm scared! Help!

This sesame seed bun is perfectly toasted.

And this is a Carl's Jr Western Bacon Cheeseburger.

The Western Bacon Cheeseburger is a great idea.

I like the hamburgers from Carl's Jr., but I'll eat this later.

(Putting it into his sleeve)

And a Whopper ... later.

A Super Star with Cheese ... later.

(Putting them into his sleeve)

What's this?

A Ramen burger?

I've never seen this before.

The buns are made of ramen noodles.

How can I eat it?

Oh, this is the best hamburger in the world!

A Sasebo jumbo.

I tried a lot of them when I visited Sasebo on business last week.

Help. I'm scared!

(Eating)

J: Don't you think it's strange?

He is screaming "help" and "I'm scared," but there is a pause in between.

Why don't you look in on him?

L: *(Sliding the door slightly open)*

John, he got us.

He's eating them.

And he is putting some of them inside his sleeves.

He loves hamburgers.

J: Really?

(Opening the door)

Henry! You are eating them.

You lied to us!

What is it that really scares you?

H: Now, I'm scared of a glass of Coca Cola.

Japan Milk Corporation (*Nihon Miruku Kosha*)

Characters:

    C: Customer
    G: Government Official(s)
    D: Doctor

The word "milk" can be used in various ways. As a noun, it is a liquid, milk itself. As a verb, it means to "take" or to "squeeze." For example, "milk the cow" means to squeeze milk from the cow; "milk the company" means to squeeze money from the company. Please keep this usage in mind because it appears at th)e end of the story.

The Japanese government collects plenty of taxes from alcohol and cigarette sales. In this story, when it was faced with a decline in tax revenue, the government decided to tax non-alcoholic drinks, too. Not long afterwards, they established the Japan Milk Corporation or Nihon Miruku Kosha.

C: *(Looking through the newspaper)*
      Japan Milk Corporation?
      What is that?
      It sounds interesting.

Hmm, I'd like to try their milk.

Honey, I'm going out to have some milk.

I'll be back soon.

(He goes out)

This is the Japan Milk Corporation's building.

There's the reception desk over there.

Excuse me.

 I would like a cup of milk.

G: You want to try our milk?

Would you like plain milk or deluxe?

C: Excuse me?

G: I said, would you like plain milk or deluxe?

C: So, you have two kinds of milk.

What is the difference?

G: Well, the deluxe milk comes from special cows born and raised in the southern district.

They eat special plants that are free of agricultural chemicals. Plus, we use special sugar taken from special sugar canes in Okinawa to sweeten the milk.

C: You mean, if I order plain milk, it contains agricultural chemicals?

G: That's not what I mean.

We are a governmental organization, so we care about environmental issues.

You don't have to worry about that.

C: I see.

Then, I'll order the deluxe milk.

How can I get it?

G: You can it order here.

Do you have any ID?

Anything that you can identify yourself with, such as your driver's license or health insurance card.

C: No, I don't.

G: You don't.

Then you have to fill out a form first and then sign the contract.

So please go to window 3 on the third floor and follow all the procedures.

C: I see. (*Going up the stairs*)

Oh, it's a government organization.

I hate all the red tape.

But you can't fight city hall.

Here's window 3.

Excuse me, I would like a cup of milk.

G: I see.

Please fill out this form.

List your name, address, age, the numbers of your landline and your cell phone, email address, and the names of your wife and your children if you have a family.

Also, please include your job title, hobbies, specialties, and the reason why you want to have milk here.

C: Do I have to write all those things down in order to have milk?

I will if you insist, but I don't know why I have to provide you with all this personal information.

G: This is a public corporation.

We need to record everything as it relates to our customers.

We are required to do so when we request our budget for the next fiscal year.

C: I see. I see. I will.

(Filling out the form)

Is this all right?

G: OK. Now, read the contract and sign here.

C: OK, OK. Here's my signature.

G: Thank you.

Oh, your name is Shinzo Abe?

It's the name of our former prime minister!

Mr. Abe, are you the one who wants to try our milk?

C: Yes, of course.

G: OK then, no problem.

	If your child or your wife wanted to try our milk, you would need to fill out another form.
C:	I see.
	I'll try it myself first.
G:	All right.
	Here we certify that Mr. Shinzo Abe will have a cup of deluxe milk.
	Here's our stamp.
	Please go to window 1 on the first floor and pay for the form, and come back here with the receipt.
C:	I see.
	How troublesome!
	Excuse me, I would like to pay for the form to have milk.
	What! It costs 800 yen? It's too expensive.
	I completed this form by myself.
	(He reluctantly pays and goes back to window 3)
	Excuse me, I made the payment.
	Here's the receipt.
	Is this all right?
G:	Well, let me see it.
	Next you have to pay for the milk.
	You have to go down to window 1, pay, and come back.
C:	Window 1 again?

Then why didn't you tell me to pay both for the form and the milk at the same time?

I have to go back and forth.

How much is the deluxe milk?

G: Two thousand yen.

C: What? I've never heard of such expensive milk!

I paid 800 yen for the form.

So the total cost is 2,800 yen.

I want to cancel my order.

I'll have milk at home.

I'll give up the 800 yen I paid a while ago.

G: You want to cancel the agreement?

C: Yes, I want to cancel it.

G: I don't mind if you cancel it, but you have to pay for the cancellation.

According to the second paragraph of Article 9 of our agreement, the cancelation fee is 3,000 yen.

C: What! Three thousand yen!

I see. I see. I'll go to window 1 and pay for the milk.

(He goes down to window 1)

Excuse me, I came to pay for the deluxe milk.

Give me a receipt.

(He goes back to window 3)

Excuse me. Here's a receipt.

G: Let me see it.

OK, do you want some sugar too?

C: Yes, I like sweets.

I want it sweet.

G: I see.

Please go to window 1 again and pay for the sugar.

C: What! Do I have to pay for sugar?

I've never heard of such a thing.

I went to window 1 twice already.

If I have to pay for something else, tell me now.

It's on the first floor.

I don't want to go back and forth so many times.

I'm tired.

G: I see. I have one more question.

Do you want it cold or hot?

If you want it cold, you don't have to pay extra money,

but if you want it hot, you have to pay for gas.

C: What? Do I have to pay for gas, too?

How much is sugar and gas?

G: They're 100 yen each.

C: I see.

I want it hot with sugar, so the total will be 3,000 yen!

It's exactly the same as the cancellation fee.

OK, OK, I'll pay for both.

(He goes down to window 1.)

	Excuse me, I came to pay for sugar and gas.
G:	OK, that's 200 yen, sir.
	Here's a receipt.
C:	I'm back.
	Here's a receipt for the sugar and gas.
G:	Thank you.
	I'm sorry but I forgot to ask you one thing.
	We would like to confirm your physical condition.
	If something happens after you've had our milk, we'll be in a big trouble.
	So please go to the doctor's office on the fifth floor, and take a physical examination.
C:	Could anything happen to me after I've had your milk?
G:	So far, nobody has died or fallen sick.
	Since we are a governmental organization, we would like to eliminate all possibilities for problems to occur.
C:	I see.
	How much is the physical examination?
G:	Three thousand yen.
C:	Another 3,000 yen?
	The total is 6,000 yen for a cup of milk!
G:	Yes. Everything is for your safety.
C:	I see. I see. I'll go to the doctor's office on the fifth floor.
	Excuse me, I came for the physical exam.
D:	Mr. Abe, I've been waiting for you.

	Let me take an X-ray first.
	Mr. Abe, please stand here.
	Breathe in, breathe out.
	Breathe in, breathe out, breathe out, breathe out, and breathe out.
C:	I can't. Are you trying to kill me?
D:	I'm sorry.
	I just wanted to know how many times you can breathe out.
	Hold your breath for a second. Good.
	It's finished.
	Next, let me take your blood pressure.
	(The doctor takes his blood pressure)
	It's 120 over 80. OK. Good.
	You have no problem with your X-ray or your blood pressure.
	Now, I'm going check your blood.
C:	Do you have to check my blood?
D:	Yes, if your blood sugar level is high, you'd better stop putting sugar in your milk.
C:	I see. You are so thoughtful.
	(The doctor examines his blood)
D:	There is no problem with your blood sugar level.

	Go back to window 3 with this certificate and enjoy your milk.
C:	Thank you very much.
	(He goes back to window 3)
	Here's the doctor's certificate.
	I have no problem.
G:	I see. This certificate is valid for a year, so you can come to have our milk as many times as you like without going to the doctor for a year.
C:	I see. I don't think I'll come back.
G:	Now, take this card to the café in the basement.
	Enjoy your milk.
C:	Is it in the basement?
	I want to have milk on the top floor, enjoying the view outside.
G:	If an earthquake occurs, you may not be able to return to the first floor.
	The basement is the safest place when an earthquake occurs.
	Everything is for your safety.
C:	I see.
	(He goes down to the basement)
	Finally, the time has come for my milk.
	I've been waiting for this moment for a long time.
	Excuse me, here's my card.

G: Thank you.

You are Mr. Abe.

Please wait at a table with your card placed in front of you.

C: I see.

(Looking at his watch)

It is already 2 o'clock. I came here at 10.

I have been kept waiting for four hours.

I paid 6,000 yen.

It should be the best milk I've ever had in my life.

G: Here you are.

C: Thank you.

(Looking at a cup)

It says something on the cup.

"Drinking too much milk can affect your health."

What does that mean?

I'm not smoking a cigarette.

Let me sip a little. And a little more.

Oh, it doesn't taste like milk at all.

It's not hot enough nor sweet enough.

Excuse me, the milk doesn't taste like milk at all.

Besides, it's not hot enough nor sweet enough.

G: Well, if you have any complaints, go to window 3.

C: OK.

Excuse me.

I tried your milk, but it doesn't taste like milk at all.

Besides, it's not hot enough nor sweet enough.

I want my money back.

G: Sorry, you can't milk our corporation.

We will milk you!

Appendix

Rakugo Associations of Japan

ಬಿಲ್ಲ

Rakugo Kyokai (Rakugo Association)
1-9-5 Ueno, Taito-ku, Tokyo
Website: http://rakugo-kyokai.jp/

—

Rakugo Geijutsu Kyokai (Rakugo Arts Association)
6-12-30 Nishi-Shinjuku, Shinjuku-ku, Tokyo 160-0023
Entertainment Kadensha 2nd floor
Website: http://www.geikyo.com/index.php

—

Enraku Ichimonkai (Enraku Association)*
Email: ryougokuyose@gmail.com
Website: http://ryougokuyose.html.xdomain.jp/

(*) *Established on February 1, 1980 as the Dai Nippon Rakugo Sumirekai by Sanyutei Enraku V and his disciples. It has been called Enraku Ichimonkai since 1990. As of 2020, it is the only group among the five major Rakugo groups that does not have female members.*

—

Rakugo Tatekawa-ryu Association
Email: rakugotatekawaryu@gmail.com
Website: https://tatekawa.info/
(*) *Established by Tatekawa Danshi V and his disciples in 1983.*

Kamigata Rakugo Association
4-12-7, Tenma, Kita-ku Osaka-shi, Osaka, 530-0043, Japan
Website: https://kamigatarakugo.jp/english/

—

English Rakugo Association
1-10-4 7F, Minami-Aoyama Minato-ku Tokyo, 107-0062, Japan
Email: contact@englishrakugo.com
Website: https://www.englishrakugo.com

Rakugo on the Radio (*In Japanese*)

☙❧

Radio Yose **(TBS Radio)** ◆ **Sundays**
https://www.tbsradio.jp/yose/

Shinuchi Kyoen **(NHK Radio Dai-ichi)** ◆ **Saturdays**
https://www4.nhk.or.jp/P632/

Yose Appli **(Radio Nikkei Dai-ichi)** ◆ **Sundays**
http://www.radionikkei.jp/yose/

Kamigata Engei Kai **(NHK Radio Dai-ichi)** ◆ **Saturdays**
https://www4.nhk.or.jp/P83/

Radio Sinya-bin Wagei 100-sen **(NHK Radio Dai-ichi)**◆ **Sundays**
https://www4.nhk.or.jp/P83/

Sinosuke Radio de Date **(Bunka Hoso)** ◆ **Sundays**
http://www.joqr.co.jp/blog/rakugo/

Rakugo on Television (*In Japanese*)

☙❦

Rakugo on SkyperfecTV

Channel 542 寄席チャンネル

(Rakugo performances broadcast on Saturdays and Sundays)

https://www.skyperfectv.co.jp/channel/premium/detail.html?cid=542

—

Baynet Yose

Baynetwork Cable TV

(Limited to the Koto and Chuo Wards only)

http://www.baynet.ne.jp/tv/commu/yume/

—

NHK 日本の話芸 (Japanese storytelling)

https://www.nhk.jp/p/ts/DQM2J31K4N/

—

Asakusa Ochanoma Yose

Chiba TV

https://www.chiba-tv.com/program/detail/1021?hl=en

—

Rakugo Kenkyu-kai

TBS (Tokyo Broadcasting System)

https://www.tbs.co.jp/rakuken/

—

Engei Zukan (Performing arts book)

NHK (Broadcast on Sunday mornings)

https://www.nhk.jp/p/ts/YRZG3YWKKJ/

Yose Directory

❦

Kobe

Kobe-Shinkaichi Kirakukan (Founded in 2018)
2 Chome-4-13 Shinkaichi, Hyogo Ward, Kobe, Hyogo 652-0811, Japan
☏ +81 78-335-7088
https://kobe-kirakukan.jp/

—

Nagoya

Osu Engeijo Entertainment Hall (Founded in 1965)
2 Chome-19-39 Osu, Naka Ward, Nagoya, Aichi 460-0011, Japan
☏ +81 577-62-9203
http://www.osuengei.nagoya/

—

Osaka

Dourakutei (Founded in 2008)
1 Chome 17-6 Sanno, Nishinari War, Osaka 557-0001
☏ +81 6-6365-8281
http://www.beicho.co.jp/rakugo/動楽亭

—

Temma Tenjin Hanjo Tei (Founded in 2006)
2 Chome-1-34 Tenjinbashi, Kita Ward, Osaka, 530-0041, Japan
☏ +81 6-6352-4874
https://www.hanjotei.jp/

Tokyo

Asakusa Engei Hall *(Founded in 1964)*
1 Chome-43-12 Asakusa, Taito City, Tokyo 111-0032, Japan
☏ +81 3-3841-6545
https://www.asakusaengei.com/

—

Ikebukuro Engeijo (Founded in 1951)
1-23-1 Nishi-Ikebukuro, Tokyo, Japan
☏ +81 3-3971-4545
http://www.ike-en.com/

—

Shinjuku Suehirotei (Founded in 1946)
3 Chome-6-12 Shinjuku, Shinjuku City, Tokyo 160-0022, Japan
☏ +81 3-3351-2974
http://suehirotei.com/

—

Suzumoto Engeijo (Founded in 1857)
Tokyo Taitou-ku Ueno 2-7-12
☏ +81 3-3834-5906
http://www.rakugo.or.jp/

Glossary

Chuza	A Kamigata rakugo hierarchical ranking (equivalent to a second level or futatsume rakugo performer in Tokyo, not used any longer).
Debayashi	Background music played before a storyteller appears on stage.
Edo rakugo	Rakugo repertory of the Kanto region (Tokyo).
Eigo rakugo	English rakugo.
Futatsume	Professional rakugoka (second level performer).
Gakuya	Backstage area.
Geza	A shamisen player who plays debayashi.
Hamemono	Music used during the story, often appearing in Kamigata rakugo.
Hanashi (rakugo)	Stories.
Hanashika (rakugoka)	A storyteller.
Hiza Gawari	Performer who appears before the *tori* (the last performer).
Hizakakushi	A small screen placed in front of the kendai to cover the performers knees used by Kamigata performers.
Hondai	Main story.
Ichiban daiko	A drum beaten when the doors open.
Iromono	Variety acts which accompany rakugo storytelling.
Kaidanbanashi	Scary ghost stories.
Kaiko ichiban	The first story of a rakugo performance.
Kamigata rakugo	The rakugo repertory of the Kansai region (Osaka, Kyoto).
Kamigata Rakugo Kyokai	Kamigata Rakugo Association.

Kamishimo	Shifts right and left to distinguish between characters.
Kamite	Stage left.
Kendai	A small wooden table used by storytellers of the Kamigata style.
Kidosen	Admission fee.
Kin-en rakugo	Banned rakugo stories.
Kobanashi	Short stories with a punchline in the end.
Kobyoshi	Small wooden clappers used by storytellers of the Kamigata style.
Kodan	Another style of traditional Japanese storytelling which focuses on heroes and heroines of history.
Kokkeibanashi	Funny stories.
Kokusaku rakugo	National policy rakugo performed during the war.
Koten rakugo	Rakugo's classical repertory.
Koza	Elevated stage or platform.
Koza gaeshi	Turning over the zabuton (floor cushion) between acts.
Kozamei	A rakugoka's stage name.
Kuitsuki	Performer who appears after the intermission.
Kuruwabanashi	Stories about the pleasure quarters.
Kusuguri	Small jokes in the story.
Makura	Prologue.
Manzai	Japan's two-person standup comedy.
Mekuri	Paper signage on which the performers' names are written.
Minarai	Apprentice rakugoka (entry level).
Myoseki	Important stage names succeeded for generations.

Nakairi	Intermission.
Narimono	Musical instruments such as a drum, chime, and clappers.
Niban daiko	Drum beaten right before the show.
Ningen kokuho	Living national treasure.
Ninjobanashi	Tragicomic human-interest stories.
Ochako	Part-time female employee at the yose in Kamigata, who takes care of the stage.
Ochi (Sage)	A punchline or a summary of the narrative utilizing wordplay, a plot surprise, or a gesture. (Often called sage in Kamigata.)
Ochiken	Literally rakugo study group. The rakugo club at college/ university.
Ogiri	Verbal entertainment performed by several rakugoka, originally presented at the end of the day's performance.
Oidashi daiko	Drum beaten right after the show.
Ongyokubanashi	Musical stories.
Otogishu	Entertainers in the service of the feudal lords of Japan during the 16th century.
Otoshibanashi	Stories with a punchline.
Rakubi	The last day of a show.
Rakugo Geijutsu Kyokai	Rakugo Art Association in Tokyo.
Rakugo kai	Rakugo show.
Rakugo Kyokai	Rakugo Association in Tokyo.
Sandaibanashi	Stories made using three words provided by the audience.
Seiyo ninjobanashi	Western human-interest stories.

Seiza	The position in which a Rakugoka sits on stage. It involves sitting with your knees together, back straight, and buttocks resting on the ankles.
Seki	Another name for the vaudeville-type theaters where rakugo is performed.
Sensu	Paper fan.
Shibaibanashi	Stories derived from Kabuki plays.
Shimote	Stage right.
Shinsaku rakugo	Rakugo's new repertory.
Shinuchi	The highest level attainable in rakugo, the headliner.
Shisho	The designation of rakugo master/ teacher/ mentor, used for a shinuchi.
Shitenno	The four most important performers of rakugo.
Shumei	Succession of a previous stage name.
Sokkibon	Written transcription of rakugo stories.
Sosaku rakugo	New stories.
Tabi neta	Stories about travels in Kamigata, particularly from Osaka to Ise.
Teigo	Rakugoka's group name, similar to a surname of an individual.
Tenguren	Amateur rakugoka.
Tenugui	Small hand towel.
Tori	The established and highly anticipated headliner who appears last in the program.
Tsuyabanashi (Enshobanashi)	Erotic rakugo stories.
Wari	Performance fee.
Yoichi kai	Rakugo show held on 31st of the month at the yose.

Yose	Vaudeville type theater where rakugo stories are performed.
Yose bayashi	Rakugo theater music which includes debayashi.
Yotarobanashi	Funny stories in which a fool, Yotaro, plays a major role.
Zabuton	Floor cushion for the rakugoka to sit on.
Zenza	Apprentice rakugoka (first level).

Illustrations and Photos

The Story of Shinigami (*Kei Ohsuga*) ....
Panels from Shunshoku Sandaibanashi
illustrated by Ikkeisai Yoshiiku (*Tokyo Metropolitan Library*).................. 8-9
Ichikawa Danjuro V in the play Shibaraku
(Los Angeles County Museum of Art *Public domain*) 19
Sanyutei Encho (*Public domain*).. 33
Wakayagi Enjo (*Public domain*) 34
Yanagiya Kosan V (*Public domain*) 48
Katsura Beicho III (*Public domain*) 49
Yanagiya Kosanji X (*Mainichi Shimbun/ AFLO*) 50
Kairakutei Black depicted in Au Japon
Les Raconteurs Publics (Hasegawa Takejiro, 1899, *Public domain*).......... 67
Grave of Kairakutei Black in Yokohama (*Kanariya Eiraku*) 68
Hanashi Zuka monument in Tokyo (*Kanariya Eiraku*) 75
Storytellers' Wall (*Kanariya Eiraku*).. 76
Kokontei Shinsho V (*Yomiuri Shimbun/ AFLO*)... 83
Sanyutei Ensho VI (*Yomiuri Shimbun/ AFLO*) 84
Katsura Utamaru hosting Shoten (*Yomiuri Shimbun/ AFLO*) 92
Tatekawa Danshi V in 1986 (*Kanariya Eiraku*)... 108
Sanyutei Enraku V (*Yomiuri Shimbun/ AFLO*).. 116
Kokontei Shincho III (*Yomiuri Shimbun/ AFLO*)....................................... 123
Kamishibai storyteller in Asakusa (*Kanariya Eiraku*).............................. 125
Tachibanaya Enzo VIII (*Mainichi Shimbun/ AFLO*)................................. 131
Hayashiya Sanpei (*Yomiuri Shimbun/ AFLO*)... 138
Kokontei Kikuchiyo (*Mainichi Shimbun/ AFLO*) 159
Katsura Sunshine (*Russ Rowland*) 208
Sanyutei Koseinen (*Shimamura Ryota*)... 217
Tatekawa Shinoharu (*Shimomura Shinobu*).. 230

Yanagiya Tozaburo *(Izima Kaoru)* 238
Kanariya Eiraku *(Kanariya Eiraku)* 246
Kanariya Eishi *(Kanariya Eishi)* 255
Kanariya Ichirin *(Kanariya Eiraku)* 261
Jugemu *(Kei Ohsuga)* 262
Another Bottle of Sake *(Kei Ohsuga)* 270
Foxes in Oji *(Kei Ohsuga)* 310
Okiku's Dishes *(Kei Ohsuga)* 339
Toki Soba *(Kei Ohsuga)* 369

Works Cited

Works in Japanese:

"明石家さんま"(**"Akashiya Sanma"**). Wikipedia. Wikimedia Foundation, January 9, 2021.
https://ja.wikipedia.org/wiki/%E6%98%8E%E7%9F%B3%E5%AE%B6%E3%81%95%E3%82%93%E3%81%BE.

"戎橋松竹 (**Ebisubashishōchiku**)," Wikipedia (Wikimedia Foundation), accessed March 16, 2022,
https://ja.wikipedia.org/wiki/%E6%88%8E%E6%A9%8B%E6%9D%BE%E7%AB%B9#%E8%90%BD%E8%AA%9E.

Gomi, Makoto. 『藝能懇話』第二十一号 特集 上方落語史考—橋本礼一論文集 (2016(平成 28) 年 大阪藝能懇話会) / "Gei Nō Konwa" Dai Nijūichigō Tokushū Kamigata Rakugo-Shi Kō — Hashimoto Reiichi Ronbun-Shū. August 2021.

"咄本とは (**Hanashibon to Wa**)." ブリタニカ国際大百科事典 小項目事典 (Britannica International Encyclopedia Small Item Encyclopedia). コトバンク (Kotobank). Accessed March 16, 2022.
https://kotobank.jp/word/%E5%92%84%E6%9C%AC-115641#E3.83.96.E3.83.AA.E3.82.BF.E3.83.8B.E3.82.AB.E5.9B.BD.E9.9A.9B.E5.A4.A7.E7.99.BE.E7.A7.91.E4.BA.8B.E5.85.B8.20.E5.B0.8F.E9.A0.85.E7.9B.AE.E4.BA.8B.E5.85.B8.

"噺家を夢見た青春時代　落語家・柳家蝠丸さん" (**"Hanashika Wo Yumemita Seishun Jidai- Rakugoka Yanagiya Fukumaru"**). The Mainichi, October 12, 2018.

"林家三平 (初代)" (**"Hayashiya Sanpei I"**). Wikipedia. Wikimedia Foundation, January 20, 2021.
https://ja.wikipedia.org/wiki/%E6%9E%97%E5%AE%B6%E4%B8%89%E5%B9%B3_(%E5%88%9D%E4%BB%A3).

"堀の内 (落語)"("**Horinouchi (rakugo)**").Wikipedia. Wikimedia Foundation, December 2, 2020.

https://ja.m.wikipedia.org/wiki/%E5%A0%80%E3%81%AE%E5%86%85_%28%E8%90%BD%E8%AA%9E%29.

"Kagekiyo." 能・演目事典：景清：あらすじ・みどころ, 2022.

https://www.the-noh.com/jp/plays/data/program_066.html.

"快楽亭ブラック (初代) (**Kairakutei Black (1st Generation)**)," Wikipedia (Wikimedia Foundation, October 30, 2021),

https://ja.wikipedia.org/wiki/%E5%BF%AB%E6%A5%BD%E4%BA%AD%E3%83%96%E3%83%A9%E3%83%83%E3%82%AF_(%E5%88%9D%E4%BB%A3).

"上方落語史"("**Kamigata Rakugo-Shi**"). YouTube, 2017.

https://www.youtube.com/watch?app=desktop&v=R6MWif8kZQk&t=45s.

小項目事典，"軽口露がはなしとは (**Karukuchitsuyugahanashi to Wa**)," ブリタニカ国際大百科事典 (Britannica International Encyclopedia) (コトバンク (Kotobank), accessed March 16, 2022,

https://kotobank.jp/word/%E8%BB%BD%E5%8F%A3%E9%9C%B2%E3%81%8C%E3%81%AF%E3%81%AA%E3%81%97-47619.

"桂米朝 (3代目)"("**Katsura Beicho III**"). Wikipedia. Wikimedia Foundation, November 22, 2020.

https://ja.wikipedia.org/wiki/%E6%A1%82%E7%B1%B3%E6%9C%9D_(3%E4%BB%A3%E7%9B%AE)#%E6%99%A9%E5%B9%B4.

"桂米朝、海原小浜の上方笑芸繁盛記 2" ("**Katsurabeichō, Unabarakohama No Kamigata Shōgei Hanjō-Ki 2**"). YouTube, 2016.

https://www.youtube.com/watch?app=desktop&v=Ss5V6HLtH3w.

"桂文枝：リアルタイム多言語字幕付きで落語を披露" ("**Katsura Bunshi: Rakugo with Real-Time Multilingual Subtitles**"). MANTANWEB（まんたんウェブ）. MANTANWEB, June 5, 2016. https://mantan-web.jp/article/20160605dog00m200030000c.html.

"桂かい枝" ("**Katsura Kaishi**"). Wikipedia. Wikimedia Foundation, February 14, 2021.
https://ja.wikipedia.org/wiki/%E6%A1%82%E3%81%8B%E3%81%84%E6%9E%9D.

"桂枝雀 (2代目)" ("**Katsura Shijaku II**"). Wikipedia. Wikimedia Foundation, December 7, 2020.
https://ja.wikipedia.org/wiki/%E6%A1%82%E6%9E%9D%E9%9B%80_(2%E4%BB%A3%E7%9B%AE).

"古今亭志ん朝" ("**Kokontei Shincho**"). Wikipedia. Wikimedia Foundation, November 14, 2020.
https://ja.m.wikipedia.org/wiki/%E5%8F%A4%E4%BB%8A%E4%BA%AD%E5%BF%97%E3%82%93%E6%9C%9D.

"古今亭志ん生 (5代目)" ("**Kokontei Shinsho (5th Generation)**"). Wikipedia. Wikimedia Foundation, November 28, 2020.
https://ja.wikipedia.org/wiki/%E5%8F%A4%E4%BB%8A%E4%BA%AD%E5%BF%97%E3%82%93%E7%94%9F_(5%E4%BB%A3%E7%9B%AE).

"前田武彦" ("**Maeda Takehiko**"). Wikipedia. Wikimedia Foundation, December 31, 2020.
https://ja.wikipedia.org/wiki/%E5%89%8D%E7%94%B0%E6%AD%A6%E5%BD%A6.

Kinoshita, Masaki. "What Kind of Person Is Hikohachi Yonezawa, the Founder of Kamigata Rakugo?" 神戸っ子 | 神戸・芦屋・西宮の上質で厳選した情報をお届けするサイト, September 2018. https://kobecco.hpg.co.jp/34133/.

Kishida, Shigeru. "『唯幻論＜岸田秀＞』(**Tada Maboroshi-Ron Taizen**) 可い長の寝床ブログ (Ka i-chō no nedoko burogu). Ameba, January 11, 2010.
https://ameblo.jp/hansyouteikaichou/entry-10430657203.html.

"Meaning of 辻噺, つじばなし, **Tsujibanash**i: Japanese Dictionary," JLearn.net, accessed March 16, 2022,
https://jlearn.net/dictionary/%E8%BE%BB%E5%99%BA.

"明治～平成 新撰 芸能人物事典.若柳 燕嬢とは.コトバンク" ("**Meiji ~ Heisei shinsen geinojin-mono jiten. Wakayanagi Tsubame jo to wa**"). Kotobanku/Meiji ~ Heisei shinsen geinojin-mono jiten. https://kotobank.jp/word/%E8%8B%A5%E6%9F%B3%20%E7%87%95%E5%AC%A2-1674783.

"明治時代に活躍した'元祖 快楽亭ブラックの人生 (**Meiji Jidai Ni Katsuyaku Shita Ganzo Kairakuteiburakku No Jinsei**)," Yokohama History Salon, March 26, 2018, https://yokohamasalon.link/wp-content/uploads/2018/06/tokushu201803.pdf.

Minobe, Mitsuko. *Sanninbanashi: Shinshō bashō shinchō*. Tōkyō: Fusōsha, 2002.

"人間的な成長が芸に磨きをかける" ("**Ningen-tekina seicho ga gei ni migaki o kakeru**"). Let's Enjoy Tokyo, 2020. https://ranking.enjoytokyo.jp/fp/kizuna/1201.html?__ngt__=TT1119cd39a002ac1e4a5a19oFRghChYehL50OLSwpIVIA.

Ogita, Kiyoshi and Sadao Osada. "Intabyu: Shitenno Wagashi o Kataru." *Kamigata geino 93* (November 1986): 24.

"落語「通」検定粋に楽しむ落語: Yahoo!インターネット検定公式テキスト" ("**Rakugo `tsū' kentei iki ni tanoshimu rakugo: Yahoo! intānetto kentei koshiki tekisuto**"). Japan: インプレスジャパン, 2006.

"**Rakugoka's Daily Life Verification Site Learned by Teaching 'Disciple Is a Master' ⇒ Rakugoka, Karoku Yanagiya**." ダイヤモンド・オンライン, August 18, 2015. https://diamond.jp/articles/-/76841?page=4.

"作家別作品リスト：No.989." 作家別作品リスト：三遊亭 円朝" ("**Sakka betsu sakuhin risuto: Nanbā 989. " (Sakka betsu sakuhin risuto: Sanyutei Encho. " (List of works by artist: No.989. List of works by artist: Sanyutei Encho)**). https://www.aozora.gr.jp/index_pages/person989.html.

"三遊亭圓朝" ("**Sanyutei Encho**"). Wikipedia. Wikimedia Foundation, November 28, 2020. https://ja.wikipedia.org/wiki/%E4%B8%89%E9%81%8A%E4%BA%AD%E5%9C%93%E6%9C%9D.

"三遊亭圓楽 (5代目)" ("**Sanyutei Enraku V**"). Wikipedia. Wikimedia Foundation, November 12, 2020.
https://ja.wikipedia.org/wiki/%E4%B8%89%E9%81%8A%E4%BA%AD%E5%9C%93%E6%A5%BD_%285%E4%BB%A3%E7%9B%AE%29.

"三遊亭圓生 (6代目)" ("**Sanyutei Ensho VI**") . Wikipedia. Wikimedia Foundation, December 21, 2020.
https://ja.wikipedia.org/wiki/%E4%B8%89%E9%81%8A%E4%BA%AD%E5%9C%93%E7%94%9F_(6%E4%BB%A3%E7%9B%AE).

"Shōfukutei Kakushō Kōshiki Saito."【笑福亭鶴笑公式サイト】笑う門には福来る, 2009. http://kakushow.jp/e-profile.htm.

"笑福亭鶴瓶"("**Shofukutei Tsurube**"). Wikipedia. Wikimedia Foundation, January 2, 2021.
https://ja.wikipedia.org/wiki/%E7%AC%91%E7%A6%8F%E4%BA%AD%E9%B6%B4%E7%93%B6.

"笑福亭笑瓶"("**Shohei Shofukutei**").Wikipedia. Wikimedia Foundation, November 30, 2020.
https://ja.wikipedia.org/wiki/%E7%AC%91%E7%A6%8F%E4%BA%AD%E7%AC%91%E7%93%B6.

"笑点 web (**Shoten**)." 日本テレビ. https://www.ntv.co.jp/shoten/encyclopedia/index.html.

"春風亭柳朝 (5代目)"("**Shunpūteiryūcho (5-daime)**"). Wikipedia. Wikimedia Foundation, September 25, 2020.
https://ja.wikipedia.org/wiki/%E6%98%A5%E9%A2%A8%E4%BA%AD%E6%9F%B3%E6%9C%9D_%285%E4%BB%A3%E7%9B%AE%29.

"橘家圓蔵 (8代目)" ("**Tachibanaya Enzo VIII**"). Wikipedia. Wikimedia Foundation, January 24, 2021.
https://ja.wikipedia.org/wiki/%E6%A9%98%E5%AE%B6%E5%9C%93%E8%94%B5_(8%E4%BB%A3%E7%9B%AE).

"橘家圓蔵 (8代目)" ("**Tachibanaya Enzo VIII**"). Wikiwand. Accessed February 14, 2021.

https://www.wikiwand.com/ja/%E6%A9%98%E5%AE%B6%E5%9C%93
%E8%94%B5_(8%E4%BB%A3%E7%9B%AE).

"立川談志" ("**Tatekawa Danshi**"). Wikipedia. Wikimedia Foundation, November 4, 2020.

https://ja.m.wikipedia.org/wiki/%E7%AB%8B%E5%B7%9D%E8%AB%87%E5%BF%97.

"天狗連" ("**Tenguren**"). Wikipedia. October 4, 2020.

https://ja.wikipedia.org/wiki/%E5%A4%A9%E7%8B%97%E9%80%A3.

"東京かわら版" ("**Tokyo Kawara-ban**"). June 28, 2020.

"若柳燕嬢" ("**Wakayanagi Enjo**"). Wikipedia. September 21, 2020.

https://ja.wikipedia.org/wiki/%E8%8B%A5%E6%9F%B3%E7%87%95%E5%AC%A2.

"露の五郎兵衛 (**Tsuyu No Gorobei**)." Wikipedia. Wikimedia Foundation, January 2, 2022.

https://ja.wikipedia.org/wiki/%E9%9C%B2%E3%81%AE%E4%BA%94%E9%83%8E%E5%85%B5%E8%A1%9B.

"露の五郎兵衛とは (**Tsuyunogorobee to Wa**)." 日本大百科全書(ニッポニカ) (Encyclopedia Nipponica (Nipponica))/ 朝日日本歴史人物事典. コトバンク (Kotobank). Accessed March 16, 2022.

https://kotobank.jp/word/%E9%9C%B2%E3%81%AE%E4%BA%94%E9%83%8E%E5%85%B5%E8%A1%9B-572694#%E5%88%9D%E4%BB%A3.

"桂米朝 (3代目)" ("**Yanagiya Kosanji**"). Wikipedia. Wikimedia Foundation, November 22, 2020.

https://ja.wikipedia.org/wiki/%E6%A1%82%E7%B1%B3%E6%9C%9D_(3%E4%BB%A3%E7%9B%AE)#%E6%99%A9%E5%B9%B4.

"全日本学生落語選手権・策伝大賞" ("**Zen'nihon gakusei rakugo senshuken・Sakuden taisho**"). Wikipedia. https://ja.m.wikipedia.org/wiki/全日本学生落語選手権・策伝大賞

Works in English:

"Aka Medaka." MyDramaList. TBS, 2015. https://mydramalist.com/15936-aka-medaka.

Allred, Laurie. "Rakugo Master Utazo Katsura to Share Traditional Japanese Storytelling in English." Daily Bruin, February 24, 2012. https://dailybruin.com/2012/02/24/rakugo_master_utazo_katsura_to_share_traditional_japanese_storytelling_in_english.

Asakura-Ward, Toshiki. "A Bridge to the Near North: The 1980s Resurrection of Henry Black (1858-1923)," (master's thesis, Western Sydney University, Australia, 2017), https://researchdirect.westernsydney.edu.au/islandora/object/uws:45295/data)

"Benshi." Wikipedia. Wikimedia Foundation, November 22, 2021. https://en.wikipedia.org/wiki/Benshi.

"Biwa Hōshi." Wikipedia. Wikimedia Foundation, December 25, 2021. https://en.wikipedia.org/wiki/Biwa_h%C5%8Dshi.

"Botan Dōrō," August 2, 2020. Wikipedia. https://en.wikipedia.org/wiki/Botan_D%C5%8Dr%C5%8D.

Brau, Lorie. Rakugo: Performing Comedy and Cultural Heritage in Contemporary Tokyo. Lanham, MD: Lexington Books, 2008.

Braun, John. "Rakugo and HOE International." English rakugo, July 10, 2013. https://englishrakugo.wordpress.com/rakugo-and-hoe-international/

Canuck, J. Hachidai Nakamura -- Theme from Shoten (笑点）, January 1, 1970. http://kayokyokuplus.blogspot.com/2012/12/hachidai-nakamura-theme-from-shoten.html.

Chaiklin, Martha. "Treaty Ports." Treaty Ports | Japan Module. University of Pittsburgh. Accessed March 21, 2022. https://www.japanpitt.pitt.edu/essays-and-articles/history/treaty-ports.

"Danjuro Dictionary - D-F." NARITAYA, 2009. http://www.naritaya.jp/english/compendium/dictionary_02.html.

DeHaven, Shawn. "Sanyūtei Aiba: A Rising Female Voice in the Rakugo World." It's Funny in Japanese, 2019.
http://www.itsfunnyinjapanese.com/interviews-sanyutei-aiba.

"Descending Stories: Showa Genroku Rakugo Shinju." Wikipedia. Wikimedia Foundation, January 23, 2021.
https://en.wikipedia.org/wiki/Descending_Stories:_Showa_Genroku_Rakugo_Shinju.

"Fallen Words." Wikipedia. Wikimedia Foundation, November 30, 2020.
https://en.wikipedia.org/wiki/Fallen_Words.

"Female 'Rakugo' Narrator Packs Bags to Spread Mirth on Korean Peninsula." The Japan Times, June 28, 2001.
https://www.japantimes.co.jp/news/2001/06/28/national/female-rakugo-narrator-packs-bags-to-spread-mirth-on-korean-peninsula/.

"Godfather Death." Grimm 044: Godfather Death. University of Pittsburgh, 2006. https://www.pitt.edu/~dash/grimm044.html.

Groves, Alison. "A Ventriloquist, a Rakugo Performer, and a Puppet Walk into a Bar…." Japan Art Directory in Australia, 2019.
https://artdirectory.jpf.org.au/showko-showfukutei/.

"Hakuen Shorin." prabook.com.
https://prabook.com/web/hakuen.shorin/3747055.

"Hakone Gora Hotel Playhouse." Hakone Gora Hotel, 2005.
https://www.nntt.jac.go.jp/english/season/s265e/s265e.html.

Hayashi, Tetsuya, and Mieko Nakajima. "Interview Series 'People': Rakugoka Kokontei Komako." Asahi Gunma, March 8, 2019.
https://www.asahigunma.com/%E8%90%BD%E8%AA%9E%E5%AE%B6-%E5%8F%A4%E4%BB%8A%E4%BA%AD%E9%A7%92%E5%AD%90-%E3%81%95%E3%82%93/.

Heinz, Morioka, and Sasaki, Miyoko. "The Blue-Eyed Storyteller: Henry Black and His Rakugo Career." Monumenta Nipponica 38, no. 2 (1983): 133.
https://doi.org/10.2307/2384558.

Heinz, Morioka and Sasaki, Miyoko. Rakugo, the Popular Narrative Art of Japan. Cambridge, MA: Council on East Asian Studies, Harvard University, 1990.

"HIS MASTER'S VOICE." JFDB, 2014. https://jfdb.jp/en/title/4304.

Hotes, Cathy Munroe. "Talk Talk Talk (しゃべれどもしゃべれども, 2007)." Nishikata Film Review, 2009. https://www.nishikata-eiga.com/2009/05/talk-talk-talk-2007.html.

"Idaten (TV Series)." Wikipedia. Wikimedia Foundation, January 17, 2021. https://en.wikipedia.org/wiki/Idaten_(TV_series).

"Implementation of 'AEON MALL Rakugo.'" AEON MALL/ CSR, 2018. https://www.aeonmall.com/en/csr_2017/feature/feature1/page3.html.

"Japan Foundation Los Angeles: Japanema Rakugo Eiga." Japan Foundation Los Angeles | Japanema Rakugo Eiga, 2017. https://www.jflalc.org/ac-japanema-110817.

Japan Today, "Henry Black (1859-1923): Japan's First Gaijin Talent," Japan Today, September 13, 2011, https://japantoday.com/category/features/opinions/henry-black-1859-1923-japan%25e2%2580%2599s-first-gaijin-talent.

"Japanophiles: Johan Nilsson Bjoerk - Japanology Plus: NHK WORLD-JAPAN on Demand." NHK WORLD, August 4, 2020. https://www3.nhk.or.jp/nhkworld/en/ondemand/video/2032211/

John Reddie black. Biglobe. Accessed March 14, 2022. http://www2s.biglobe.ne.jp/matu-emk/black.html.

"Joshiraku." MyAnimeList.net. https://myanimelist.net/anime/12679/Joshiraku.

Joshua Hammer, "The Great Japan Earthquake of 1923," Smithsonian.com (Smithsonian Institution, May 1, 2011), https://www.smithsonianmag.com/history/the-great-japan-earthquake-of-1923-1764539/.

"J. R. Black." Wikipedia. Wikimedia Foundation, December 1, 2021. https://en.wikipedia.org/wiki/J._R._Black.

K, Anthony. "Rakugo Musume." AsianWiki. Accessed February 7, 2021. https://asianwiki.com/Rakugo_Musume.

"Kairakutei Black I." Wikipedia. Wikimedia Foundation, May 4, 2020. https://en.wikipedia.org/wiki/Kairakutei_Black_I.

"Kamigata." Wikipedia. Wikimedia Foundation, January 17, 2022. https://en.wikipedia.org/wiki/Kamigata.

"Kamishibai." Wikipedia. Wikimedia Foundation, December 29, 2020. https://en.wikipedia.org/wiki/Kamishibai.

"Kodan." Wikipedia. Wikimedia Foundation, October 12, 2018. https://en.wikipedia.org/wiki/K%C5%8Ddan.

Larsen, Brooke. "What Is Kabuki? 6 Things to Know About Kabuki Theater." Japan Objects. Japan Objects, February 1, 2021. https://japanobjects.com/features/kabuki/#elements.

"List of Living National Treasures of Japan (Performing Arts)," June 28, 2020. https://en.wikipedia.org/wiki/List_of_Living_National_Treasures_of_Japan_(performing_arts).

"Living National Treasure (Japan)." Wikipedia. Wikimedia Foundation, April 11, 2020. https://en.wikipedia.org/wiki/Living_National_Treasure_(Japan).

Markus, Andrew L. Journal of Japanese Studies 18, no. 2 (1992): 623-28. doi:10.2307/132855.

Martin, Alex. "Spectral Sightings at Zenshoan Temple." The Japan Times, August 4, 2019. https://www.japantimes.co.jp/culture/2019/08/04/arts/spectral-sightings-zenshoan-temple/.

Murakami, Asako. "'Rakugo' Artist Takes Sit-down Shtick to Edinburgh Festival, with Subtitles." The Japan Times, August 6, 2000.

"Mainichi Broadcasting System." Wikipedia. Wikimedia Foundation, February 14, 2022. https://en.wikipedia.org/wiki/Mainichi_Broadcasting_System.

Maruko, Mami. "Canadian Has English-Language Rakugo Dream." The Japan Times, January 14, 2013.
https://www.japantimes.co.jp/community/2013/01/14/our-lives/canadian-has-english-language-rakugo-dream/.

Miller, J. Scott. "SANYUTEI ENCHO." Academic Dictionaries and Encyclopedias, 2009.
https://japan_literature.enacademic.com/343/SAN%E2%80%99YUTEI_ENCHO.

Mimizuka, Kayo. "Storyteller Broadens Appeal of 'Rakugo'." The Japan Times, January 24, 2012.

"Negishi Sanpei-Do." Hello Japan - Japan Travel Guide. Accessed February 16, 2021. http://www.hellojapan.asia/en/travel-guide/negishi-sanpeido.html.

Oshima, Kimie. "Japanese Sit-Down Comedy." Rakugo. Humor & Health Journal (Vol XII, Number 3), May 1998.
http://www.angelfire.com/vamp/shoopshoop/Rakugo.html

"Rakugo." languagehatcom, November 24, 2018.
http://languagehat.com/Rakugo/.

"Rakugo." Wikipedia. Wikimedia Foundation, August 22, 2020.
https://en.wikipedia.org/wiki/Rakugo.

"Rakugo Classic Comic Storyteller Beicho Dies at 89." The Japan Times, March 20, 2015.
https://www.japantimes.co.jp/news/2015/03/20/national/rakugo-classic-comic-storyteller-beicho-dies-89/.

"Rakugo Girls." rakugogirls. Accessed April 17, 2021.
https://mgsdp835.wixsite.com/rakugogirls.

"Rakugo Performed in Sign Language." "Rakugo" performed in sign language (long version), 2007.
https://www.dinf.ne.jp/doc/english/resource/rakugo.html.

"Rakugo Storyteller, TV Personality Katsura Utamaru Dies at 81." The Mainichi, July 4, 2018.
https://mainichi.jp/english/articles/20180702/p2a/00m/0na/008000c.

"Rakugo Storytelling Master Kosan Dies." The Japan Times, May 17, 2002.
https://www.japantimes.co.jp/news/2002/05/17/national/rakugo-storytelling-master-kosan-dies/.

"Rakugo (The Art of Storytelling)." nippon.com, May 30, 2020.
https://www.nippon.com/en/features/jg00045/.

"Rakugo: Traditional Comic Story Telling." Rakugo: Learn Japanese - Japanese language and Culture, September 12, 2007.
http://www.gaikoku.info/japanese/rakugo.htm.

"Rakugoka Katsura Utamaru Dies at 81." Manila STV, July 2, 2018.
https://manila-stv.ph/lifestyle/rakugo-storyteller-katsura-utamaru-dies-at-81.html.

"The Roots of Edo Rakugo: Rakugo Special: EDO TOKYO Digital Museum - Historical Visit, New Wisdom." TOKYO METROPOLITAN LIBRARY.
https://www.library.metro.tokyo.lg.jp/portals/0/edo/tokyo_library/english/rakugo/page1-1.html.

"Sandai-Banashi: Impromptu Rakugo Based on Three Themes: Rakugo Special: Edo Tokyo Digital Museum - Historical Visit, New Wisdom." Tokyo Meetropolitan Library.
https://www.library.metro.tokyo.lg.jp/portals/0/edo/tokyo_library/english/rakugo/page2-1.html.

"Sanma Akashiya." Wikipedia. Wikimedia Foundation, January 20, 2020.
https://en.wikipedia.org/wiki/Sanma_Akashiya.

"Sanyutei Encho." Wikipedia. Wikimedia Foundation, October 4, 2020.
https://en.wikipedia.org/wiki/San%27y%C5%ABtei_Ench%C5%8D.

"Sanyutei Enraku V." Wikipedia. Wikimedia Foundation, October 4, 2020.
https://en.wikipedia.org/wiki/San%27y%C5%ABtei_Enraku_V.

Seth Jacobowitz and Ranpo Edogawa, in The Edogawa Rampo Reader (Fukuoka: Kurodahan Press, 2008), p. 24.

"Shijaku Katsura II." Wikipedia. Wikimedia Foundation, December 26, 2019. https://en.wikipedia.org/wiki/Shijaku_Katsura_II.

"Showko Showfukutei." Wikipedia. Wikimedia Foundation, July 28, 2020. https://en.wikipedia.org/wiki/Showko_Showfukutei.

"Shōten." Wikipedia. Wikimedia Foundation, December 11, 2020. https://en.wikipedia.org/wiki/Sh%C5%8Dten.

"Something Like It." MyDramaList. Accessed February 7, 2021. https://mydramalist.com/51563-something-like-it.

"Something Like, Something Like It." AsianWiki. Accessed March 7, 2021. https://asianwiki.com/Something_Like,_Something_Like_It.

"Taikomochi." Wikipedia. Wikimedia Foundation, May 31, 2020. https://en.wikipedia.org/wiki/Taikomochi.

"Television in Japan." Academic Dictionaries and Encyclopedias. Accessed March 13, 2022. https://en-academic.com/dic.nsf/enwiki/11643185.

"Tiger and Dragon." AsianWiki, 2005. https://asianwiki.com/Tiger_and_Dragon.

Tokuhashi, Isao. "If I Made an Unfunny Joke, I Could Say, 'I Guess It's 'Cause I'm from Sweden'. Do You Know Why?" My Eyes Tokyo, April 23, 2017. https://www.myeyestokyo.com/johan-nilsson-bjork/.

"VOX POPULI: 'Rakugo' in Wartime Japan Still Serves as a Cautionary Tale." The Asahi Shimbun, August 15, 2020. http://www.asahi.com/ajw/articles/13638016.

Yoneda, Melynie. "Shinoharu Tatekawa Makes Sure That 'Rakugo' Isn't Lost in Translation." The Japan Times, January 14, 2016. https://www.japantimes.co.jp/culture/2016/01/14/stage/shinoharu-tatekawa-makes-sure-Rakugo-isnt-lost-translation/.

Yu, A. C. "Kamigata Rakugo (Comic Storytelling in Kyoto and Osaka) (上方落語)" - Japanese Wiki Corpus. https://www.japanese-wiki-corpus.org/culture/Kamigata%20Rakugo%20(Comic%20Storytelling%20in%20Kyoto%20and%20Osaka).html.

Yu, A. C. "Karukuchi" - Japanese Wiki Corpus. https://japanese-wiki-corpus.github.io/culture/Karukuchi.html.

Yu, A. C. "Ochi (the punch line of a joke)" - Japanese Wiki Corpus. Accessed March 10, 2021. https://www.japanese-wiki-corpus.org/culture/Ochi%20(the%20punch%20line%20of%20a%20joke).html.

Yu, A. C. "Ogiri (Professional Rakugokas play on words.) (大喜利)." Japanese Wiki Corpus. https://japanese-wiki-corpus.github.io/culture/Ogiri%20(Professional%20rakugo%20storytellers%20play%20on%20words.).html.

Yu, A. C. "Rakugoka (Rakugoka) (落語家)." Japanese Wiki Corpus. https://japanese-wiki-corpus.github.io/culture/Rakugoka%20(Rakugo%20Story%20Teller).html.

Interviews:

Kanariya Eiraku. Email interview with author, September 17, 2020.
Kanariya Eishi. Email interview with author, September 24, 2020.
Kanariya Ichirin. Email interview with author, September 21, 2020.
Katsura Sunshine. Zoom interview with author, September 18, 2020.
Sanyutei Koseinen. Email interview with author, September 11, 2020.
Tatekawa Shinoharu. Email interview with author, September 9, 2020.
Yanagiya Tozaburo. Email interview with author, August 28, 2020.

About Us

KRISTINE OHKUBO is a Los Angeles-based author whose work emphasizes topics related to Japan and Japanese culture. While growing up in Chicago, she developed a deep love and appreciation for Japanese culture, people, and history. Her extensive travels in Japan have enabled her to gain insight into this fascinating country, which she shares with you through her books.

Her first book, a travel guide to Japan, was published in 2016. In 2017, she released a historical study of the Pacific War written from the perspective of the Japanese people, both those who were living in Japan and in the United States, when the war broke out. Two years later, she supplemented her earlier releases with the story of an infamous twentieth century geisha, who was both a victim and an aggressor, struggling amidst a strict patriarchal culture and a rapidly changing social system. In 2019, she followed up her 2017 release, *The Sun Will Rise Again*, with a book titled *Sakhalin*. The work examines the far-reaching impact the island changing hands had on its inhabitants and resources, and culminates with the tragic events which took place in August 1945.

Kristine's most recent work is quite a departure from her previous releases. Still focusing on Japan's history and culture, the series introduces readers to rakugo, Japan's 400-year-old art of storytelling. Through a succession of biographical information, anecdotes, interviews, and rakugo scripts, the author explains why this traditional art form has endured for many years.

As an author, Kristine believes that writing from other cultural perspectives encourages empathy and understanding, and at the same time it broadens our knowledge of the events that have unfolded over the years.

You can find Kristine's work on: A*mazon.com/author/kristineohkubo* as well as other major online book retailers.

KANARIYA EIRAKU is an English rakugo storyteller based in Tokyo. He participated in the Tatekawa-ryu in 1984 to learn about the essence of rakugo from the legendary Tatekawa Danshi. He began offering Japanese rakugo classes in Tokyo in 1991; in 2007, he established his English rakugo classes.

He has translated and performed over sixty classical and contemporary rakugo stories. Since 2007, he has performed in front of enthusiastic audiences in Japan, the United States, the United Kingdom, Denmark, Australia, New Zealand, Georgia, Kazakhstan, and Laos.

Eiraku is one of the founding members of the English Rakugo Association in Tokyo. The organization was established in 2020 with the mission to spread rakugo all over the world.

He also offers English performance classes at universities.

You can learn more about Eiraku by visiting his website: *https://kanariyaeirakuweb.wixsite.com/my-site.*

Talking About Rakugo 2: The Stories Behind the Storytellers

Rakugo, with its stories rooted in everyday life, is currently experiencing a boom in popularity not just in the country where it originated, but also in places where until just recently the word rakugo was an unfamiliar term. The art form, which was once confined to the traditional yose theaters, has expanded to a variety of media, including radio, television, internet, CDs, DVDs, film, drama, manga, and anime.

It owes its success to its practitioners, the RAKUGOKA. The contemporary storytellers, who shifting away from the norms and rules guiding them in their treatment of the narratives, have diversified and developed personas based on their individual lifestyles and personalities. Each one brings his or her own experiences, eccentricities, and authenticity to the unique world of rakugo. Sometimes the stories behind the storytellers entice the public as much as the ones they tell on stage.

You were introduced to the traditional Japanese art of storytelling in **Talking About Rakugo**, now venture into the private world of the storytellers in **Talking About Rakugo 2: The Stories Behind the Storytellers.**

Product details

Published : February 7, 2022

Language : English

Paperback : 298 pages

ISBN-10 : 1087984599

ISBN-13 : 978-1087984599

www.ingramcontent.com/pod-product-compliance
Lightning Source LLC
Chambersburg PA
CBHW070521010526
44118CB00012B/1042